Native and Immigrant Entrepreneurship

Simone Guercini · Gabi Dei Ottati
Loretta Baldassar · Graeme Johanson
Editors

Native and Immigrant Entrepreneurship

Lessons for Local Liabilities in Globalization from the Prato Case Study

Springer

Editors
Simone Guercini
Department of Economics and Management
University of Florence
Florence
Italy

Gabi Dei Ottati
Department of Economics and Management
University of Florence
Florence
Italy

Loretta Baldassar
School of Social Sciences
The University of Western Australia
Crawley, WA
Australia

Graeme Johanson
Faculty of Information Technology
Monash University
Caulfield East, VIC
Australia

ISBN 978-3-319-44110-8   ISBN 978-3-319-44111-5   (eBook)
DOI 10.1007/978-3-319-44111-5

Library of Congress Control Number: 2016959803

Printed on acid-free paper

This Springer imprint is published by Springer Nature
The registered company is Springer International Publishing AG
The registered company address is: Gewerbestrasse 11, 6330 Cham, Switzerland

Acknowledgements

The editors thank the reviewers that participated to the revision process of chapters included in this book. The list of reviewers includes the followings: Johnatan Benney, Monash University, Australia; Tom Dennison, Monash University, Australia; Laura Grassini, University of Florence, Italy; James Jupp, Academy of Social Sciences, Australia; Narelle McAuliffe, Monash University, Australia; Roberta Raffaetà, University of Lousanne, Switzerland; Silvia Ranfagni, University of Florence, Italy; and Andrea Runfola, University of Perugia, Italy.

Contents

Editors and Contributors

About the Editors

Simone Guercini is a professor of management at the University of Florence and visiting professor at the Grenoble Graduate School of Business. His research interests include business marketing, heuristics in business, entrepreneurship in communities, and internationalization, with a special focus on the Italian fashion industry. Simone received his Ph.D. in economics from Sant'Anna School of Advanced Studies, Pisa. He collaborated with many academic journal in management and marketing both as author, member of the editorial board and reviewer, including Industrial Marketing and Management, Management Decision, and Journal of Business Research. He can be contacted at simone.guercini@unifi.it.

Gabi Dei Ottati is a professor of applied economics at the University of Florence and a member of the European Research Centre on Regional and Local Development. Her main research interests include industrial organization and economic development, with a special focus on Italy and industrial districts. Having collaborated for many years with Giacomo Becattini, the revitalizer of the Marshallian industrial district concept, she is part of the Florence school of local development.

Loretta Baldassar is a professor of anthropology and sociology at the University of Western Australia and adjunct principal research fellow at the School of Political and Social Inquiry, Monash University. Her research interests focus on transnational migrants, families, and caregiviers, including the question of generations. Loretta received her Ph.D. from the University of Western Australia.

Graeme Johanson recently retired as associate dean research training in the Faculty of Information Technology at Monash University, Melbourne, Australia. His research interests focus on the uses of information and communications technologies for developing countries, and marginalized social groups, including migrants. He teaches research methods and supervises postgraduate students. His publications include books and many journal articles. He undertakes consultancies.

Contributors

Eduardo Barberis (Ph.D. Sociology) is researcher in urban sociology at the University of Urbino Carlo Bo, Italy, where he lectures on immigration policy and coordinates the Research Centre on Applied Transcultural Research (CIRTA). His research interests include the territorial dimension of immigration and social policy, and antidiscrimination practice. He published several articles in Italian and English on issues such as immigrant entrepreneurship, social work, and immigration, and rescaling social policy.

Stefano Becucci is an associate professor of sociology at the Department of Social and Political Sciences, University of Florence (Italy). His research interests include organized crime, trafficking in human beings, smuggling of migrants, and migrants process of integration and exclusion in the hosting society. His research has been published in monographs, collected books, and scientific reviews such as Global Crime, Quaderni di Sociologia, and European Journal on Criminal Policy and Research. E-mail: stefano.becucci@unifi.it.

Francesco Beghelli holds a master's degree in development economics from the University of Florence. He is a professional working in the integration of migrants in Prato and cofounded Finyx, a company delivering audit services to foreign firms established in Prato and supporting public institutions and private organizations to reach migrants.

Paola Biasi (Ph.D., University of Florence) is a research grantholder at the University of Siena. She was a visiting researcher at IRPET and collaborated with the Econometrics and Applied Statistics Unit, at the European commission, DG Joint Research Centre. Her research interests include development economics, sustainability, regional development, and policy evaluation.

Francesco Capone (Ph.D., University of Florence) is an assistant professor in management at the Department of Economics and Management of the University of Florence. He is the member of the Doctorate Programme in Development Economics and Local Systems of the University of Florence and Trento. His recent research interests deal with firms and networks innovation and competitiveness in cluster and industrial districts. He published in Journal of Business Research, Industry and Innovation, European Planning Studies among others. He recently edited the book Tourist clusters, destinations, and competitiveness with Rutledge (2016).

Anja Fladrich is the associate dean, Holmes Institute, Melbourne. She has many years of experience working in the insurance and education sectors with large multinational companies, a government agency, and a family business in Germany, China, and Australia. Her Ph.D. at Monash University's Asia Institute investigated Chinese enterprises in Prato.

Susan Freeman (Ph.D., Monash University, Australia) is a professor of International Business at the University of South Australia Business School, Adelaide, Australia. Her research investigates the strategies of internationalizing entrepreneurial firms, as well as multinational companies and the development of autonomy by subsidiaries, from both advanced and emerging economy perspectives. Her work has been published in Management International Review, Journal of World Business, and Journal of International Marketing, among others.

Luciana Lazzeretti is a professor of economics and management of firms and founding director of the postgraduate programme in 'Economics and Management of Cultural Goods and Museums', University of Florence, and vice-coordinator of the doctorate programme Developing Economics and Local Systems of the University of Trento and Florence. According to multidisciplinary approaches, her current research interests deal with innovation networks, creative industries and clusters in local and global perspective, fashion industries and fashion city, urban and regional resilience, city and cluster transformation, and digitalization of cultural heritage and museums. She recently published in Journal of Economic Geography, International Journal of Urban and Regional Research, and Regional Studies, among others.

Matilde Milanesi is a research fellow at the University of Florence. She received her Ph.D. in economics in March, 2015, from the University of Florence with a thesis on liabilities in internationalization. Her research interests lie in the area of international business and international marketing, industrial marketing and buyer–supplier relationships, and fashion and luxury companies. She can be contacted at matilde.milanesi@unifi.it.

Xander Ong (Ph.D., Monash University, Australia) is an emerging international business researcher at Monash University. His research interests include the growing impact of the ethnic Chinese diaspora, ethnic entrepreneurship, cross-cultural management, and international strategy.

Adua Paciocco undertook graduate and undergraduate studies in Australian universities and completed a Ph.D. on the social identity construction of Chinese migrants in Prato through Monash University. She began her teaching career as a second language teacher of foreign languages and English language teacher in secondary schools in Melbourne (Australia), before taking up lecturing appointments in Australian tertiary institutions. She subsequently relocated to Italy where she has been lecturing in English in the Italian university system. She is an independent researcher in social identity formation, in particular migrant identity formation, and linguistic anthropology.

Stefano Rosignoli is a statistical researcher at IRPET (Regional Institute for Economic Planning of Tuscany). His main field concerns economic statistics and econometrics, national and regional economic accounts, building of regional input/output tables, Supply&Use and SAM (Social Accounting Matrices) and building of macroeconometric models for short-term forecast, and policy macroevaluation. He has worked also as econometrician in many economic national and international research project for UNICEF (United Nation Children's Fund), University of Ottawa (Canada), University of Florence, SVIMEZ (South-Italy Economic Development Association) and RES (Research Institute for the Sicilian Economy and Society).

Alberto Violante (Ph.D., Università Bicocca—Milan) is actually employed as researcher at the National Institute of Statistics (Istat). He had a postdoc grant at Università Sapienza—Rome. His areas of interest covered the interconnections between economic processes and urban territorial development. His work about Rome's urban development was published in a book, and he was the coauthor of many articles and chapters in edited books.

Min Zhang obtained her Ph.D. in management from the University of Huazhong University of Science and Technology (China). Her research used quantitative and qualitative techniques to capture the internal mechanism of Wenzhou immigrant entrepreneurs embedded in the overseas industry.

Yili Zhang (Ph.D., Xiamen University) is a professor of economics at the School of Business, Wenzhou University, in China. He has research interests in entrepreneurship and entrepreneur social network. His recent research work focuses on Wenzhounese businessmen around the world. He has published papers in the Journal of Sociological Studies (China).

Introduction

**Simone Guercini, Gabi Dei Ottati, Loretta Baldassar
and Graeme Johanson**

Abstract The international business and economics literature investigates the concepts of *foreignness* and *outsidership* as a source of liabilities for foreign firms. This introductory chapter discusses the genesis of this book and its structure, explaining the reasons for its multidisciplinary approach to studying the liabilities emerging in local contexts and relating to the separation between the immigrants and the native firms and communities. Immigrant entrepreneurship is an increasingly important phenomenon driven by growing immigration, entrepreneurial attitude diffusion among the immigrants, and the globalization of markets and supply chains. Immigrant entrepreneurs can experience liabilities similar to the liabilities of foreignness and of outsidership in their local networks, while being insiders to the global networks that are dominant in their specific industries and markets. Native entrepreneurs can experience a relative outsidership from the new global networks dominated by international entrepreneurship. The focus on local liabilities affords a unique perspective on the nature of globalization. Although the book applies the theme in reference to the case of Prato in Italy, the goal is to provide useful information to address a global phenomenon.

Keywords Foreignness · Outsidership · Native entrepreneurship · Immigrant entrepreneurship · Multidisciplinary approach

---

S. Guercini (✉) · G. Dei Ottati
University of Florence, Florence, Italy
e-mail: simone.guercini@unifi.it

G. Dei Ottati
e-mail: gabi.dei@unifi.it

L. Baldassar
University of Western Australia, Perth, Australia
e-mail: loretta.baldassar@uwa.edu.au

G. Johanson
Monash University, Melbourne, Australia
e-mail: graeme.johanson@monash.edu

© Springer International Publishing Switzerland 2017
S. Guercini et al. (eds.), *Native and Immigrant Entrepreneurship*,
DOI 10.1007/978-3-319-44111-5_1

1

> In the absence of special features, the enterprises operating in a country are likely to be national firms; for national firms are likely to have advantages over foreigner...National firms have the general advantage of better information about their country: its economy, its language, its law, and its politics. To a foreigner the cost of acquiring this information may be considerable. But note that it is a fixed cost, once incurred by establishing a foreign operation it need not be incurred again
>
> Hymer (1960, pp. 38–39).

> A firm that does not have a position in a relevant network is an 'outsider'. If a firm attempts to enter a foreign market where it has no relevant network position, it will suffer from the liability of outsidership and foreignness, and foreignness presumably complicates the process of becoming an insider
>
> Johanson and Vahlne (2009, p. 1415).

We live in an era of significant social challenges resulting from increasingly diverse migration movements that require the ability to deal with complex integration issues from different perspectives. The relationship between native and immigrant entrepreneurship is one such issue that has important local and global implications for businesses, the economy, and society. This book deals with the relationship between native and immigrant entrepreneurship in local contexts, examining the effects of cultural separation conditions, acculturation stress, and the outsidership of actors from social and business networks. These phenomena produce specific liabilities at the local level, but also bring opportunities that can deliver both business growth and economic development.

The authors examine these opportunities and challenges from various perspectives, as experts of different disciplines, including management, economics, sociology, and anthropology. Specifically, this book adopts a multidisciplinary approach to elucidate the problems, or liabilities, associated with outsidership in the sense not only of foreignness, but also of the exclusion from the most effective international social and business networks. The focus on local liabilities affords a unique perspective on the nature of globalization. Importantly, immigrant entrepreneurs can experience a liability of outsidership from local networks, yet may be insiders to the global networks that are dominant in specific industries and markets. Conversely, native entrepreneurs can experience a relative outsidership from the new global networks dominated by immigrant entrepreneurs. Although we address the outsidership theme with reference to specific regional and local contexts—especially the local system in Prato, Italy—the goal is to provide information that is widely applicable to this global phenomenon.

This book's genesis helps to explain the approach adopted. The book is the result of over 3 years of collaboration that began with the organization of a conference held in Prato (29–30 October 2013), titled *Chinese migration, entrepreneurship and development in the new global economy*. That conference combined the sixth *Chinese in Prato* and the fourth *Wenzhounese Diaspora Symposia* events: the Monash University Prato Centre, the University of Florence, and the European University Institute of Fiesole jointly organized the conference. The conference papers covered a variety of disciplines, including applied economics, industrial marketing, the sociology of migration, and the anthropology of migration.

The resulting collection of papers that emerged from the conference were as interesting as they were diverse, highlighting important disciplinary and method- ological differences that are not easily integrated into a single volume. This said, the challenge of finding common themes, analytical approaches, and conceptual frameworks only added to a shared appreciation for the richness of the overall results. This appreciation stimulated the ambition of the editors of this book to give life to an organic work on a focused theme.

In the months following the conference, as editors we thought it more useful to identify the main emerging themes and results of the presented research and to construct a volume to feature these, rather than simply publishing the conference's proceedings. We identified the most significant subject of focus as the comparison between native and migrant communities and entrepreneurship. This comparison is particularly evident in the case of the community of Chinese Wenzhounese immigrants and their relationship with the native Italian community in the industrial district of Prato.

Deliberation on the conference results continued through 2014 and 2015, with ongoing contact between the organizers and the authors. These deliberations led to the organization of a workshop designed to compare and develop a specific set of research themes, facilitated by the careful selection of the papers presented at the initial conference. This workshop, held from 3–4 December 2015 at the Monash University Prato Centre, was titled *Liabilities of native and immigrant entrepre- neurs in globalization: The case of Prato*. The workshop papers represented aca- demic advances around a central idea, focused on a paradox in the relationship between native entrepreneurship and migrant entrepreneurship: a paradox generated by the contrast between the two terms. On the one hand, strong liabilities are evident for both the people and the businesses of migrant communities in their relationship with the native-born Italian population. These liabilities are also apparent for the businesses and the people of native Italian communities in their relationship with migrants. On the other hand, there are concurrent clear signs of significant business and growth opportunities for all (both native and migrant) firms, and of more general socio-economic and human development. The latter outcomes can arise if the identified liabilities are resolved, or at least partly over- come. Each chapter of this book engages with the concept of liability: the liability that arises from the separation between the (so-called) native communities and the migrant communities who share the same territory. Our collaborative discussions and workshops highlighted how this liability results, in part, from the effects of the outsidership of the individual actors from the social and business networks in which the members of the other community (native or migrant) are embedded. Examining the liability of outsidership concept is a key theme of this book. The editors decided that additional inputs from specialists around the globe would demonstrate the importance of this theme.

The outsidership concept borrows from the literature of management and international business (Johanson and Vahlne 2009). Outsidership links with the well-studied liability of foreignness concept in the theory of multinational enter- prises (Hymer 1960). The liability of foreignness is the difficulty, or the burden, that those in contexts other than their own cultural and national milieu must address (Zaheer 1995; Johanson and Vahlne 1977). Generally, this liability features in contexts where business actors move into a foreign territory. Recent international business literatures stress the growing importance of the liability of outsidership phenomenon (Johanson and Vahlne 2009; Håkansson and Snehota 1995; Hilmersson and Jansson 2012). This liability is defined as the difficulties that must be addressed by those who are external to the most effective and important international networks, which are often more complex than the simple foreigner/local distinction.

By definition, the liability of foreignness refers to foreign actors who come from a different national context to their current settled context (either as multinational organizations or as entrepreneurs). The liability of outsidership refers to the actors (both local/native and foreign/migrant) and their connections (or lack of them) with the prominent social and business networks (including both local/native and foreign/international), that lead to a distinction between the outsiders and the insiders. Globalization makes it increasingly important for businesses to belong to a diversity of networks, some of which may be stronger than the networks of the dominant nationality in the market (Vahlne and Johanson 2013). Outsider liability is strongly linked to the study of the migrant business communities settled in different territories, and affects social and business networks, as highlighted in the literature on the role of weak ties (Granovetter 1973), and on the industrial district (Becattini 1990).

Given the increasing diversity of global migration flows and worker mobility, we believe that this book addresses a key issue for the corporate actors and for the policy makers at local, national and global levels. A case study can apply substantive observation and analysis to a more general phenomenon (Woodside 2010). In cases such as Prato, the immigrant entrepreneurs can experience a social local outsidership, while being insiders to the global networks that are dominant in the specific industries and markets. This situation is not new historically; however, it assumes a new importance in today's global business environment. In cases like Prato, the entrepreneurs rooted in the native cultures can experience a relative outsidership from the new global networks dominated by the community of immigrant entrepreneurs settled in their territory.

These different forms of local liabilities are central to the analyses and discussions that comprise this book. We consider that the local liabilities phenomenon is of central relevance beyond the specific case of Prato and of the Wenzhounese immigrant entrepreneurs. However, we also believe that Prato provides an excellent case to understand the relationships between various levels of the economy and society, and that it offers a prime example of current forms of globalization.

The book provides a rich and insightful content that clarifies what constitutes the local liabilities experienced in a local context by two different communities of people and businesses. The theme of local liabilities, its antecedents and its consequences, is clearly transdisciplinary. Hence, the book's chapters have a multidisciplinary frame, even when partly integrated by a shared research context. The thesis that emerges from the book is that local liabilities are not only an empirical phenomenon, but that they also correspond to a concept interwoven with the well-studied individual components (foreignness, outsidership).

The liabilities related to local liabilities point to pressing contemporary concerns. Such liabilities may be strong enough to prevent the integration—not only in terms of social networks, but also in terms of business networks—of both the native and the migrant populations. At the same time, it is important that we understand that local liabilities are central to harnessing the opportunities offered by globalization itself.

This book comprises 12 chapters, including this introduction and the final remarks. In the next chapter, the editors discuss some central ideas (liabilities, separation, outsidership, and integration opportunities). The following three chapters examine some of the central issues that shape the Chinese community in Italy, and the specific case of Prato. These chapters provide useful data for the interpretation of the phenomenon at an economic and sociological level, switching from Barberis and Violante's national frame, to Biasi and Rosignoli's focus on the local economy, and finally to Becucci's ethnographic study of the immigrant business community active in the manufacture of clothing in Prato.

Paciocco and Baldassar and Johanson, Beghelli and Fladrich provide two different sociological perspectives of separation between immigrant Chinese and native Italians. The chapters focus, respectively, on the friendship networks and the associations of the new generation of (school age) immigrants, and on the use and impact of mobile communication technologies (smartphones) on the relationship networks. Both chapters explore the practices and processes that facilitate intra-ethnic versus inter-ethnic communication and exchange, from local and transnational perspectives.

The subsequent chapters examine managerial and international business issues. Guercini and Milanesi deal with the liabilities of foreignness and of outsidership in the international business literature, and their local implications. Lazzeretti and Capone examine the results of a survey on the demographics of the population of failed firms in Prato. Zhang and Zhang and Ong and Freeman explore the relational and business issues of Chinese migrant entrepreneurship. They address the role of *guanxi* (the Chinese network of interpersonal relationships) on the sustainability, importance, and evolution of migrant entrepreneurship, as well as on the development of new competences and relationships with native entrepreneurship.

Finally, the last chapter (authored by the editors) takes stock of the relationship between native and immigrant entrepreneurship from the studies presented in the book. The chapter considers what is actually happening in practice, as well as the aspirations and hopes for future developments. Achieving improved outcomes for both migrant and native communities requires the active participation by the business community and by political actors. We need such participation to challenge the paradox inherent in the local liabilities, and to address successfully a common challenge faced by many places experiencing globalization.

References

Becattini G (1990) The Marshallian industrial district as a socio-economic notion. In: Pyke F, Becattini G, Sengenberger W (eds) Industrial districts and inter-firm co-operation in Italy. International Institute for Labour Studies, Geneva, pp 37–51

Granovetter MS (1973) The strength of weak ties. Am J Sociol 78(6):1360–1380

Håkansson H, Snehota I (eds) (1995) Developing relationships in business networks. Routledge, London

Hilmersson M, Jansson H (2012) International network extension processes to institutionally different markets: entry nodes and processes of exporting SMEs. Int Bus Rev 21(4):682–693

Hymer SH (1960) The international operations of national firms: a study of direct foreign investment. Ph.D. dissertation, published in 1976, MIT Press, Cambridge

Johanson J, Vahlne JE (1977) The internationalization process of the firm-a model of knowledge development and increasing foreign market commitments. J Int Bus Stud, 23–32

Johanson J, Vahlne JE (2009) The Uppsala internationalization process model revisited: from liability of foreignness to liability of outsidership. J Int Bus Stud 40(9):1411–1431

Vahlne JE, Johanson J (2013) The Uppsala model on evolution of the multinational business enterprise-from internalization to coordination of networks. Int Mark Rev 30(3):189–210

Woodside AG (2010) Case study research: theory, methods and practice. Emerald Group Publishing, Bingley

Zaheer S (1995) Overcoming the liability of foreignness. Acad Manag J 38(2):341–363

Liabilities of Native and Immigrant Entrepreneurship in the Processes of Globalization

Simone Guercini, Gabi Dei Ottati, Loretta Baldassar
and Graeme Johanson

Abstract This chapter introduces the main issues addressed in the book by examining the liabilities of native and immigrant entrepreneurship in local contexts from a multidisciplinary perspective. Immigration leads to the presence of different cultures in the same place of settlement. This may push immigrant entrepreneurship into ethnic enclaves because of discrimination and racism. However, through globalization, native entrepreneurship can also lose centrality and become peripheral in global markets compared with the transnational networks. Both groups (immigrants and natives) can experience liabilities of outsidership, and acculturation stress. The local liabilities are associated with costs, competitiveness losses, and missed business opportunities. These liabilities may significantly affect the development of Prato's industrial district, on which the city's economic prosperity relies. The liabilities of native and immigrant entrepreneurship are so many and so varied, that they do not solely concern market relationships. Considering the second generation of immigrants adds another layer of complexity to analyzing the local liabilities. The second generation hold great promise for the improved integration of the Chinese community in Prato in the future. The radical social transformation provided by smartphones and similar technologies, can help immigrants to maintain contacts and business with their community of origin. We propose examining the local liabilities of native and immigrant entrepreneurship in terms of degrees of outsidership, rather than from clearly bounded positions of insidership or

S. Guercini (✉) · G. Dei Ottati
University of Florence, Florence, Italy
e-mail: simone.guercini@unifi.it

G. Dei Ottati
e-mail: gabi.dei@unifi.it

L. Baldassar
University of Western Australia, Perth, Australia
e-mail: loretta.baldassar@uwa.edu.au

G. Johanson
Monash University, Melbourne, Australia
e-mail: graeme.johanson@monash.edu

© Springer International Publishing Switzerland 2017
S. Guercini et al. (eds.), *Native and Immigrant Entrepreneurship*,
DOI 10.1007/978-3-319-44111-5_2

7

outsidership. Finally, we compare the disciplinary points, providing a broad context for the chapters that follow.

Keywords Local liability · Native entrepreneurship · Immigrant entrepreneurship · Outsidership · Industrial district · Chinese migration · Italian immigration

1 Introduction

Significant and increasing global migration flows and the spread of entrepreneurial propensity among migrants have resulted in the coexistence of native entrepreneurship and migrant entrepreneurship in many local contexts. The native entrepreneurship concept refers to the business activities of the so-called native population (also known as the host-country nationals) already settled in a territory.[1] The growth of the number of migrant entrepreneurs present in a territory and the success achieved by migrant businesses in markets not only locally, but nationally and globally, make migrant entrepreneurship an important phenomenon from an economic and managerial point of view as well as sociologically and anthropologically (Waldinger 1986). In local contexts, migrant entrepreneurship can coexist with native entrepreneurship. Native entrepreneurship traditionally benefits from its position as the incumbent embedded in the settlement. However, native entrepreneurship may see its central position become peripheral in globalizing markets, while the migrant firms may have less psychological distance from the emerging markets and the high insidership in the transnational networks (Johanson and Vahlne 2009).

As a concept, entrepreneurship is linked to the notions of: entrepreneur, innovation, organization creation, creating value, profit or no profit, growth, uniqueness, and being the owner-manager (Gartner 1990). The term *entrepreneurship* is distinct from the terms *firm* and *entrepreneur* (Schumpeter 1934), and is used here to define a general phenomenon involving individuals linked to communities and networks of relationships. Distinguishing native entrepreneurship from migrant entrepreneurship does not automatically imply different business models or entrepreneurial profiles. The characteristics of the native companies can differ from, as well as be similar to, those of the migrant businesses, as can the profiles of the entrepreneurs belonging to each group.

There are frequent debates on the complex convergences and divergences of entrepreneurship in migrant settings, and recent research on different cultural contexts highlights the importance of the cultural dimension in entrepreneurship theory (Thomas and Mueller 2000). Such entrepreneurship converges (or diverges)

---

[1]Given the multidisciplinary approach adopted in this book, the term *native* has different meanings and connotations in the various disciplines that comprise the social sciences. This book uses *native* to refer to the local majority host-country settler population. In the case of Prato, native refers to those people who consider themselves Pratese. This said, such groups are often far from homogeneous, and can include diverse provincial, regional, urban, rural, and even national divisions.

because the characteristics of the native companies can be similar to, as well as different from, those of the migrant companies, as can the profiles of the entrepreneurs belonging to each group. The role and characteristics of entrepreneurship in different cultures is complex, and is beyond the scope of this book. Culture's characteristics can be indicators of the community's entrepreneurial role, even if only for the ways in which a particular cultural community responds to the uncertainty related to innovation, or experiences an individualism-collectivism relationship (Hofstede 1980).

Immigration leads to the presence in the same territory of different cultures of entrepreneurship that can generate a process of acculturation. This acculturation process influences both the migrants and the natives, especially when there is a close relationship between the migration and the spread of entrepreneurship among migrants (as is the case in Prato). In migration contexts, the business environment is affected by the presence of actors from different cultural backgrounds—implying a diversity of opportunities, resources, and actual or potential customers with varying degrees of psychological and cultural distance—not unlike those that can be found in foreign markets (Shenkar 2001; Sousa and Bradley 2006).

There is a greater predisposition or propensity toward entrepreneurship in some national communities and ethnic groups than in others. This is particularly important in migrant settings in which the entrepreneurial attitude of the migrants influences the profile of the ethnic firms (Aldrich and Waldinger 1990). Research in this area is more focused on the sociological dimension of this phenomenon than on its management dimension, although some research considers the entrepreneur profiles with reference to specific ethnic groups (Weidenbaum 1996) and to national communities (Siu 1995).

It is possible to link the growth of immigrant entrepreneurship to the development of an ethnic economy that has the essential resources for the development of the ethnic community (labor, financing, market outlets), as in the case of ethnic enclaves (Portes and Jensen 1987). Migrant entrepreneurship can be a self-employment choice in response to the difficulties of integration and the lack of employment opportunities. This is especially evident in the case of migrants who have a cultural background characterized by a psychological distance from the host nation, and/or by difficulties in communicating with the native actors. This said, migrant entrepreneurship can also be competitive outside of ethnic enclaves and the community market. However, even in these cases, the migrant community tends to be a vital pool of resources, and a source of advantage to access transnational networks and opportunities that are often difficult for the native counterparts to secure (Riddle and Brinkerhoff 2011). This phenomenon often materializes as a middleman (Bonacich 1973) or a cultural mediator (Reynolds and Zontini 2014).

The ethnic or migrant community factor can facilitate connections and continuous interactions between people who share a cultural background, because they belong to a particular national reality and share common experiences of migration. These connections can be especially important to the development of entrepreneurial roles, favoring the recognition and exploitation of opportunities both in terms of the settlement context and in larger contexts, owing to the transnational nature of community relationships. There are many migrant entrepreneurship studies, not only from the perspective of the migrant actors but also from the perspective of the host society. However, as globalization intensifies, this phenomenon now requires the simultaneous consideration of both migrants and natives. As this book highlights, both of those groups experience liabilities of outsidership and forms of acculturation stress.

The community's boundaries (both migrant and native) may limit the identification, and especially the realization, of the opportunities generated through migration. This can generate competition between cultural groups arising from a combination of factors, including access to resources and success in the export markets (Bruderl and Schussler 1990; Guercini 2010). The entrepreneurship phenomenon is particularly relevant here, because it highlights the difficulties related to the conditions of separation, distance, and outsidership, produced in local contexts because of massive flows of immigrants (Schweizer 2013; Smans 2012).

To study the relationship between native and immigrant entrepreneurship, we propose the notion of local liability; a notion we develop from the international business literature, with conceptual links to sociology and anthropology. Studying the local liability notion requires a consideration of its possible resolution, and includes an appreciation of its antecedents and its consequences.

2   Acculturation and Liabilities in Relationships Between Native and Immigrant Entrepreneurship

Globalization processes not only create bridges between distant places, but they also change the face of businesses and socio-economic systems at the local level. This book proposes the concept of local liabilities that may emerge when two (or more) separate communities (of persons and firms) exist in the same place. Generally, the greater the separation between the communities, the greater the local liabilities. While this is a commonly recognized aspect of globalization, it is inadequately studied (Guercini 2016).

The liability concept comes from the international business literature, where notions of foreignness, and more recently outsidership, are widely addressed (Zaheer 1995; Johanson and Vahlne 2009). Local liabilities refer to the separation between natives and immigrants in the development of local networks of people and firms. Such separation, and the problems that it causes, hinders the process of integration and the development of thriving economies. Liabilities are experienced by the individual actors (micro level), but have antecedents and consequences at economic and societal levels (macro level). This book proposes a multidisciplinary approach to the issue of local liabilities by analyzing the case of Chinese migrants in the Italian district of Prato. It offers a framework through which to view the problems involved, as well as possible paths for their analysis and transformation.

We first examine more closely what local liability means. To do this we must consider the implications of the coexistence of native and migrant entrepreneurship. A useful starting point is an examination of the acculturation process (drawing on Berry's classic thesis—Berry 1969) and its impact on business processes.

2.1 Acculturation Process and Entrepreneurship

What impact does the presence of native entrepreneurship and immigrant entrepreneurship have on the generation and exploitation of opportunities for the development of the local system and its firms? It is possible to address this question both conceptually and empirically. For example, at a conceptual level, the structural holes concept locates the missing steps in networks that may correspond to the creation of opportunities and new combinations (Burt 1990). The separation between communities in the same place may correspond to the presence of structural holes, creating challenges and opportunities at the same time.

During the acculturation process, entrepreneurs and businesses need to learn and adapt, and must meet the accompanying costs and difficulties. Acculturation is a "*culture change which results from continuous, first hand contact between two distinct cultural groups*" (Berry et al. 1987, pp. 491–492; Redfield et al. 1936). Acculturation can also affect business processes. Entrepreneurs are interested in, and impacted by, acculturation processes at both personal and professional levels. We can also identify an organizational level of acculturation, such as the settlement of multinational subsidiaries in culturally distant contexts (Perlmutter 1969). Although their institutional framework is that of their country of origin, local businesses may have fewer material resources and knowledge to address acculturation compared with multinational companies. Thus, acculturation may offer opportunities; however, it can also be a source of stress at the individual, group, and organizational levels.

The concept of stress arises in the psychology and medicine disciplines (Berry et al. 1987). Stress influences both the physiological and psychological state of an organism. The normal functioning of the organism requires a reduction of stress, through the removal of the conditions that generate it, or through a satisfactory adaptation to the new situation. In acculturation, stress can be positive or negative, based on the antecedents of the acculturation and its implications. In fact, a condition of stress can support an intense learning phase, but can also absorb resources and generate costs. Acculturative stress is a particular stress "*...in which the stressors are identified as having their source in the process of acculturation*" (Berry et al. 1987, p. 492).

The changes brought about by acculturation can have a physical and a biological impact on the individuals involved. Further, the changes can have a psychological impact at the social and cultural level, with implications for the relationships between the actors involved. The impact of acculturative stress can be moderated by several factors, including: the nature of the larger society; the type of acculturating group; the mode of acculturation; the demographic and social characteristics of the individual (for example, young and old people may respond to the acculturative process differently); and the psychological characteristics of individuals (Berry et al. 1987, p. 493).

Specifically considering acculturation groups, it is possible to recognize different types. Berry and Kim (1987) identify five acculturation group types: (1) immigrants, (2) refugees, (3) native (local) peoples, (4) ethnic groups, and (5) sojourners. There are two dimensions for analyzing these groups: the *voluntariness of contact* and the *degree of mobility*. Here, *contact* means the interface with components of other cultural (ethnic) groups. Immigrants correspond to a high degree of both voluntariness of contact and degree of mobility (migrants). However, the natives (locals) seem to experience a low degree of voluntariness of contact (involuntary) and a low degree of mobility (sedentary). Hence, the immigrants have certain similarities with the sojourners. However, the sojourners have a temporary perspective, while the immigrants have a relatively permanent approach to the context of settlement (Fig. 1).

We examine acculturation stress at the level of the individuals and of the groups belonging to a culture. With reference to entrepreneurial activity, this can also relate to the voluntariness of contact and the degree of mobility, because the search for a context in which to do business can result in a certain degree of mobility and a desire to connect with other individuals and groups. In this sense, from the moment that the migration process begins, the migrant's aim is to start an enterprise. Similarly, there are also native (local) people who exhibit a high entrepreneurial attitude, but may not be involved in a search for a new context. The relationship between migration and entrepreneurship can be particularly important in the case of the sojourners. For sojourners, the entrepreneurial attitude, or at least the search for business opportunities, leads to a continuous migration, given the relatively temporary nature of their stay (Berry and Kim 1987).

Many sociology studies of immigrant businesses examine the factors that affect migrant entrepreneurship. We can summarize these factors as a combination of

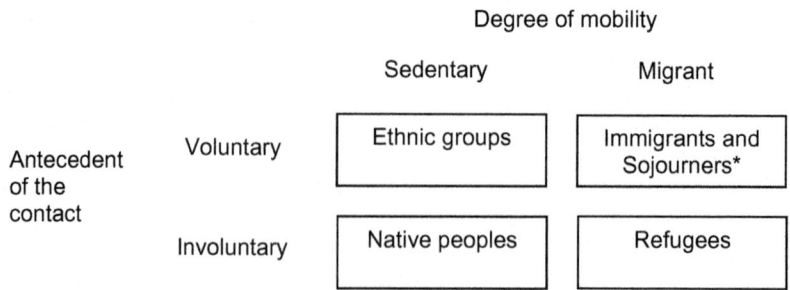

*The immigrants are relatively permanent, while the sojourners are temporary

Fig. 1 Acculturative groups (adapted from Berry et al. 1987, p. 495)

choice, chance, or no option (also known as survival, or opportunity entrepreneurship, cf. Chrysostome 2010). Depending on the political, social, and economic context of the receiving society, the immigrants may have little or no choice but to develop work opportunities within their own community (see, for example, Light and Bachu 1993; Kloosterman et al. 1998). The mixed embeddedness theory explores the migrants' integration in both the social networks of migrants and of the receiving society (Kloosterman and Rath 2001; Aliaga-Isla and Rialp 2013).

The barriers to the job market can include racism and discrimination from the native population, often because of the perceived or real threat of competition. These barriers are often compounded by migration and social policy that might, for example, limit the recognition of qualifications, essentially forcing migrants into self-employment ventures. Difficulties with the language, no creditworthiness, and poor access to bank loans are further factors that increase ethnic segregation in particular occupational niches. Migrant entrepreneurship and small business ownership can often provide the only opportunities for economic advancement. Families and community members can pool their resources so that they do not need a bank loan, and they often work for low (or even no) pay or entitlements to keep their running costs to a minimum. These processes increase the likelihood of migrant residential segregation (the development of enclaves). In turn, enclaves facilitate the establishment of niche markets, providing culturally appropriate services to the migrant community. In this environment, the host-country language and cultural skills are not essential, and the migrants can thrive in a relatively closed community.

Further, the degree to which the migration is voluntary can influence the conditions of contact, in the sense that the migration precedes the contact and is the result of an actor's choice. However, this does not mean that maintaining relationships with other groups is not valuable. Various acculturation pathways account for the value that migrants place on maintaining or generating relationships with their (ethnic) community of origin and with the native (and other) communities of the settlement area. This value depends on the social and political context of settlement, and on how the receiving society perceives the migrants, which also influences the degree of agency the migrants may have to foster ties. There may be situations where the value of a relationship with the other groups is considered limited, and situations where a relationship with the other groups is highly valued (Fig. 2). The mixed embeddedness theory explores the migrants' integration both in the social networks of migrants as well as in those of the receiving society (Kloosterman and Rath 2001; Aliaga-Isla and Rialp 2013).

In addition to the value of the relationship with the other groups, the mode of acculturation may depend on the perceived value of sustaining the identity and cultural characteristics of the group of origin. That given value, both at the individual and group level, may be high or low. Both the value of maintaining relationships with the other groups and the value of maintaining cultural identity and characteristics are important elements. These elements are important not only in cross-cultural studies, but also for the development of entrepreneurship, where the value of the

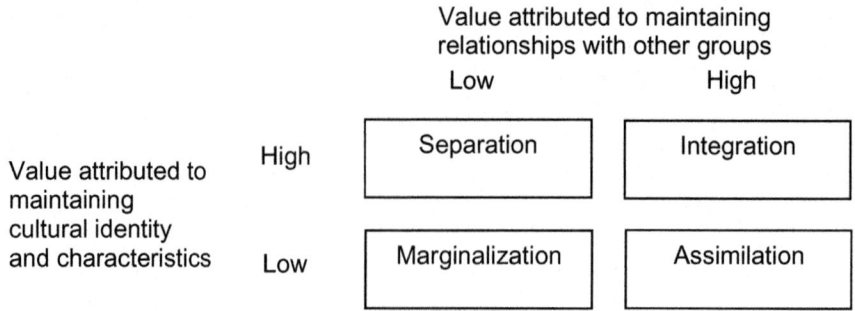

Fig. 2 Mode of acculturation (adapted from Berry et al. 1987, p. 496)

elements can significantly affect the resources, relationships, and business networks. This aspect can be true at both the group level and at the individual level (Fig. 2).

Therefore, acculturation stress links in various ways to the role of entrepreneurship in the migration process, as well as to the specific conditions of the host nation and of the native (local) people. Accordingly, the study of acculturation stress should include both the immigrants and the natives, particularly where there is intense migration and intense economic competition in the business community between migrants and natives, as is the case in Prato.

The acculturation model offers an interesting framework with which to examine the separation of psychological and cultural distance and outsidership, which is characteristic of a place and its migration history. Therefore, this book carefully examines the liabilities associated with the presence of a range of entrepreneurial communities in the same local context. We do this because, just as for the conditions of acculturation stress, there may be a need for adaptation that will imply costs related to the conditions of foreignness and outsidership, as discussed in this book in the chapter authored by Guercini and Milanesi.

2.2 Liabilities Between Native and Immigrant Entrepreneurship

The term liability is associated with disadvantages that determine specific costs and that reduce competitiveness. The term is particularly used in the field of international business studies, in connection with the ecology of organizations, as highlighted in this book by Lazzeretti and Capone. Specifically, in management literature liability is associated with additional costs and with the probability of failure, starting from the antecedents that qualify the type of liability.

Liabilities in internationalization can be defined as difficulties faced by firms when they internationalize in search of new markets. Such liabilities include the liability of foreignness and the liability of outsidership (Johanson and Vahlne 2009).

The chapter authored by Barberis and Violante, in this book, analyzes the international business literature on this issue. In this current chapter, we describe the general characteristics associated with the concept of local liabilities.

Local liabilities refer to the higher costs and/or the lower competitiveness that emerge in contexts in which there are two or more separate communities (people and/or companies). Thus, the conditions for local liability include the presence of other separate communities, and that the acculturation mode corresponds mainly to separation. If there are other forms of acculturation (such as integration or assimilation), then the conditions that generate costs and/or lack of competitiveness can be significantly different, and the local liabilities may be wholly or partially overcome. Another case is the marginalization mode of acculturation, where individuals or groups are not valued, also exhibits the loss of value for the identity and the culture of origin. This leads to the weakening of (if not to the absence of) separate communities, because individuals or marginalized groups can create social costs, but do not form distinct communities that are active in the local context.

Hence, in studying the difficulties associated with the presence of local liabilities, the contexts characterized by separation are the most interesting of the many forms of acculturation. Further, the contexts characterized by significant immigrant entrepreneurship success are especially interesting. In these situations, the native entrepreneurs also feel the local liabilities, not just the immigrant entrepreneurs.

The local liabilities concept relates to the generation of specific costs (Grant 1991) and to the loss of competitive capability (Porter 1986). Particularly, local liabilities produce at least three categories of costs. (1) The additional costs of adapting to an environment where interactions may occur, and where there are cultural elements other than those already learned in the immigrants' culture of origin. (2) The figurative costs related to the non-achieved, but existing, opportunities for the local actors; such opportunities are not accessible because of difficulties communicating and cooperating with elements of the other culture. (3) Other costs, such as those related to resolving the conflicts produced by the coexistence of different cultural groups, and more generally to resolving the difficulties produced by the presence of different cultural groups in the same place. The other modes of acculturation also contain forms of stress; however, for separation acculturation, the local liabilities related to the figurative costs for unrealized opportunities are particularly high. This is because separate networks form inside each community, and everyone remains an outsider to at least one network.

The relative loss of the competitive capacity connected to the occurrence of local liabilities has at least three sources: (1) low competitiveness owing to high costs; (2) low competitiveness in relation to gaps in the exchange of creative contributions; and (3) low competitiveness in relation to closing the networking of relationships. The loss of competitiveness stems primarily from the aforementioned higher cost conditions that the actors in the local environment are bearing, relating to the conditions of separation between communities and between native and immigrant entrepreneurship. These high costs derive from the cost of communicating in foreign languages, and from investing in the necessary resources to overcome the difficulties in understanding the rules and implications of the other culture. Moreover, a competitive capacity loss can occur because of the barriers relating to an exchange of content, and to realizing the opportunities that derive from the particular separation situation. Accordingly, a locally made offer will be less differentiated than an offer made elsewhere. Local liabilities produce a barrier to the combination of local elements from separate communities as a means to differentiate offering. This implies that such a local liability is a weakness in global markets (Cavusgil and Guercini 2014).

This loss in competitiveness related with local liabilities is a source of disadvantage in comparison with situations where there is no plurality of separate communities. However, it can also be a source of disadvantage in comparison with situations where plural business communities have overcome the condition of separation. The separation condition can limit the creative capacity for various reasons. (1) A low level of communication between the actors of the two communities. (2) The lack of acceptance by the business actors of the creative products resulting from the communication between the different cultures. (3) The lack of legitimization of such hybrid results by the local networks and by the community market. The lack of a relationship or a partnership between local actors (intra-local but inter-community) that could generate contacts and opportunities also affects competitiveness. Figure 3 synthesizes the costs and the competitive impact of local liabilities.

The liability related to having several entrepreneurial communities in the same local area, concerns both the cultural distance perceived locally and the relevant outsidership from the other community networks. Foreignness is a fundamental concept in multinational enterprise theory, where it relates to the additional costs sustained by a multinational's subsidiaries in foreign markets (Zaheer 1995). Both liabilities (foreignness and outsidership) are relevant to the conditions of outsidership occurring (Johanson and Vahlne 2009). The presence of separation does not exclude the possibility that there are significant transactions between native and immigrant entrepreneurship. Such transactions can correspond to weak ties (Granovetter 1973) at a local cluster level; however, the ties are often weaker than the ethnic ties within the immigrant and transnational communities (Zaheer et al. 2009).

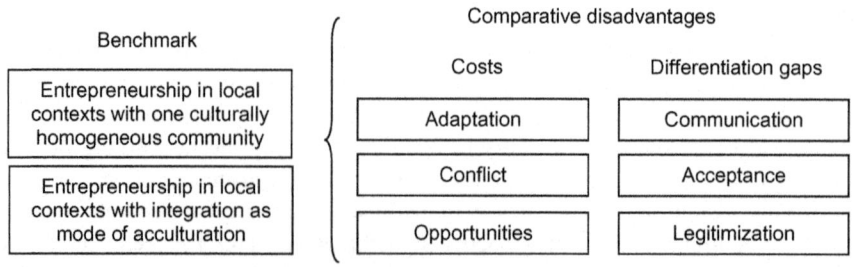

Fig. 3 Disadvantages of local liabilities (authors' synthesis)

The presence of several communities in the same local environment is not just the product of immigration. Historical reasons can generate local liabilities perceived at the entrepreneurial level: for example, in areas where two (or more) communities are historically separate (such as in Balkan regions). In that case, if the separation also produces entrepreneurship-wide effects, then it produces additional costs—or at least the loss of access benefits to other community resources because of psychological distance or outsidership. In that case, there are many communities with different cultures in the same territory, each with (relatively, because of weak ties) separate networks. Such networks can be at the transaction level or at the individual relationship level.

The presence of two (or more) communities in a territory not only produces liabilities, but is also a source of advantage for both native and migrant entrepreneurship. The sources of advantage arise from access to human resources at low costs, an additional specific market (because migrants can be suppliers or customers of other businesses), and a broader local market than before immigration.

3 Impact of Migrant Entrepreneurship on the Evolutionary Processes of the Industrial District

Giacomo Becattini rediscovered the Marshallian industrial district concept during his research on the industrialization of Tuscany in the 1970s. He defines the industrial district as:

> …a socio-territorial entity which is characterized by the active presence of both a community of people and a population of firms in one…area. In the district, unlike in other environments such as manufacturing towns, community and firms tend to merge.
>
> Becattini (1990, p. 38).

Drawing on 18 years of research on Prato (Becattini 1997), he concludes that the study of the district, because of its complexity and continuous change, can be categorized into several evolutionary processes. The most important evolutionary processes of the industrial district are: (1) the division of labor among enterprises; (2) the flexible integration of the division of labor; (3) the integration of the contextual knowledge with the new external knowledge; and (4) the conscious governance by the formal institutions so that there is coherence between the evolution of the district's production system and the local society (Becattini 2001, pp. 51–54; Dei Ottati 2002). This coherence is necessary to encourage the social forces to cooperate with the economic forces (Marshall 1920, p. 276), so that the many specialized firms integrate into an organic whole. Hence, the district firms can enjoy economies of scale, of learning, and of innovation in the form of external economies.

Globalization means exponential increases in the international flows of capital and goods, and in the movement of people. Thus, foreign migration affected the Italian industrial districts, especially after the 1990s. The presence of many immigrant entrepreneurs in an industrial district influences the division of labor, because the immigrant entrepreneurs tend to enter the local economy as the sub-contractors to the district's final firms (that is, those firms specialized in marketing the district's products) in the most labor-intensive activities of the main industry. This insertion of immigrant businesses exacerbates the price competition in the local markets, because the migrant entrepreneurs are willing to work for conditions that are unacceptable to the native subcontractors. Such insertion increases the local liabilities, because it gives rise to costs of adaptation to a different culture. It also fosters costs relating to social conflicts between immigrants and natives, and between those natives positively affected by the presence of immigrants versus those adversely affected. Moreover, unbridled competition in the local markets undermines the balance between competition and cooperation. An equal balance underpins the flexible integration of the division of labor in the industrial district (Becattini 1990; Dei Ottati 1986), and the possible reproduction over time of the district as a competitive form of organization.

In specific cases, such as in the Prato district, the immigrant entrepreneurs enter a market niche that differs to the main local industry. This gives rise to the immi-grants' own ethnic niche (Waldinger 1994) and to a socio-economic system with few and weak ties with the native entrepreneurship.

The production system of an industrial district is formed by many small firms specialized in the various phases of a main industry and in related activities. The division of labor among the firms means that they must interact frequently, and must cooperate with one another. This mode of integration, and the large number of operators that share the same industrial and social culture, generate an environment in which information, knowledge, and tacit knowledge circulate easily among the many subjects involved in production and exchange. Therefore, the environment of a thriving industrial district is rich in contextual knowledge. Alfred Marshall introduced what he called an industrial atmosphere to describe this setting: *"The mysteries of the trade become no mysteries; but are as it were in the air, and children learn many of them unconsciously"* (Marshall 1920, p. 156). The industrial atmosphere is very important for the competitiveness of a district and of its firms: it facilitates reciprocal learning and innovations in products, processes, and organi-zations. However, to generate the positive effects of an industrial atmosphere, it is necessary to integrate the contextual knowledge with the new external knowledge (Becattini and Rullani 1993). The need for such integration has increased with the global economy, because the pace of change in demand and technology has accelerated, and competition has become global.

We see how the presence of immigrant entrepreneurship generates social con-flicts within the district, fierce competition in local markets, and an almost separate socio-economic system. These phenomena hamper the normal working of the evolutionary processes, and hence the successful development of the district.[2] This outcome magnifies the local liability and prevents the circulation of knowledge and information not only between the immigrant and the native entrepreneurs, but also among the native entrepreneurs themselves, because of the erosion of trust. In the medium term, this situation can result in a lock-in and a decline of the entire district, even if in the short term some local enterprises can take advantage of the presence of immigrant subcontractors. Additionally, if the immigrant entrepreneurs remain separate from the native entrepreneurship networks, then they cannot upgrade their products and technology; consequently, they also risk lock-in in the longer term (see the chapter authored by Zhang and Zhang in this book).

Contrastingly, if the local and immigrant liabilities are overcome and the two populations (firms and people) integrate, than a new, more complex, and trans-national socio-economic system might form; a system that is more suited to the global economy. However, the liabilities of native and immigrant entrepreneurship are so many and so significant that it is not possible to deal with them by market relations alone. It needs the conscious governance by the formal institutions of both communities to address the liabilities. Political institutions and trade associations must deliberately help the process of acculturation. They can do this by creating opportunities for economic and social interactions, and by mediating any conflicts between the two populations. If integration occurs, than the best developmental processes of the district will revitalize and competitiveness will eventually regain. It is also possible, as in the case of the Silicon Valley-Taiwan connection, that a trans-national industrial district can be established (Hsu and Saxenian 2000).

4   Immigrants, Second Generation and Integration: Liabilities from a Sociological Perspective

Considering the second generation adds another layer of complexity to the analysis of local liabilities, not least because it further complicates the distinction between native and immigrant entrepreneurs and businesses. The second-generation category is itself heterogeneous. The second generation includes those individuals born in the sending areas but who arrived in the host country at a young age (the so-called 1.5 generation), as well as those individuals who were born and raised in the receiving society. In Prato, the second-generation Chinese self-identify is a mix of Italian-Pratese and Chinese-Wenzhounese, particularly those who are educated in the Italian school system and who make regular and lengthy visits to their extended family in China (Marsden 2014; Pedone 2013a, b; Paciocco 2015; Paciocco and

---

[2]In Prato's case, its local textile industry had already lost competitiveness mainly because of cost competition from products made in new industrializing countries. This caused difficulties in the processes of reproduction of the industrial district as a model of organization, independently from the massive inflow of Chinese immigrants to the area.

Baldassar in this book). This said, the dominant politics of identity in Italy is such that despite their self-ascribed mix of identities, the broader immigrant population tend to define them as exclusively Chinese (Raffaetà et al. 2015; Baldassar and Raffaetà 2017).

Recent research by Paciocco (2015) shows that many second-generation Chinese in Prato aspire to occupy middle or senior management roles in both Chinese and Italian-run businesses in the region and beyond (for a fuller discussion, see the chapter authored by Paciocco and Baldassar in this book). In her study, the so-called 1.5 individuals intend to become translators and interpreters, drawing on their multilingual competencies to achieve a degree of upward social mobility by occupying white-collar positions. The second-generation individuals who complete all of their schooling in Italy and who have a high command of Italian are even better placed than the 1.5 generation to become cultural brokers (Reynolds and Zontini 2014). They have the necessary skills and network ties to operate in both Italian and Chinese businesses. In terms of the liabilities of outsidership, these second-generation individuals could potentially be insiders in both native and immigrant entrepreneurial endeavors. Their mix of identities and double cultural competences suggest the need to examine the liabilities of entrepreneurship in terms of degrees of outsidership, rather than from clearly bounded positions of insider or outsider.

The degree of insider-outsider status is also relevant to the analysis of the acculturation processes. Presumably, the second generation have a different, and perhaps more intensive, experience of acculturation (through their schooling) than their parents. Certainly, their role as cultural mediators is evident at a macro level in the form of the very active Chinese-Italian second-generation association, *Associna*. Associna promotes cultural understanding and awareness through its website and its public initiatives. Contrastingly, the Prato Province and the Monash University Prato Centre jointly published two collections of youth stories. These publications contain submissions from Prato second-generation Chinese who describe the parental pressure to leave school so that they can help the family businesses using their Italian language skills; a pressure not necessarily welcomed by the young people (Liao 2013, p. 135; Wu 2014, p. 49). In other submissions, Chinese teenagers complain that their parents—and first-generation Chinese migrants in general—do not speak Italian. This suggests that the second generation may experience the role of cultural mediator as a challenging one, foisted upon them by community expectations rather than by personal choice. While they are capable of acting as a bridge between Chinese and native Italian business networks, they may find this role limiting in terms of alternative career aspirations.

These complex identity and cultural configurations reveal that second-generation individuals may claim and experience a degree of insidership to both Chinese and Italian networks. However, they may simultaneously experience a degree of outsidership from both, given their specific identity positions as a mix of both Chinese and Italian. Sociology studies define the ambiguity of the second-generation subject position as a hybrid, or a third, space. That is, a cultural space that differs from the networks and spaces in both the host and the home countries. Alejandro Portes and colleagues' classic work (Portes and Jensen 1987) on segmented assimilation examines similar issues of belonging and identity for various migrant groups in the United States. They highlight the factors that facilitate and impede social mobility, including those outlined above (Haller et al. 2011; Alba and Waters 2011).

The fundamental question is whether the presence of the second generation can help to resolve or to overcome the liabilities of outsidership in Prato. This question is particularly relevant in the future, when presumably greater numbers of bilingual and bicultural Chinese-background individuals will be fully ensconced in various sectors of the Italian labor market. There may also be a mediation role for the young Italians who have grown up and gone to school with young Chinese-background individuals. Those Italians have developed relationships and accumulated cross-cultural knowledge about their Chinese counterparts. Certainly, the second generation, along with their ties and their relationships with young Italians, hold great promise for the improved integration of the Chinese community in Prato.

5   Sociology of the Economics of Outsidership/Insidership and of Networks

The early theorists on human development frequently had both economic and sociological interests, sharing common foundational concerns. There were many such theorists, including Adam Smith, Jeremy Bentham, John Stuart Mill, Harriet Martineau, Karl Marx, Friedrich Engels, Beatrice Webb, Arnold Toynbee, and Max Weber (Merton 1972; Swedberg 1990). For Marx, the outsiders were persons who had nothing to sell other than their labor power.

In the twentieth century, the realms of *homo economicus* and the study of society moved apart, and followed separate specializations. The economic human stereotype was depicted as behaving in consistently in rational ways, and as a narrowly self-interested individual. Typically, individuals were considered as imbued with innate talent and skills, but needing to work hard to achieve personal success and wealth. Humans came together to foster market places, to form businesses, and to harmonize supply and demand.

Other scholars were more humanist, and believed that people were not simply economic units. For example, the sociologist Mark Granovetter pointed out that (from the outset) people were embedded in webs of significant social relationships and institutions that gave them security, identity, and access to many essential resources (interviewed in Swedberg 1990). Culture broadly provided rich contexts for human activities, and it was assumed that individuals had a degree of choice, and that their lives were not entirely predetermined.

Sociologists with an interest in migration wrote of social remittances, whereby, not only was cash exchanged from far away to home countries, but also ideas, norms, and social practices (Garip and Asad 2015; Levitt and Lamba-Nieves 2011). Mutual cultural interaction continued from a distance. Sociologists also took an interest in differences, for example, between social classes, between the labor of women and men, between ethnic groups, and between sojourners and settlers. An insider usually belonged to an identifiable community (Kersen 2016). The groups of insiders and outsiders each had distinctive advantages and disadvantages, and also opportunities and temptations (Crocker 1991, p. 159).

Thus, both economists and sociologists are interested in outsiders and insiders for a range of reasons, but primarily because of the power imbalances that keep them apart (Barberis and Aureli 2010). Broadly, an outsider does not belong to a well-defined group, is isolated, and has less chance of success than an insider has. The term outsider is often complemented by the use of social descriptors that indicate other identifying features, such as, stranger, other, deviant, alien, illegal, free-floating (Kersen 2016; Merton 1972), isolate, casual link (Geser 2004), marginalized, homeless, stateless, nomad, and itinerant (Hall et al. 1996).

In sociology, there is a long-running methodology debate about whether researchers who are inside the mainstream (for example, white academics) can hope to understand a particular outside social group (for example, Afro-Americans) (Carling et al. 2014; Crocker 1991; Hage 2006). The questions raised are about the ethics and the potential objectivity of the insider presuming to investigate the outsider. We mention this debate because of its considerable body of sociological literature, even although the methodological question is peripheral to the main themes of our discussion.

Sociologists tell us that a tendency to think in narrow ethnocentric ways means that people assume the superiority of their own cultural heritage, often wishing it for deprived outsiders (Crocker 1991). Insidership can be tacit, implicit, and unarticulated until a crisis erupts, at which event the outsiders can be implicated in and blamed for radical change (Merton 1972). A philosophical perspective is that, in theory, the insider-outsider distinction only exists because the insiders choose to propagate it. Without insiders, no such barrier would survive. Sociologists also argue that multiple realities exist within each person, but that historical paths of personal experience tend to foster the predominance of one reality. Yet at the same time, each person can empathize with the other (the outsider), and may have had contact with them in varying degrees in the form of an imagined *mirror image* (Hage 2015, p. 216).

There is a practical reason to question the value of the insider-outsider distinction. In the case of migrants, social media may break down the barriers between the insiders and the outsiders. Smartphones are a personal talisman, a social tool, and an essential business device (Bunmak 2012; Hage 2015). A key question for the contemporary sociologist is whether modern information and communication technologies are changing society. Such technologies assist migrants in four ways: (1) they enable the maintenance of strong ties with the community at home after migration; (2) they provide ties for making personal economic progress; (3) they create new networks in the host country; and (4) they supply vital insider knowledge to assist with the migration process (Dekker and Engbersen 2014; Geser 2004).

A key difference between the economic and the sociological approaches to migration studies relates to agency. Contrasting predictions about behavior result from philosophical differences about how independent a human actor can be. For example, the economist may argue that self-interest and rationality are the main drivers of the migrant entrepreneur. In contrast, the sociologist hones in on the social influences that affect the individual choices of the migrants, such as the drawing power of communities of earlier migrants (Wilding 2012), and key social features of the host countries. The personal choices of migrants increase with the use of smartphones, and person-based systems may replace the influence of centralized agencies of communications and social control (Geser 2004).

Generally, the rigidity of established networks and institutions affects the interplay between human action and social structures. The relationships of insider to outsider (and vice versa) are affected by the levels of objective behavior allowed within structures, as observed by economists, and/or by the personal freedoms and empowered social networks, as noted by sociologists (Garip and Asad 2015). Insiders are supposed to control structure, while outsiders must have fuller agency because of the risks that they take (Barberis and Aureli 2010).

There is a considerable body of research on the relationships between individuals and structures. Marx and Engels argue that they were in constant flux throughout history (Hall et al. 1996), and Swedberg notes that economic institutions can be interpreted as social constructions like any other (Swedberg 1990). Therefore, the separation of economic and sociological explanations for migration is not helpful. Functioning together, both disciplines provide a more powerful lens than separately:

> It is worth approaching both sides (local and immigrant people) with similar tools and methods, so [as] to prevent essentialism and an asymmetric understanding of social bonds.
>
> Barberis and Aureli (2010, p. 7).

By way of illustration, recent research into the Chinese labor market in Prato indicates that there are both structural and social reasons for the perpetual low pay rates and poor working conditions among Chinese migrants. Structurally, there is a lack of government migration regulations, the Italian trade unions are unable to engage with the Chinese workers, and there is sometimes a difficult interaction between ethnic migrants and Italian authorities. Socially, Chinese norms and Wenzhou business customs dictate that Chinese firms hire Chinese workers first, and sustain a pool of insider (guanxi) laborers (Lan 2015).

Giddens's (1984) theory of structuration describes the role of the individual within structures, and the transforming and constraining effects that the pair have on each other. Giddens believes that a focus on one at the expense of the other led to distortions in our understanding of social change and global development. There are several criticisms of Giddens's theory. For example, he over-emphasizes the rationality of agents and their social action, and does not acknowledge sufficiently the support of the extensive social networks behind the individual agents (De Haas 2010). Others criticize him for under-playing the latitude of human actors (Bessant and Watts 2007). Commentators argue about how to interpret the degree of inter-activity between agency and structure, and appropriate avatars, but they do not totally reject Giddens's perspectives. His theory provides a viable working hypothesis for the study of migration, not least because Giddens successfully explicates globalization as a joint economic-sociological endeavor. Most scholars would agree with the fundamental proposition that the space and time distances have shrunk considerably in recent times, with the advent of cheap and widespread physical and telecommunications mobility. Such changes have serious economic and social consequences, including the dislocation of the traditional structures (Hall et al. 1996). Several sociologists comment on the role of social media in bringing about the *annihilation of space* and the *death of distance* (Frouws et al. 2016, p. 2).

Giddens's ideas are useful for the specific element of social behavior that affects migrants and the economics and sociology of a place; namely, inward-looking adherence to local identity, to the insider way, to the tribe over and above national or global forces (Merton 1972). An example of such behavior in Prato is the clash between the insider Pratesi loyalty and the guanxi (the network of ethnic relationships) of outsider Chinese migrants. Each group strives to maintain their own local economic and social order, and their attendant memories, values, norms, traditions, hopes, trust, and mutual obligations (Crocker 1991). Newly arrived laborers or entrepreneurs tend to stick together, eventually creating a self-sustaining flow of compatriot labor, and an ethnic branch of a local economy. The Chinese community in Italy is labelled as exemplary communitarianization (Barberis and Aureli 2010, p. 6), having imported their network habits (for business and social connections) with their people (Garip and Asad 2015). Clearly, mobile phones function like an umbilical cord to consolidate and sustain migratory commitments (Geser 2004, p. 12).

The importance of networks cannot be overestimated:

> Most treat [migrant] networks as hubs of information or help from prior migrants, while others view them as conduits for normative pressures or other institutionalized resources

Garip and Asad (2015, p. 9).

The networks evolve and adapt over time, and can become self-sustaining, regardless of the economic causes that began them in the first place. Hans Geser is one sociologist who advocates further research into the effects of mobile phone networks on individual actors, on local networks, on groups, and on organizational processes and structures.

> Despite the basic bilaterality of its communication channels, the mobile phone can eventually act as a catalyzer of collectivization, at least in situations where many receivers are ready to forward the message[s] … so that they spread in a tree-like fashion

Geser (2004, p. 29).

Thus, immigrant networks may be more effective and speedy than the official channels for migrants to find jobs in new countries (Lan 2015). Flexible networks can assist in many ways:

The transnational social space ... is constantly reworked though migrants' embeddedness in the sending and receiving contexts. This embeddedness, in turn, shapes familial, social, economic, religious, political, and cultural processes

Garip and Asad (2015, p. 4).

Networked communications allow current migrants to take their roots with them (Hage 2015). The migrants negotiate two worlds at a time—the world of their country of origin and the world of their new settlement (Bunmak 2012).

In the past, economists and sociologists undervalued the influence of migrant group connectivity (Barberis and Aureli 2010). Poor migrant laborers (some of them illiterate) have little time off work to meet face-to-face with their compatriots, let alone established locals, and for them the mobile phone becomes a lifeline (Bunmak 2012). The mobile phone links their home and foreign experiences. The Prato workplace—where they also rest and eat—forms their social center. From an economic perspective, the migrant entrepreneur-employers see price competition, fast production, high risk, and self-exploitation as normal features of any small business, having witnessed that situation in Wenzhou, China, before arrival in Italy (Barberis and Aureli 2010). As well as a forum for socialization, mobile phones are also an essential business tool. Often family members work alongside the cheap imported laborers in Prato (Lan 2015), for the expectation of a *postponed reward* (Barberis and Aureli 2010, p. 32). The markets in Italy operate as *"sets of rules and social relations in which immigrant entrepreneurs [are] embedded"* (Barberis and Aureli 2010, p. 9). Market networks are thus co-constructed.

The Prato experience demonstrates important elements of economic and sociology theories. Previously, the American sociologist Robert Merton pointed to an interrelated society status, showing the co-existence of insider and outsider characteristics (Merton 1972, p. 22). David Crocker argues that *"we can be both insiders and outsiders"* at the same time (Crocker 1991, p. 156); he considers that the categories are not mutually exclusive, but are on a continuum. Crocker quotes Salman Rushdie, who testified that he reinvents himself, taking on some values of the new homeland *"without giving up insider status in the old country"* (Crocker 1991, p. 158).

In 1996, Stuart Hall et al. argued that difference and social antagonism are the norm of everyday life, to permit fresh changes in identity (Hall et al. 1996, p. 600). Outsider and insider tensions are a common part of social change, and with globalization:

...economies and cultures [are] thrown into intense and immediate contact with each other – with each 'Other' (an 'Other' that is no longer simply 'out there', but also within).

Hall et al. (1996, p. 622).

More recently, Ghassan Hage pointed to insecure insiders with stakes in over-emphasizing the insider or outsider identity. For example, the *parvenus* or *nouveau riches* portray themselves as well integrated inside a desirable economic milieu, even if they have belonged to that milieu for only a short time. In the Prato case, the migrant laborers or servants must remain at arm's length, classified by insiders as being outside the economy and the culture of the mainstream host, so that they maintain their economic value to the employers. To be a needed outsider in Italy—with a small income and a limited work role—is better than remaining a worthless insider in rural China (Hage 2006; Lan 2015).

This section reviews the degree of freedom with which the individual laborer and entrepreneur is able to act, and suggests that mobile phones constitute a catalyst that widens personal choices. Portable online technologies extend the depth and breadth of relationships. The structuration theory of Anthony Giddens is a useful middle-range theory—with both economic and sociological implications—for clearly understanding the interactions between structures and individual actors. The structuration theory helps to theorize the mobile phone experiences in China and Italy. Johanson, Beghelli and Fladrich in this book argue that mobile phones and social media in combination break down structural barriers, and that the economy and society of Prato have to adjust accordingly. With modern global communications, it is easy to belong to two worlds at once.

This book more fully explores the links between economics, sociology, and the role of networks in the context of Prato. We conclude that outsiders and insiders are not binary opposites, but are part of a continuum on which migrants choose spaces of their own. Economic survival demands that the Prato insider takes advantage of the complicit Chinese outsider. Wenzhounese laborers and entrepreneurs have migrated into Prato for at least three decades, both disrupting and stimulating the local economy. For survival, the Wenzhounese adhere to pre-existing networks of relationships, and develop these networks for profit and for their own narrow insider advantage.

References

Alba R, Waters MC (eds) (2011) The next generation: immigrant youth in a comparative perspective. NYU Press

Aldrich HE, Waldinger R (1990) Ethnicity and entrepreneurship. Annu Rev Sociol 16:111–135

Aliaga-Isla R, Rialp A (2013) Systematic review of immigrant entrepreneurship literature: previous findings and ways forward. Entrepreneurship Reg Dev 25(9–10):819–844

Baldassar L, Raffaetà R (2017) "It's complicated, isn't it?": citizenship and ethnic identity in a mobile world. Ethnicities (forthcoming)

Barberis E, Aureli S (2010) The role of Chinese SMEs in Italian industrial districts. University of Urbino, Italy. http://www.academia.edu/3160896/The_role_of_Chinese_SMEs_in_Italian_Industrial_Districts_with_S._Aureli_. Accessed 2 Aug 2016

Becattini G (1990) The Marshallian industrial district as a socio-economic notion. In: Pyke F, Becattini G, Sengenberger W (eds) Industrial districts and inter-firm co-operation in Italy. International Institute for Labour Studies, ILO, Geneva, pp 37–51

Becattini G (ed) (1997) Prato storia di una città. Il distretto industrial (1943–1993). Comune di Prato-Le Monnier, Firenze

Becattini G (2001) The caterpillar and the butterfly. An exemplary case of development in the Italy of the industrial districts. Felice Le Monnier, Firenze

Becattini G, Rullani E (1993) Sistema locale e mercato globale. Economia e Politica Industriale 80:25–48. English translation in Becattini G (ed) (2004) Industrial districts. A new approach to industrial change, Edward Elgar, Cheltenham, pp 48–66

Berry JW (1969) On cross-cultural comparability. Int J Psychol 4(2):119–128

Berry JW, Kim U (1987) Acculturation and mental health. In: Dasen P, Berry JW, Sartorius N (eds) Cross-cultural psychology and health: towards applications. Sage, London

Berry JW, Kim U, Minde T, Mok D (1987) Comparative studies of acculturative stress. Int Migrat Rev, 491–511

Bessant J, Watts R (2007) Sociology Australia. Allen & Unwin, Sydney

Bonacich E (1973) A theory of middleman minorities. Am Sociol Rev 38(5):583–594

Bruderl J, Schussler R (1990) Organizational mortality: the liabilities of newness and adolescence. Adm Sci Q, 530–547

Bunmak S (2012) Cell phone networks and migrant networks: the case of Nayu migrant workers in Malaysia. Malays J Soc Space 8(1):38–49

Burt RS (1990) Structural holes. The social structure of competition. Harvard University Press, Cambridge

Carling J, Erdal ME, Ezzati R (2014) Beyond the insider-outsider divide in migration research. Migrat Stud 2(1):36–54

Cavusgil T, Guercini S (2014) Trends in middle class as a driver for strategic marketing. Mercati & Competitività 3:7–10

Chrysostome E (2010) The success factors of necessity immigrant entrepreneurs: in search of a model. Thunderbird Int Bus Rev 52(2):137–152

Crocker DA (1991) Insiders and outsiders in international development. Ethics Int Aff 5(1):149–173

De Haas H (2010) Migration and development: a theoretical perspective. Int Migrat Rev 44 (1):227–264

Dei Ottati G (1986) Distretto industriale, problemi delle transazioni e mercato comunitario: prime considerazioni. Econoomia e Politica Industriale 51:93–131. English translation (1991) The economic bases of diffuse industrialization. Int Stud Manag Organ 21(1):53–74

Dei Ottati G (2002) Social concertation and local development: the case of industrial districts. Eur Plan Stud 10(4):449–466

Dekker R, Engbersen G (2014) How social media transform migrant networks and facilitate migration. Glob Netw 14(4):401–418

Frouws B, Phillips M, Hassan A, Twigt M (2016) Getting to Europe the 'WhatsApp' way; the use of ICT in contemporary mixed migration flows to Europe. Regional Mixed Migration Secretariat Briefing Paper 2, Nairobi

Garip F, Asad AL (2015) Migrant networks. In: Scott R, Kosslyn S (eds) Emerging trends in the social and behavioural sciences: an interdisciplinary, searchable, and linkable resource. Wiley Online Library, pp 1–13

Gartner WB (1990) What are we talking about when we talk about entrepreneurship? J Bus Ventur 5(1):15–28

Geser H (2004) Towards a sociological theory of the mobile phone. University of Zurich. http://socio.ch/mobile/t_geser1.htm. Accessed 3 Aug 2016

Giddens A (1984) The constitution of society. Outline of the theory of strcuturation. Polity, Cambridge

Granovetter MS (1973) The strength of weak ties. Am J Sociol, 1360–1380

Grant RM (1991) Contemporary strategy analysis: techniques, applications. Blackwell, Oxford

Guercini S (ed) (2010) Marketing e management interculturale. Il Mulino, Bologna

Guercini S (2016) Local liabilities between immigrant and native entrepreneurship in industrial districts and global value chains. Paper presented at the workshop on evolving industrial districts within global and regional value chains and the role of manufacturing and innovation capabilities, University of Padova, Padova, 7 April

Hage G (2006) Insiders and outsiders. In: Beilharz P, Hogan T (eds) Sociology: place, time and division. Oxford University Press, Melbourne, pp 342–345

Hage G (2015) Alter-politics. Critical anthropology and the radical imagination. Melbourne University Press

Hall S, Held D, Hubert D, Thompson K (1996) Modernity; an introduction to modern societies. Wiley-Blackwell, Oxford

Haller W, Portes A, Lynch SM (2011) Dreams fulfilled, dreams shattered: determinants of segmented assimilation in the second generation. Soc Forces 89(3):733–762

Hofstede G (1980) Culture's consequences: international differences in work-related values. Sage, London

Hsu J, Saxenian A (2000) The limits of guanxi capitalism: transnational collaboration between Taiwan and the USA. Environ Plann A 32:1991–2005

Johanson J, Vahlne JE (2009) The Uppsala internationalization process model revisited: from liability of foreignness to liability of outsidership. J Int Bus Stud 40(9):1411–1431

Kersen TM (2016) Insider/outsider: the unique nature of the sociological perspective and practice. J Appl Soc Sci, 1–9, Online. http://jax.sagepub.com/content/early/2016/01/21/1936724415626961.full.pdf+html. Accessed 12 Aug 2016

Kloosterman R, Rath J (2001) Immigrant entrepreneurs in advanced economies: mixed embeddedness further explored. J Ethn Migrat Stud 27(2):189–201

Kloosterman R, van der Leun J, Rath J (1998) Across the border. Immigrants' economic opportunities, social capital and informal business activities. J Ethn Migrat Stud 24(2):249–268

Lan T (2015) Industrial district and the multiplication of labour: the Chinese apparel industry in Prato, Italy. Antipode 47(1):158–178

Levitt P, Lamba-Nieves D (2011) Social remittances revisited. J Ethn Migrat Stud 37(1):1–22

Liao X (2013) 'Quali occhi a mandorla?' in Provincia di Prato (eds) Seconda Generazione, vol 1. Piano B, Prato

Light I, Bachu P (eds) (1993) Immigration and entrepreneurship, culture, capital and ethnic networks. Transaction Publishers, New Brunswick

Marsden A (2014) Chinese descendants in Italy: emergence, role and uncertain identity. J Ethn Racial Stud 37(7):1239–1252

Marshall A (1920) Principles of economics, 8th edn. London, Macmillan

Merton RK (1972) Insiders and outsiders: a chapter in the sociology of knowledge. Am J Sociol 78 (1):9–47

Paciocco A (2015) Constructing social identity through language: the case of Italian-schooled Chinese migrant youth in Prato. Unpublished thesis, Monash University, Melbourne

Pedone V (2013a) A Journey to the West. Observations on the Italian migration to Italy. Firenze University Press, Firenze

Pedone V (2013b) Chugo, uscire dal Paese: breve quadro dei flussi migratori dalla Cina verso l'estero. In: Bert F, Pedone V, Valzania A (eds) Vendere e comprare. Processi di mobilità sociale dei cinesi a Prato. Pacini Editore, Pisa, pp 59–84

Perlmutter HV (1969) The tortuous evolution of the multinational corporation. Columbia J World Bus 4(1):9–18

Porter ME (1986) Competition in global industries. Harvard Business Press

Portes A, Jensen L (1987) What's an ethnic enclave? The case for conceptual clarity. Am Sociol Rev 52(6):768–771

Raffaetà R, Baldassar L, Harris A (2015) Chinese immigrant youth identities and belonging in Prato, Italy: exploring the intersections between migration and youth studies. Identities: Glob Stud Cult Power. http://dx.doi.org/10.1080/1070289X.2015.1024128

Redfield R, Linton R, Herskovits MJ (1936) Memorandum on the study of acculturation. Am Anthropol 38:149–152

Reynolds T, Zontini E (2014) Care circulation in transnational families: social and cultural capitals in Italian and Caribbean migrant communities in Britain. In: Baldassar L, Merla L (eds) Transnational families, migration and the circulation of care: understanding mobility and absence in family life. Routledge Transnationalism Series

Riddle L, Brinkerhoff J (2011) Diaspora entrepreneurs as institutional change agents: the case of Thamel.com. Int Bus Rev 20(6):670–680

Schumpeter JA (1934) The theory of economic development. Harvard Econ Stud, Cambridge

Schweizer R (2013) SMEs and networks: overcoming the liability of outsidership. J Int Entrepreneurship 11(1):80–103

Shenkar O (2001) Cultural distance revisited: towards a more rigorous conceptualization and measurement of cultural differences. J Int Bus Stud 32(3):519–535

Siu W (1995) Entrepreneurial typology: the case of owner-managers in China. Int Small Bus J 14:53–64

Smans M (2012) The internationalisation of immigrant ethnic entrepreneurs. Ph.D. thesis, University of Adelaide

Sousa CM, Bradley F (2006) Cultural distance and psychic distance: two peas in a pod? J Int Mark 14(1):49–70

Swedberg R (1990) Economics and sociology: redefining their boundaries: conversations with economists and sociologists. Princeton University Press

Thomas AS, Mueller SL (2000) A case for comparative entrepreneurship. Assessing the relevance of culture. J Int Bus Stud 31(2):287–301

Waldinger R (1986) Immigrant enterprise. Theory Soc 15(1):249–285

Waldinger R (1994) The making of an ethnic niche. Int Migrat Rev 28(1):3–30

Weidenbaum M (1996) The Chinese family business enterprise. Calif Manag Rev 38(4):141–156

Wilding R (2012) Migrants. In: Beilharz P, Hogan T (eds) Sociology: antipodean perspectives. Oxford University Press, Melbourne, pp 436–442

Wu WD (2014) 'Sono di Nuovo Qui'. in Provincia di Prato (eds) Seconda Generazione, vol II. Tipografia La Moderna, Prato

Zaheer S (1995) Overcoming the liability of foreignness. Acad Manag J 38(2):341–363

Zaheer S, Lamin A, Subramani M (2009) Cluster capabilities or ethnic ties? location choice by foreign and domestic entrants in the services offshoring industry in India. J Int Bus Stud 40 (6):944–968

Chinese Immigration to Italy and Economic Relations with the Homeland: A Multiscalar Perspective

Eduardo Barberis and Alberto Violante

Abstract The chapter characterizes the Chinese migrant economic integration in Italy in three ways. First, in a globalized world, migration flows are not discrete processes, but create permanent international links through different economic channels. We identify investments, remittances, and international trade as examples of these ties. Second, migrant integration occurs at different territorial scales, with the local level being the most interesting. Chinese firms and migrant remittances are embedded in a local context, and follow the geography of territorial change. Third and most important, liabilities and outsidership are ambivalent. The statistical analysis shows that Chinese communities would not have filled the gap left in Italian industrial districts by the industrial decline in the textile sector without their connection to their homeland. The growth of second-generation migrants and their embeddedness in the local communities of the receiving country is strategic, drawing a picture of a transilient migrant community.

Keywords Ethnic entrepreneurship · Industrial districts · Liabilities · Transilient migration · Chinese diaspora · Middleman theory · Globalization flows

1 Introduction

This chapter analyzes Italian-Chinese bilateral relations, and the role played by Chinese migrants in Italy. We examine the role that immigration plays in the transformation of the local, national, and international socio-economic systems. We place the in-group network effects and the effects arising from the transnational relationships among migrants and those left-behind, in both institutional contexts

E. Barberis (✉)
University of Urbino Carlo Bo, Urbino, Italy
e-mail: eduardo.barberis@uniurb.it

A. Violante
ISTAT, Rome, Italy
e-mail: alberto.violante@istat.it

© Springer International Publishing Switzerland 2017
S. Guercini et al. (eds.), *Native and Immigrant Entrepreneurship*,
DOI 10.1007/978-3-319-44111-5_3

and place-based industrial networks. Hence, we challenge the commonsense idea of a self-referential, bounded Chinese community, and try to disentangle the ties between network openings and closures and the dynamic interactions with local contexts. To do this, we first theoretically frame the relationship between globalization, immigration, and context-based incorporation (Sect. 1). We then introduce the literature that analyzes bilateral relations (trade, investments, and remittances) and immigration (Sect. 2). We analyze the specificity of the Italian context and its Chinese migration (Sect. 3), and the bilateral trade and remittances between Italian local economies and China (Sect. 4). Finally, we conclude by focusing on the factors affecting the development of bilateral relations brokered by migrants (Sect. 5).

2 National Models and Rescaling Processes: Immigration and Globalization

2.1 Changes in Migration

In the twentieth century, scholars frequently viewed immigrant incorporation within a nationalist paradigm, with insiders and outsiders defined by state-level labor and welfare and immigration policies, resulting in national models of incorporation (Heckmann and Schnapper 2003). Scholars linked migration flows to a wave of globalization related to decolonization processes and Fordist economies (Castles and Miller 1993): a mass migration of unskilled labor entered mass production in the Global North. Migration studies mirrored this territorial bias. Early research focused on the spatial concentration of migrants in local contexts (Park et al. 1925). However, some studies considered the (urban) areas of arrival as containers for social relationships, replicating features of the countries of origin and destination. The main issue was the time needed to assimilate the new populations in the host (national) society. The place of origin was nonetheless present (Thomas and Znaniecki 1920), although simply to explain the causes of migration, and not as a focal context for a persistent relationship.

From the 1970s, this migration model changed for various reasons (Sciortino 2000). State transformations and the post-Fordist economic transition were related to the new roles played by super- and sub-national arenas, while most European countries enacted a closed-door policy toward migration. The increasing globalization of value chains, the role of local clusters in opening up the intra-national competitive gap between strong and weak regions, and the revolutions in transport and communications all played a role in changing migration flows, in ways beyond national control. Migration shifted from temporary labor to settlement, and new migrants bypassed the *stop policies* in the traditional gateways by entering new destinations. The functional role of these new waves of migrants was somewhat blurred because they were dispersed in fragmented post-Fordist economies (Ambrosini 1999).

Hence, immigration became increasingly destandardized. Migration shifted from large, organized communities from a definite number and type of origin areas (also reified in public and policy discourse) to small and fragmented (by gender, class, areas of origin, and destination) flows, which challenged national labeling practices. The increasing interest in these changes encouraged a holistic approach to migration studies. This approach attempted to identify the links between the sending and the receiving countries, shifting the focus from places to interconnections (Sassen 1988).

2.2 Rescaling Processes

Along with this new research agenda, came criticisms of methodological nationalism (Smith 1983) that paved the way for approaches analyzing the relationships between national and other territorial levels. The emerging concept of rescaling (Brenner 2004) stressed that the territorial redistribution of power and economic processes is a continuing interplay between social and economic forces and related institutional processes. In this respect, regions represent an engine of new wealth in the knowledge-based economy. The need to overcome information asymmetries is essential in these economic processes; hence, personal networks can play a relevant role in circulating information and knowhow (Storper and Scott 1995). This also explains the success of some European regions (including Third Italy),[1] where manufacturing is embedded in the local handicraft traditions and the personal networks. This new economic centrality of places reshaped national powers: local policies gained momentum.

At first, this approach focused on urban governance and on local development. Later, analysis looked at other fields, migration included (Glick Schiller and Caglar 2010). Glick Schiller and Caglar (2010) consider that mobility challenges state boundaries, and participates in the social and economic transformation of territorial relationships. They see context as fundamental in value chains and in power hierarchies, because immigration profiles and roles differ in global and regional gateways, and in downscaled or shrinking territories.

2.3 Rescaling and Transnationalism

The embeddedness and social capital of migration-related networks is context-based, according to the scale-making processes that link origin and destination areas and their positions in the global system. Such networks also affect

---

[1]Third Italy refers to an area of the country characterized by a production model different from the large industries in North-West Italy and the under-industrialized Southern Italy. Hence, North-Eastern and Central Italy—the Third Italy—is characterized by clusters of small and medium size businesses. That is, industrial districts specializing in one or more traditional manufacturing sectors (see Bagnasco 1977; Becattini 2000).

cross-national ties: the shifting focus from unidirectional flows to migration systems forms the basis of categories such as diaspora and transnationalism (Faist 2010). Transnationalism focuses on the fluid relationships taking place across boundaries, beneath the formal relationships among states. In this perspective, migrant networks themselves create a long-lasting, self-regenerating connection between sending and receiving areas.

Some consider Chinese migration to be a typical transnational diaspora (Ma Mung 2000). Historically, Chinese migration filled entrepreneurial niches in the garment industry and in catering, while maintaining economic ties with the homeland (for example, via the imports of food or of semi-manufactured goods). This structure had two effects: the strengthening of bilateral trade, and the strengthening of the relationships between the overseas Chinese and the mainland Chinese. This idea challenges the concept of a state monopoly on social regulation: the denizenship position of those not sharing ab initio the same language, culture, history, and social ties produces social identities—belonging neither completely to one or the other country—in which socio-economic processes are embedded.

However, Chinese migration to Italy is a special case regarding both transnational networks and local contexts, since community closure seems to be coupled with integration into local economies. The share of Chinese firms in the total number of firms usually grows more than proportionally as Chinese migrants concentrate in local areas. For example, Rome's population is 0.4% Chinese, and yet 1.5% of its firms are Chinese-owned. In Milan, these figures are 0.8 and 2.5%, respectively, and in Florence 1.6 and 4.0%, respectively.[2] These numbers indicate how inserting labor into the local value chains connects to wider-scale, transnational processes. Chinese migrants are part of the globalization of the local production systems, although in a contested way (Barberis 2008; Baldassar et al. 2015).

2.4   Foreignness and Outsidership? Migration and Liabilities in Global Interconnections from a Sociological Perspective

Section 2 thus far focuses on the global connections among different countries and locales. This implies a mid-level network-aware analysis, rather than a simple micro-macro analysis (Ambrosini 2009). The links between the homeland and the diaspora (including international trade, investments, and remittances) are, as much as self-employment and other forms of social integration, relevant to showing the network position of a minority (the Chinese community in this instance). Focusing on the persistence of ties between the sending and the receiving countries does not simply relate to the renewed importance of networks in sociological analysis

---

[2]The percentage of residents is calculated using data from the Municipal Register. Data on Chinese-owned firms are from the Chamber of Commerce Register.

(Granovetter 1985). German sociology classics (Simmel and Sombart among others) focus on foreignness as a constraint and a resource, assuming Jewish history as a reference. Further, American migration studies (Bonacich 1973; Light 1980) mainly examine Asian self-employment.

To understand the middleman minority, we first analyze the destination society. If there is a structural hole (Burt 1992) between the elites and the lower social classes, then some outsiders may become middlemen to fill the hole. In this regard, Italy is a perfect case study. Italy has one of Europe's most uneven income distributions (Italy's income ratio between its first and the last quintile is 5.5, compared with 4.1 in Germany, and 4.0 in France). Further, Italy has Europe's highest share of self-employed people in manufacturing (2.36%).[3] Italy's many micro-firms face threats from market internationalization, and feature by a high rate of employee turnover. In turn, this affects the in-group and out-group network relationships. For example, the former may be strengthened (bounded solidarity) with a regulated competition, and by the provision of startup capital. Thus, a position of foreignness turns out to be a resource.

Foreignness is also at the center of the Uppsala model in management studies (Johanson and Vahlne 1977). Much of that debate focuses on the strategic decisions and the constraints that the first-movers face. Initially, the focus was on psychic distance (Hymer 1976), maintaining that the constraint related to a lack of adequate awareness of the context. More recently, conceptualizing markets as networks and the liability of outsidership (Johanson and Vahlne 2009), the focus shifted to the relationship with customers and suppliers to understand the feasibility of internationalization. Contrary to the above-mentioned sociological literature, for this strand of literature being part of a recognized minority does not usually represent potential success. Though, it is not the greatest obstacle, because the ties that transnational networks can provide and the kind of connections that firms are able to establish in the host countries are more relevant. In this respect, the sociological literature—with its attention to the structure of the receiving society (the way it shapes the opportunity to enter a market; the relationship between economic and social inclusion; and the issues of power and discrimination) and to the ties with sending countries—can positively feed business studies on the liability of outsidership.

3   Trade, Investments, and Remittances: Linking Countries Through Immigration

We first focus on the links between immigration, trade, investment, and remittances. Historically, studies underrated the economic role of immigration in linking countries, in favor of a focus on the gains and the drains within either country. Research on capital flows, investments, and institutions tends not to highlight the active role of

---

[3]Income data are from 2006, and self-employment data are from 2008 (source: Eurostat).

immigration in increasing interactions and in supporting co-development (Portes and Zhou 2012), although the transnational perspective does address this issue. The links between globalization from below [transnational small and medium enterprises (SMEs)], and globalization from above [foreign direct investment (FDI) flows] are still unexplored. These links are particularly important where remittances, trade, and migration seem to show an increasing integration between two areas, as in the case of Wenzhou and Italy (Wu 2007). In the last two decades, a growing literature on remittances and on immigrant-related trade and FDI is changing the historical viewpoint.

3.1 Immigration and Trade

When analyzing trade and immigration, a scale-careful approach can support the focus on the role of networks and embeddedness in world trade by the new international economics of migration (Rauch 1999). According to neoclassical economics, countries with an excess of labor send the labor to countries with an excess of capital. This mobility should reduce the pressure on the countries with excess capital, leading to an equilibrium (Harris and Todaro 1970). However, according to the Heckscher-Ohlin-Samuelson trade model, the *indifference of factor mobility* means that trade and migration are substitutes (Samuelson 1948; Mundell 1957). If there are no trade barriers, then a country can specialize in the commodity where it retains a comparative advantage, either by raising its employment level and improving its exports, or by exporting the surplus labor.

In that model, migration and bilateral trade have no positive correlation: a trade increase should limit migration. However, evidence from the last twenty years supports the opposite hypothesis (Genc et al. 2011). Knowledge of both the receiving and the sending contexts and the social networks that can fill the structural holes between the different markets can reduce the transaction costs for exports. Further, the migrants' preference for goods from their origin countries increases the import levels of those goods, as does promoting such goods to the natives for *exotic consumption* (White 2010). The trade enhancement is particularly strong when the migrants come from low-income and distant countries, and when the product dissimilarity is high. When relationships between the nations are asymmetric and the information flows are scanty, then the middlepersons play a fundamental role in filling the structural holes, through bicultural skills and trust building (Girma and Yu 2002; White 2007; Murat and Pistoresi 2009). To date, these hypotheses are partially confirmed empirically. The leading research on these issues focuses primarily on countries such as the United States, Canada, Australia, and New Zealand, whose political culture, nation-making, and state-making concepts rely on the role played by migrants. However, European migration studies maintain that the concepts and the interpretations based on liberal extra-European countries do not fit the situation in Europe, because of the different political cultures, immigration histories, and types of regulation (Engelen 2001; Esser 2004).

The same European traits can also affect trade and immigration analyses. A long immigration history with established international and transnational links makes it difficult to observe the trade creation effect of actual immigration (Peri and Requena-Silvente 2010). Currently, this issue is particularly relevant in Southern Europe, where the migration flows are recent and not necessarily linked to former colonies.

3.2 Immigration and Foreign Direct Investment (FDI)

Globally, FDI has increased significantly in recent decades, both in the form of capital transfers and of buyouts. For buyouts, China attracts many productive investments by corporations. In the general equilibrium model described in Sect. 3.1, the cost of investing abroad must be less than the cost of exporting (unless there are other organizational reasons, such as technology or expertise). Generally, studies consider that labor migration is non-influential in the decision to invest in a foreign country. At most, some scholars analyze the effect of FDI in causing emigration flows in the long-term, in contrast with trade integration that is supposed to lessen international mobility (Sanderson and Kentor 2008).

FDI usually connects developed economies and fails to involve developing countries. Migrants can support transnational networks, helping the expansion of FDI in their origin countries. This process seems particularly relevant in the destination countries with a long migration history and with high-skilled migrants (Flisi and Murat 2011; Javorcik et al. 2011). SMEs—often unable to outsource at an international level—may opt for doorstep internationalization via international migrants (Murat and Paba 2004). Hence, low-skilled immigration can be a functional alternative to FDI.

An alternative hypothesis connects Chinese migration to Italy to inward FDI from China to Italy. This view is supported by evidence of the role played by the Chinese immigrants' networks in FDI toward other destination countries (Gao 2003; Tong 2005). However, in Italy, the flows seem largely disconnected. Chinese investors are usually very large firms that focus on manufacturing (particularly metalworking and automotive) to buy brands and market shares, and to access technology and local competitive advantages (Stanca 2009; Pietrobelli 2011). Thus, they differ significantly from the SMEs owned by Chinese migrants and, at most, they may benefit from the cultural and economic brokerage enacted by new Sino-Italian generations.

Accordingly, although Italy attracts significant Chinese migration to Europe, it seems largely unable to attract Chinese FDI, probably for two reasons. (1) The Chinese migrants to Italy are mainly low skilled and poorly capitalized, without clear upward social mobility. This is exacerbated by a restrictive Italian immigration policy and a depressed labor market (Raffaetà and Baldassar 2015; Boeri and Van Ours 2008). (2) The Italian market has little allure for investors, and is an overall laggard in inward FDI (not just in inward FDI from China).

3.3   Immigration and Remittances

Remittances can directly measure the financial flows associated with migration. Remittances are the money transferred from migrant workers to their home country. While FDI is a top-down investment, remittances travel back to the origin country through informal networks, meaning that official data underestimate the real inflows.[4] The role of remittances in maintaining transnational relationships became clear during the 2007–2009 global financial crisis, the effects of which are ongoing. In that crisis, FDI fell considerably more than remittances, so that by 2009, FDI and remittances were equal resources for developing countries (World Bank 2011). The last decade saw huge increases in the remittances toward the fast-growing emigration countries like China and India (the countries with the highest volume of remittances globally). China's remittances grew from USD $25.7 billion in 2007 to USD $62 billion in 2014. Italy is consistently in the top ten remittance-sending countries in the world, with China as its main non-EU destination. This is particularly evident in the remittances from Rome, Prato, Florence, and Milan toward Wenzhou (World Bank 2011; Fondazione ICSA 2012).

3.4   The Italian Case

Most studies on trade, FDI, and remittances find that certain conditions are necessary to give an effective social and economic advantage to the involved parties. First, there is an association between trade and demographic openness (Mosk 2005). There should be liberal and clear rules on access and associated rights. Further, there is a negative effect from the trade restrictions and the immigration policies not attracting skilled migration (Genc et al. 2011; Boeri and Van Ours 2008). Second, transnational ties are associated with a positive integration into the host country, and with a rich social capital. Well-educated, well-established, and high-skilled immigrants play a fundamental role in keeping active relationships between the origin and the destination countries (Faustino et al. 2009; Portes and Zhou 2012). Third, trade is boosted on reaching a (place-specific) threshold of immigrant participation in the manufacturing sector, and on easing socio-economic upward mobility (Blanes and Martín-Montaner 2006; Faustino et al. 2009). Most

---

[4]Italy underestimates some of its official figures. For example, the Bank of Italy only has detailed information for bank transfers over €12,500 (Giangaspero 2009). This gives rise to estimation problems, because of the small and repeated transactions that are used to avoid suspicion in the illegal or gray economy. This effects the statistical reliability of the available data (Fondazione ICSA 2012). Additionally, there are probably underestimations in the money flowing from origin to destination countries, because this money is difficult to track. The bilateral remittance matrix of the World Bank shows that the Italy-China inflows are one hundred times larger than the Italy-China outflows (see: http://www.worldbank.org/en/topic/migrationremittancesdiaspora issues/brief/migration-remittances-data).

such features are not present in the Italian case, meaning a potential negative affect on the Sino-Italian relations tied to migration.

4 Immigration and (Co-) Development: The Italian Case

To acknowledge the role of immigration in co-development processes, avoiding a zero-sum interpretation of drains and gains, we consider the socio-economic participation of labor immigration as multi-sited with mixed embeddedness (Kloosterman and Rath 2001). The local community, the in-group bounded network, and the origin country each play a role in this mix. This double embeddedness helps to frame the immigrant settlement patterns in Italy, and to explain why Italy is one of the most relevant destinations for Chinese migration.

4.1 Putting the Italian Case in Context

Immigrants play important roles in Italian local economies (Barberis 2008; Lombardi et al. 2011). The effects include a consistent complementarity, a growth in the native mid-to-high skilled jobs, and a functional role in cushioning production shocks. We hypothesize that localized institutions and networks play a basic role in the ethnicization of some economic sectors. This should be understood as the consequence of intergroup relationships, and of the disembedding and re-embedding processes.

The debate on the changes affecting Italian local production systems considers whether there is a transformation or just a decline (Solinas 2006). The evolution of the international and local contexts includes exports, the outsourcing of the most labor-intensive production activities, the buyout of district firms, and the growing role of immigrant labor. The link between exogenous and endogenous factors is frequently overlooked, forgetting the historical role of immigration in forging the present social and economic configurations (Mingione 2009).

Again, Chinese migration to Italy is relevant, because it involves rescaling transformations in both the sending and the receiving areas. The opening of China's economy to market reforms in the late 1970s created special economic zones in China and provided the evidence of a diversified China (Weber 2001). In the 1990s, the creation of joint ventures between Chinese and private foreign firms boosted FDI and exports (due to outsourced manufacturing in China, see Fu 2004). Additionally, the overseas Chinese were linked to effects of Deng Xiaoping's open door policy in the 1980s. In Italy, Chinese entrepreneurship benefited from the unintended effects of these changes. The 1985 Italy-China bilateral agreement on the mutual promotion and protection of investments made it relatively easy to amend the position of the early Chinese immigrant firms. This agreement gave those firms an advantage over migrants from other origin countries, who had to wait for the 1998 immigration law to gain easier access to business opportunities.

   Additionally, Chinese out-migration is territorially biased, with different migration networks connecting different sending and receiving areas. The Chinese
migrants to Italy come mostly from Zhejiang, and are stratified according to China's
opening strategies. Although there were early flows in the first half of the twentieth
century, the current Chinese migration to Italy started in the 1980s. This migration
took the form of main networks with hub cities and with Third Italy (for example,
Prato). In the 1990s, migration flows grew toward both the largest metropolitan areas
and the new industrial district destinations. A part of this growth tied in with trading
entrepreneurship—as the terminal manufacturing firms settled in China during the
1990s. The complexity of these flows is beyond the remit of this book. Suffice to say
that we must take a nuanced perspective, because the link is not between China and
Italy. The link is between specific Italian regions and specific Chinese regions:
regions where economic and migration processes are concentrated.
   A group of Chinese entrepreneurs filled the role left by Italian firms in some
local economies following the industrial and monetary crisis of the 1990s. Some of
the entrepreneurs in that generation of Chinese migrants both had links with their
homeland and started to gain positions in industrial districts like Prato. Figure 1
shows the Chinese population in Italy from 1992. As the Chinese population grew,
initially little changed in Italy's textile trade. After a few years, the textile
import-export trade balances started to change. The finished commodities began to
show a heavy negative net trade balance. However, the raw materials remained
balanced, and even showed a small trade surplus during the first years of the crisis.
We assume that this happened because of the intra-industry trade operated by the
Chinese firms in the industrial districts and the main urban hubs. Thanks to their
connection with their homeland, the overseas Chinese entrepreneurs started to
exchange raw and treated materials between Italy and Wenzhou. By that stage,
Wenzhou was a net exporter of finished garments to the rest of the world.

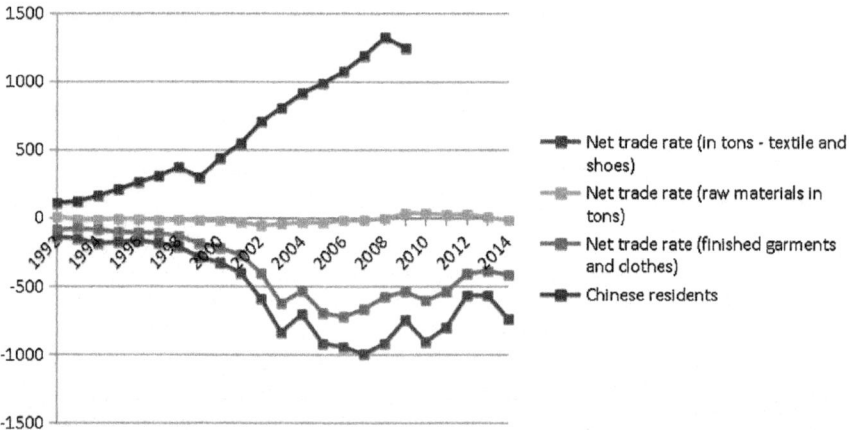

Fig. 1 Textile trade and Chinese population in Italy, 1992–2014 (authors' elaboration from Italy's
National Institute for Statistics data)

4.2 Immigration in the Italian Production System

The role played by new international migration is consistent with endogenous changes in the traditional reserves of labor. The circumstances that reduced the traditional pool of cheap native labor include (1) enhanced youth qualifications (changed expectations and the destandardization of transition paths), and (2) the changed configuration of female labor, of households, and of intergenerational solidarity. Additionally, the globalization of competition and the difficulties that small enterprises experienced in undertaking research and development made many local economies both less competitive and less able to introduce new skills.

Overall, immigration was a way to rebuild strong networks by *acquiring* trust via middlepersons with access to dense immigrant cliques. Sometimes the weak ties of isolated migrants were exploited. This structure helped to make ethnicized specializations, whose role is partly related to the marketization and informalization of local economies in their global restructuring (Panayiotopoulos 2010). The role of Chinese networks in hub and in district economies is a specific form of a more general process.

Essentially, the embedding process of immigration is bi-lateral, or even multi-lateral. The immigrant-native relationships increase because of changes in the local power and economic sets, which in turn change the socio-economic configurations in both destination and origin areas, in both migrant and in local networks. Transnational links mean also a double engagement and integration, a contribution to the economy and society of the origin and the destination (Mazzucato 2008).

Again, Italy is an interesting case because it has a business structure that is somewhat similar to that of developing countries (small firms in labor-intensive sectors). Italy also has a high level of both national and immigrant entrepreneurship, which challenges the idea of a residual role of the latter (OECD 2010).

Piore (1990) was the first to describe *ethnoindustrialization*. This notion was subsequently assumed by Murat and Paba (2001) to describe trust relations and tacit knowledge in Italian local production systems. Using this concept, two forms of ethnoindustrialization (native and immigrant) are conceivably involved in a dynamic interplay of competition and cooperation. These forms share common features with the industrial districts and the ethnic clusters described elsewhere in the literature. The features include the overlap of ownership and management, no formal division between production and management, low productivity, paternalistic management, strong personal relations between employers and employees and among competitors, family labor, poor access to credit, and a high level of informality (Panayiotopoulos 2010). In other words, while immigrant players involved in petty capitalism appear elsewhere in the West (Rath 2002), Italy has a specific value added research interest because of the embedding of immigrant firms in a system where SMEs are not marginal.

4.3   Chinese in Italy

There is a dynamic opportunity attached to the emerging role of Chinese immigrant businesses in Italy's local production systems. This is the potential to unhinge the established socio-economic relationships with a disembedding process. When the Chinese presence reaches a critical threshold, it is no longer a temporary answer, but is a structural feature steering future outcomes. Hence, it is important to consider network structures from a wider perspective than arm's length ties. The analysis of minority economies often focuses solely on strong ties and on in-group bounded solidarity, notwithstanding a long tradition in economic sociology that acknowledges the role of weak ties and of the creation of new links between separate cliques (Granovetter 1973; Burt 1992).

Thus, an in-group analysis of Chinese diaspora and transnational links, without considering intra- and inter-group asymmetries, strong and weak ties, bridges between localized cliques, and localization issues would limit our understanding. Rather, the sustainability of this asymmetric model of socio-economic participation is important, based on social segmentation and on economic inclusion. This means that long subcontracting chains relieved of social responsibility by main contractors, weak trust, high marketization, and the high frailty of socio-economic ties could pave the way to a general fading of the industrial networks. The networks would be unable to re-embed new ties and to capitalize on the structural holes made accessible by new links. In this respect, the native Italian and Chinese residents may become involved in a negative spiral of unsustainable impoverished subcontracting in the long-term. In the best case, this may be coupled with renewed transnational links.

Correspondingly, it is important to analyze any discourses on the similarity of the ethnoindustrialization paths of the local economies in Italy and in Wenzhou. A growing literature considers the Wenzhou model as similar to the Italian model of development (Wang and Tong 2005; Walcott 2007; Lombardi 2010), with Wenzhounese migrants having skills and expertise usable in Italian local economies. Such a situation could also enhance bilateral trade and investment relations.

However, there is evidence that Wenzhounese migrants to Italy are frequently low-skilled families from rural backgrounds, not necessarily having such expertise. Further, the business core in the Italian local systems are selective and thus difficult to access. Moreover, the Chinese firms are often fragile because of their small size, their low capitalization levels, and information asymmetries. These weaknesses are exacerbated by crises in some of the *made in Italy* value chains, and by the growth of fellow native competitors that reduces profitability, increases the risks of cut-throat competition, and weakens the in-group networks (Denison et al. 2010; Genova and Ricucci 2010). The segmentation of the in-group interests provides the foundation for an in-group exploitation that equals the out-group exploitation (Ceccagno 2007; Wu 2008). For every successful entrepreneur, many others simply feed a survival subcontracting economy. This situation may have consequences on the ability to retain transnational links and bilateral relations.

4.4 Socio-economic Consequences

We now consider the socio-economic consequences of this specific type of economic integration. Insertions into the labor market that are consistent with the role of informality and self-exploitation in maintaining spaces of profitability make the Chinese self-employment-centered model of labor participation successful. However, it is fragile, especially in labor intensive and mature productions. The informal arrangements produce a downward assimilation, both in the transnational channels (undocumented immigration and off-the-books trade transactions) and in the local networks (low production costs essentially demanded by the Italian buyers are only achievable by infringing labor, safety and fiscal rules).

The role of Chinese immigrants in enhancing bilateral relations can be hindered by their socio-economic integration in Italy. Stereotyping and blaming practices hide an enduring exploitation in the local business and the subcontracting networks. They attribute long-lasting and structural problems to Chinese (internal and international) competition, while using such competition in a cutthroat competition game.

Thus, if Chinese immigration is successfully used to cut production costs via price and time competition in the local production systems under stress—especially those with smaller and less innovative firms (Bigarelli et al. 2009; Murat and Paba 2004; Colombi 2002)—then we can expect a limited effect on the transnational relationships.

If we continue to analyze the Chinese business and social networks as separate and parallel, then it will be difficult to boost a successful development of the existing intergroup networks, and to overcome their present weaknesses (Hakansson and Snehota 1995). If the Chinese role is seen as transient—a stopgap solution in the development of local economies and transnational links—then it will hinder a successful networking. This is because *"an extant degree of commitment will persist and increase when partners believe that continuing a relationship is in their long-term interest"* only (Johanson and Vahlne 2009, p. 1418).

5 Bilateral Integration: Immigration, Trade, and Remittances Between Italy and China

5.1 Selecting the Factors

To analyze the role of Chinese immigrants in enhancing the links between their homeland and the Italian local economies, we focus mainly on remittances and trade. For trade, we choose a relatively specific field of relations between China and Italy—goods that are *made in Italy*. We accept that we overlook an important transnational channel by not considering the exotic and ethnic goods and services (Ambrosini 2011) that have a positive effect on the degree of bilateral relationships.

Such markets are sometimes set primarily for the migrants themselves, and the immigration-trade link seems to hold more strongly for the consumers than for the producers that use raw goods on which we focus (Gould 1994; Dunlevy and Hutchinson 1999). Nonetheless, this choice is consistent with stressing the level of economic integration and interdependence between the sending and the destination areas. Further, the choice is consistent with checking the network effect of the contribution made by the migrants to such a relationship (Rauch 1999; Blanes and Martín-Montaner 2006).

Note that we focus on intra-national variability. This is because immigration in Italy (particularly Chinese immigration, see Barberis 2014) is unevenly scattered, while the local economy features also differ substantially. This means that national data are of limited use in understanding the relationship between the sending and the receiving areas,[5] as shown in other recent studies on countries with strong regional differences (Peri and Requena-Silvente 2010).

Other studies focus on both an inter-group and a national comparison that analyzes the bilateral trade between a host country as a whole and the different immigrant national groups and their sending countries. However, we focus on an intra-national and single group perspective: the relationship between Chinese immigration and trade in different Italian local contexts.

5.2 Remittances

In the late 2000s, the remittances to China showed a progressive increase. The growing number of Chinese residents clearly helped this increase. However, the per capita remittances also progressed until recently (see Fig. 2), with the very recent collapse possibly due more to increased controls on money laundering than to the financial crisis.

The maps of Chinese residents and per capita remittances give some hints about the nature of these flows. The areas of residence overlap many of the local production systems where Chinese people settled (the Tuscany, Veneto, Adriatic regions). However, the richest sending areas are the metropolitan areas; even those in Southern Italy with few residents (see Fig. 3). We assume a cut-off between some communities because of the role of the informal resources (fiscally transparent or not).[6] Hence, the urban remittance outflows indicate that the trade in low-cost garments and in the catering economy (transiting through hub cities) is not

---

[5]The same applies to the sending regions in China. However, given the quite delimited territorial origin of the Chinese in Italy—mainly from Zhejiang, and particularly from Wenzhou—the national data on China are a sufficiently satisfactory proxy of the sending region.

[6]We controlled for the incidence of Chinese residents, the rate of concentration of Chinese residents, the per capita general income of the province, and the demographic size. None of the variables was statistically correlated to the per capita average remittance.

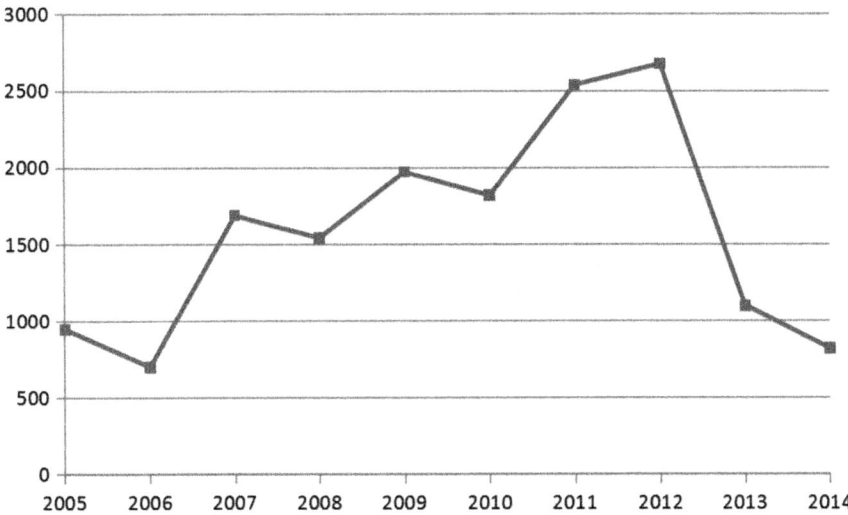

Fig. 2 Italy's remittances per capita, 2005–2014 (authors' own extrapolation from www.bancaditalia.it data)

significantly affected by the crisis. This is because those sections operate in the low-cost informal market that is fed (not hurt) by the crisis.

5.3 Trade

We tried to find significant trade links between individual Italian areas and China, exploring the determinants of the export value (measured as the export value per province), and the importance of the Chinese presence in the area. It is difficult to find evidence of a strict relationship between foreign trade and the Chinese presence at a territorial level, because many empirical factors intervene to make it more complex. On the one hand, China is a big importer from any Western industrial country, meaning that many industrial areas have a specific export relationship with China. This means that the context links between the export flows and the Chinese diaspora disappear among many other factors. On the other hand, there are concerns about data quality (for example, the port areas show high export figures because of the many commercial firms registered there).

We analyzed the export value of the textile sector, a traditional *made in Italy* manufacturing subsector,[7] for two reasons. First, the textile sector is one of the most

---

[7]To classify the economic activities we used ATECO 2007 (at a 2-digit level), which is the Italian version of the NACE Rev. 2 economic classification system. The textile industry is classified as NACE 13.

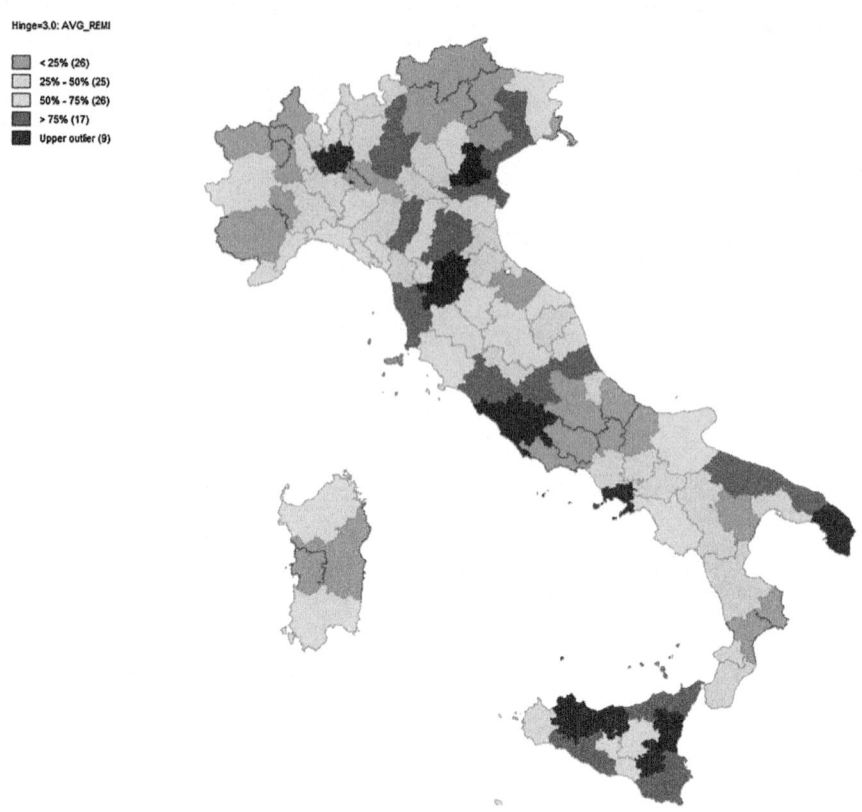

Fig. 3 Italy's mean remittance per capita per province, 2011–2014 (authors' own extrapolation from www.bancaditalia.it data)

representative industries of the so-called Third Italy. Second, the textile sector was the forerunner of Chinese SME growth in 1980s and 1990s, with the Chinese textile firms almost substituting the Italian textile firms (for example, in the metropolitan area of Florence). Moreover, for Chinese migrants the textile sector has a different entrepreneurial trajectory than other sectors. This trajectory is more connected with exports and influenced by international trade agreements than other sectors. It is less prone to subcontracting for the national Italian market (Milanesi et al. 2016).

However, we stress that the results of the regression model cannot be generalized to other economic sectors (even the similar sectors like leather and garments). We applied the same model to other *made in Italy* sectors, without significant results, or with opposite results. This is central to our reasoning, because it shows that the social networks of Chinese communities do not move in a technological vacuum. Some technology factors precondition the shape and the strength of the social ties. Interestingly, our model fits the textile sector well: the textile industry is an increasingly divided sector that operates in a high cost market niche and that has many firms that suffer from a technological lag.

Table 1 Linear regression models: Italian textile exports

Dependent variable: textile export (NACE 13)		Number of observation			101
				R2	0.6995
				R2adj	0.6902
	DF	Sum of squares	Mean of squares	Value F	Pr > F
Regression	3	5959.68540	1986.56180	75.25	<0.0001
Residual	97	2560.61731	26.39812		
Total adjusted	100	8520.30272			
Parameters estimate					
Variable	DF	Parameters estimate	Standard error	T value	Pr > |t|
Intercept	1	0.81883	0.67655	1.21	0.2291
Chinese population	1	−0.0128	0.0038006	−3.38	0.0011
Chinese under age (sq)	1	9.06	1.60089E-7	5.66	<0.0001
Decrease of textile firms	1	0.01	0.0100	8.56	<0.0001

The data on Chinese firms came from the Chamber of Commerce Registers; the data on the Chinese population came from the Municipal Registers; and the data on young Chinese people came from the Italian census.[8] A linear model is not optimal for analyzing export data, because such data tend to follow a Poisson distribution. We wanted to exclude outliers because we wanted to check for a rough relationship between some interesting variables. Hence, we used Cook's method of identifying the outliers (Cook and Weisberg 1999) and used a straightforward linear regression. We thus obtained a solid model (the F-test is positive and the R-squared shows that approximately 70% of the variance is explained by the model) (Table 1). However, this result owes something to the predicted value for some units showing high standard errors in both directions. This means that the residuals deviated from the predicted values in opposite directions and compensated for each other.

We excluded the Italian provinces of Modena and Biella as outliers. Biella hosts a strong textile district that exports (usually high-end products) to China; however, that province has very few Chinese residents. Modena has a large Chinese population and many Chinese firms; however, most of its Chinese firms are in sectors other than textiles. It is important to note such omissions when considering our model, because our general exploration of liabilities and of middlemen may not account for the specific scalar configuration in some territories.

We used a forward procedure to select the relevant variables for the model. We discounted two variables because of a lack of statistical significance, the amount of remittances from Italy to China, and (quite surprisingly) the number of Chinese

---

[8]Chinese population figures for the under 18s are not available at a county level. Therefore, we used census data from 2011 and made a linear interpolation to 2013.

firms in the textile sector. The model arising from the selection has three variables: (1) the decrease in the number of Italian textile firms between 1981 and 2001 (a proxy of the structural hole that Chinese migrants may have exploited); (2) the share of Chinese residents under 18 (a proxy of the stability of Chinese communities and of the mediating roles that the second generations may take); and (3) the number of Chinese residents. All of the variables had significant coefficients (two of them highly significant). The decrease in the number of textile firms in the previous two decades paradoxically increases the chance of exporting. The decline of the textile sector is strongly related with the presence of Chinese residents: a Pearson coefficient of over 0.70 connects the industrial decline and the Chinese arrival. There is clear evidence that the textile sector contained a social mechanism that filled the gap left by the decline of the native firms, as confirmed by the most prominent grounded analysis (Dei Ottati 2014).

The relationships between both sides of this phenomenon are insufficiently explored. We could argue that without an economic growth in China's southeastern special economic zones there would not be any meaningful flow of Chinese entrepreneurs to export, and probably also a decline. This would imply a link between the origin of the structural hole in Italy's territorial economy and China's own development.

Interestingly, a positive and extremely strong relationship links exports with the presence of Chinese residents under 18—although this variable is related by a quadratic relationship rather than a linear relationship. Its reverse U-shaped distribution relates the middle levels of Chinese minors to the highest export values, and relates the extremes (both positive and negative) of the distribution with the lowest export values. The number of Chinese residents has a less significant effect on export than the under-18 variable, and a slightly negative coefficient. This statistical effect arises because most Chinese migrants live in large metropolitan areas. Those areas export proportionally less than do the small urban centers and the areas where many Chinese families with minors live.

The most successful links between China and Italy seem to involve those provinces where Chinese SMEs are involved in traditional, labor-intensive *made in Italy* industries. Such links are not necessarily located in the traditional local production systems. Chinese SMEs not located in large metropolitan areas or in saturated industrial districts can more effectively avoid cutthroat competition.

6 Conclusion

We find an increasing (although fragmented) economic integration between Italy and China tied with the presence of Chinese immigration. Most of the contribution to the net exports relate to a mix of factors, with the Chinese presence in Italy being just one.

The result is not unexpected, given the preliminary remarks and the assumptions made in Sects. 1 and 2. Italy seems to be missing some of the conditions of reciprocal success, particularly when it comes to Chinese migration. Nonetheless, understanding the links between China and Italy means considering the complexity inside both countries, not simply the differences between the two. The liability of outsidership in Italy could act specifically in some areas rather than in some activities, because of the relevant territorial differences.

This is particularly true for a number of Chinese immigrants (self-)employed in the *made in Italy* local production systems. In our statistical model, the Chinese presence seems alternative to the Italian one in building bilateral links. The mature Italian industry is locked-in and struggles to internationalize, while the settlement of Chinese communities is able to boost the production and trade toward China. This is clear in the territories where the industrial crisis created a structural hole to fill, but in other sectors and territories there is no sign of a zero-sum game. Further, the marked effect of the new Sino-Italian generations stresses the point that settling seems a strategic element in substituting local players and in creating connections to the homeland. This does not come without social consequences. It may imply that Chinese concentrations within Italian industrial districts had to build their own version of the local industrial atmosphere, while being exploited to keep the core (native) networks alive. Notwithstanding conflicts, the links constructed by inter-generational settlements are somehow limiting a schismogenesis process, and the reciprocal isolation between natives and migrants (apparent in many industrial districts) is milder than before. The evolution of these links is an open challenge for both the reproduction of local production systems in an era of globalization and the local and transnational chances of the new Sino-Italian generations.

Developing mixed skills and increasing social interactions can help to overcome the liability of outsidership for both the Chinese investing in Italy and the Italians investing in China. Having new Sino-Italian generations as middlepersons means the ability to improve connectedness and interdependence. However, to achieve a more effective brokerage, we must resolve the symmetry of the relationships. If discrimination, conflict, and reactive bounded identities—as much as a downward market and social assimilation—prevail, if economic and social relationships are strongly detached, and if the stigma of being a foreigner (Hymer 1976, p. 35) endures for those who are no longer foreigners, then the insider position reached by the Chinese migrants and their offspring is not enough.

References

Ambrosini M (1999) Utili invasori. Franco Angeli, Milan

Ambrosini M (a cura di) (2009) Intraprendere fra due mondi. Il Mulino, Bologna

Ambrosini M (2011) Sociologia delle migrazioni. Il Mulino, Bologna

Bagnasco A (1977) Tre Italie. Bologna, Il Mulino

Baldassar L, Johanson G, McAuliffe N, Bressan M (eds) (2015) Chinese migration to Europe. Palgrave Macmillan, Basingstoke

Barberis E (2008) Imprenditori immigrati. Ediesse, Rome

Barberis E (2014) Chinese entrepreneurs in Italy. In: Sagiyama I, Pedone V (eds) Perspectives on East Asia. FUP, Florence

Becattini G (2000) Il distretto industriale. Rosenberg & Sellier, Torino

Bigarelli D, Baracchi M, Corradi S (2009) Osservatorio del settore tessile abbigliamento nel distretto di Carpi. 9° rapporto. Comune di Carpi, Carpi

Blanes JV, Martín-Montaner JA (2006) Migration flows and intra-industry trade adjustment. Rev World Econ 142(3):568–585

Boeri T, Van Ours J (2008) The economics of imperfect labour markets. Princeton, PUP

Bonacich E (1973) A theory of middleman minorities. Am Sociol Rev 38(5):583–594

Brenner N (2004) New state spaces. OUP, Oxford

Burt R (1992) Structural holes. HUP, Cambridge

Castles S, Miller MJ (1993) The age of migration. The Guilford Press, New York

Ceccagno A (2007) The Chinese in Italy at a crossroads: the economic crisis. In: Thuno M (ed) Beyond Chinatown. NIAS, Copenhagen

Colombi A (ed) (2002) L'imprenditoria cinese nel distretto industriale di Prato. Leo S. Olschki Editore, Firenze

Cook D, Weisberg S (1999) Applied regression including computing and graphics. Wiley, New York

Dei Ottati G (2014) A transnational fast fashion industrial district: an analysis of the Chinese businesses in Prato. Camb J Econ 38(5):1247–1274

Denison T, Arunachalam D, Johanson G, Smith R (2010) La comunità cinese di Prato. In: Johanson G, Smyth R, French R (eds) Oltre ogni muro. Pacini, Pisa

Dunlevy JA, Hutchinson W (1999) The impact of immigration on American import trade in the late Nineteenth and Twentieth centuries. J Econ Hist 59(4):1043–1062

Engelen E (2001) 'Breaking in' and 'Breaking out': a Weberian approach to entrepreneurial opportunities. J Ethn Migrat Stud 27(2):203–223

Esser H (2004) Does the "New" immigration require a "New" theory of intergenerational integration? Int Migrat Rev 38(3):1126–1159

Faist T (2010) Diaspora and transnationalism: what kind of dance partners? In: Bauboeck R, Faist T (eds) Diaspora and transnationalism. AUP, Amsterdam, pp 9–34

Faustino H, Peixoto J, Baptista P (2009) As Características da Imigração em Portugal e os seus Efeitos no Comércio Bilateral. *ACIDI - Estudos Observatório da Imigração*, 31

Flisi S, Murat M (2011) The hub continent. Immigrant networks, emigrant diasporas and FDI. J Soc Econ 40(6):796–805

Fondazione ICSA (2012) *Esportazione illegale di capitali: come combatterla?* Report downloadable from www.fondazioneicsa.it. Accessed 9 Oct 2012

Fu X (2004) Export, FDI and economic development in China. Palgrave Macmillan, New York

Gao T (2003) Ethnic Chinese networks and international investment: evidence from inward FDI in China. J Asian Econ 14:611–629

Genc M, Gheasi M, Nijkamp P, Poot J (2011) The impact of immigration on international trade: a meta-analysis. IZA discussion papers, 6145

Genova C, Ricucci R (2010) Abitare Torino. Percorsi, integrazione, vita quotidiana. In: Berzano L et al (eds) Cinesi a Torino. Il Mulino, Bologna

Giangaspero G (2009) Le rimesse dall'Italia in tempo di crisi. CeSPI working papers, 63

Girma S, Yu Z (2002) The link between immigration and trade: evidence from the U.K. Weltwirtschaftliches Archiv 38(1):115–30

Glick Schiller N, Caglar A (eds) (2010) Locating migration. CUP, Ithaca

Gould DM (1994) Immigrant links to the home nation. Rev Econ Stat 76(2):302–316

Granovetter M (1973) The strength of weak ties. Am J Sociol 78(6):1360–1380

Granovetter M (1985) Economic action and social structure: the problem of embeddedness. Am J Sociol 91(3):481–510

Hakansson H, Snehota I (eds) (1995) Developing relationships in business networks. Routledge, London

Harris JR, Todaro MP (1970) Migration, unemployment and development: a two-sector analysis. Am Econ Rev 60(1):126–142

Heckmann F, Schnapper D (eds) (2003) The integration of immigrants in European societies. Lucius and Lucius, Stuttgart

Hymer S (1976) The international operations of national firms. MIT Press, Cambridge

Javorcik BS, Ozden C, Spatareanu M, Neagu C (2011) Migrant networks and foreign direct investment. J Dev Econ 94(2):231–241

Johanson J, Vahlne J-E (1977) The internationalization process of the firm. J Int Bus Stud 8:23–32

Johanson J, Vahlne J-E (2009) The Uppsala internationalization process model revisited. J Int Bus Stud 40:1411–1431

Kloosterman R, Rath J (2001) Immigrants entrepreneurs in advanced economies: mixed embeddedness further explored. J Ethn Migrat Stud 27(2):189–201

Light I (1980) Asian enterprise in America. In: Cummings S (ed) Self-help in urban America. Kennikat, New York

Lombardi S (2010) Il modello di sviluppo di Wenzhou attraverso la letteratura dei distretti industriali. In: Johanson G, Smyth R, French R (eds) Oltre ogni muro. Pacini, Pisa

Lombardi S, Lorenzini F, Sforzi F, Verrecchia F (2011) Chinese entrepreneurship in context: localization, specialization and their impact on Italian industrial districts. Paper presented at the ERSA Congress 2011, Barcelona, Aug 30–Sept 3

Ma Mung E (2000) La diaspora Chinoise. Ophrys, Paris

Mazzucato V (2008) The double engagement: transnationalism and integration. J Ethn Migrat Stud 34(2):199–216

Milanesi M, Guercini S, Waluszewski A (2016) A Black Swan in the district? An IMP perspective on immigrant entrepreneurship and changes in industrial districts. IMP J 10(2):243–259. doi:10.1108/IMP-09-2015-0050

Mingione E (2009) Family, welfare and districts. The local impact of new migrants in Italy. Eur Urban Reg Stud 16(3):225–236

Mosk C (2005) Trade and migration in the modern world. Routledge, New York

Mundell RA (1957) International trade and factor mobility. Am Econ Rev 47(3):321–335

Murat M, Paba S (2001) Flussi migratori e modelli di sviluppo industriale. In: Lunghini G, Silva F, Targetti Lenti R (a cura di) Politiche pubbliche per il lavoro. Il Mulino, Bologna

Murat M, Paba S (2004) Migrazioni internazionali e sviluppo economico. Una riflessione sul caso italiano. In: Associazione Mario Del Monte (a cura di) Rapporto 2003. Immigrazione, distretti industriali e istituzioni nell'era della globalizzazione. Il caso della Provincia di Modena. Associazione Mario Del Monte, Modena

Murat M, Pistoresi B (2009) Migrant networks: empirical implications for the Italian bilateral trade. Int Econ J 23(3):371–390

OECD (2010) Open for business: migrant entrepreneurship in OECD countries. OECD, Paris

Panayiotopoulos P (2010) Ethnicity, migration and enterprise. Palgrave-MacMillan, Basingstoke

Park RE, Burgess EW, McKenzie RD (eds) (1925) The city. UCP, Chicago

Peri G, Requena-Silvente F (2010) The trade creation effect of immigrants: evidence from the remarkable case of Spain. Can J Econ 43(4):1433–1459

Pietrobelli C (2011) Chinese FDI strategy in Italy: the 'Marco Polo' effect. Int J Technol Learn Innov Dev 4(4):277–291

Piore M (1990) Work, labour and action: work experience in a system of flexible production. In: Pyke F, Becattini G, Sengenberger W (eds) Industrial districts and inter-firm co-operation in Italy. ILO, Geneve

Portes A, Zhou M (2012) The eagle and the dragon: immigrant transnationalism and development in Mexico and China. Princeton University—Centre for Migration and Development Working Papers, 3

Raffaetà R, Baldassar R (2015) Spaces speak louder than words: contesting social inclusion through conflicting rhetoric about Prato's Chinatown. In: Baldassar L, Johanson G, McAuliffe N, Bressan M (eds) Chinese Migration to Europe: Prato, Italy, and Beyond. Palgrave Macmillan, Basingstoke

Rath J (ed) (2002) Unravelling the rag trade. Berg, Oxford

Rauch J (1999) Networks versus markets in international trade. J Int Econ 48:7–35

Samuelson PA (1948) International trade and equalization of factor prices. Econ J 59(234): 181–197

Sanderson MR, Kentor J (2008) Foreign direct investment and international migration. Int Sociol 23(4):514–539

Sassen S (1988) The mobility of labour and capital. CUP, Cambridge

Sciortino G (2000) L'ambizione della frontiera. Franco Angeli, Milano

Smith AD (1983) Nationalism and social theory. Br J Sociol 34:19–38

Solinas G (2006) Integrazione dei mercati e riaggiustamento nei distretti industriali. Sinergie 69:87–114

Stanca L (2009) Investimenti diretti cinesi in Italia: da ruscello a fiume? Economia e politica industriale 1:135–144

Storper M, Scott AJ (1995) The wealth of regions: market forces and policy imperatives in local and global context. Futures 27(5):505–526

Thomas WI, Znaniecki F (1920) The Polish peasant in Europe and America, vol 4. The Gorham Press, Boston

Tong SY (2005) Ethnic network in FDI and the impact of institutional development. Rev Dev Econ 9(4):563–580

Walcott SM (2007) Wenzhou and the third Italy: entrepreneurial model regions. J Asia-Pac Bus 8 (3):23–35

Wang J, Tong X (2005) Industrial clusters in China: embedded or disembedded? In: Alvstram CG, Schamp EW (eds) Linking industries across the world. Ashgate, Aldershot

Weber M (2001) Il miracolo cinese. Il Mulino, Bologna

White D (2007) Immigrant trade links, transplanted home bias and network effects. Appl Econ 39:839–852

White R (2010) Migration and international trade. Elgar, Cheltenham

World Bank (2011) Migration and remittances. Factbook 2011. The World Bank, Washington

Wu B (2007) Exploring links between international migration and Wenzhou's development. China Policy Institute—University of Nottingham Discussion Papers, 25

Wu B (2008) Vulnerability of Chinese migrant workers in Italy: empirical evidence on their working conditions and the consequences. China Policy Institute—University of Nottingham Discussion Papers, 28

A Social Accounting Matrix for Prato: Interrelating the Chinese Migrant Community and the Provincial Economy

Paola Biasi and Stefano Rosignoli

Abstract A social accounting matrix (SAM) is a descriptive and analytical tool that records the flows occurring between all of the actors of an economic system. SAMs represent the economic process, stressing its circularity in a flexible way. The disaggregation of the individual accounting blocks in a SAM make it possible to highlight particular interdependencies. Such interdependencies would remain hidden in traditional statements (two section accounts). We analyze the 2010 SAM estimated for Prato Province, distinguishing between the Chinese migrant community and the local community (that includes other migrant communities). This distinction allows us to quantify the contribution of the Chinese community to the entire provincial economy. We consider contributions such as the production of goods and services, the income generation, and the aggregate demand addressed to the system by the community itself. Using the estimated SAM as an impact modeling tool allows us to evaluate the economic effect of the integration policies of the Chinese community (additionally, in terms of overcoming local liabilities).

Keywords Social accounting matrix (SAM) · Input output · Multiplier analysis · Structural analysis · Social integration · Impact models

1 Introduction

We estimate a social accounting matrix (SAM) for the province of Prato for 2010, to analyze Prato's economic system, the contribution provided by the Chinese community, and the network of local and transnational relations of this community. Given the particular socio-economic connotation of the province and the flexibility

P. Biasi (✉)
University of Florence, Florence, Italy
e-mail: paola.biasi@unifi.it

S. Rosignoli
IRPET, Florence, Italy
e-mail: stefano.rosignoli@irpet.it

© Springer International Publishing Switzerland 2017
S. Guercini et al. (eds.), *Native and Immigrant Entrepreneurship*,
DOI 10.1007/978-3-319-44111-5_4

of the SAM structure, we distinguish two groups in the system: the Chinese migrant community, and the local community (including other migrant communities). The SAM helps to describe the provincial economic system as a whole, and can isolate the flows of goods and services, and of income and capital between all of the actors in the economic system. This matrix can quantify the contribution of the Chinese community to the entire provincial economy in terms of both the production of goods and services and income generation, and the aggregate demand addressed to the system by the community itself.

There is an extensive literature on the particularity of Prato's economic system. Extant studies examine the relationship between the international dimension of corporate activity and the local development in the years of maximum development (Colombi 2002); the history, the actual status, and the future consequences of Chinese business developments (Dei Ottati 2014); and the evolution of the social mobility of the Chinese community in Prato (Berti et al. 2013). We contribute to the field by offering a method to measure and evaluate the economic flows between the Chinese immigrants and other communities in the territory, both in terms of businesses and of families.

In Sect. 2, we present the SAM as a descriptive tool for economic systems, and indicate its origin, content, and usefulness on a local scale. Section 3 shows how SAMs evolved to describe a system, and how they can estimate the contribution of different migrant communities to the functioning of the system itself. Section 4 presents the main economic values (supply-and-use accounts, production and value-added sectors, exports, and taxes paid) to quantify their overall levels in the province. We distinguish the contribution of the Chinese community from the other entities operating in the area. We describe an input–output model based on a SAM in Sect. 5. We use this model to estimate the contribution of the Chinese community to the local economy in terms not only of the value added but also of the indirect and induced effects that propagate through the inter-sectoral relationships between companies and migrant communities.

2 Social Accounting Matrix

A SAM is a matrix that records the flows occurring between all of the actors (production activities and institutions) in an economic system in a given time period (usually 1 year). SAMs initially appeared in traditional economic theory as an extension of the input–output matrices, and are now widely used to analyze the economies in developing countries (Pyatt and Round 1985). Specifically, SAMs can consider the problems of income distribution that are particularly acute in developing countries. In the SAM acronym, the adjective *social* links precisely to the distribution of household income. Recently, SAMs have also been used to study developed economies. This progression is because of the increased availability, reliability, and standardization of national account data; of the usefulness of reconciling all of the accounting data in a single scheme that simultaneously represents and makes them consistent; and of the importance of performing structural analyzes and building multi-sector models that simulate economic policies (Ministero dello Sviluppo Economico 2009).

SAMs represent the economic process, stressing its circularity in a flexible way. The disaggregation of the individual accounting blocks in a matrix makes it possible to highlight the particular interdependencies that would remain hidden in traditional accounting statements (accounts in two sections). Given the availability of statistical information, it is also possible to choose a suitable classification depending on the specific needs of the economic analysis.

SAMs form the basis of information for a wide range of multi-sector models, often developed within alternative theoretical frameworks (for example, linear models, general equilibrium models, and micro-macro simulation models). The flexible SAM structure allows calibrations to analyze specific parts of the economy, while remaining within a comprehensive and consistent macroeconomic framework (Scandizzo 1994). For example, SAMs facilitate the study of the macroeconomic impacts of specific sectoral policies, or the analysis of their geographical differentiation (multi-regional models, rural-urban disaggregation of the economy, migrant and autochthonous[1] groups).

The amount of statistical information available at a national level makes it relatively easy to construct a sufficiently disaggregated SAM. However, constructing a SAM at a sub-national level is more difficult, and more so again at a sub-regional level. At those levels, the lack of clear boundaries for external trade flows and the insufficient statistical coverage (often only representative at a national level) make it difficult to construct the matrices.

3 Using a Social Accounting Matrix to Describe an Economic System

The economic cycle is a set of relationships among institutional sectors. The relationships are distinct in an aggregate way in households, businesses, and in public administration.

In an economic system, the first exchange relationship in the market takes place between businesses and households (see Fig. 1). The former sell goods and services to the latter for the market price of the consumer goods; the latter provide capital and labor to the former in return for interests and salaries (representing the remuneration for the production factors). The government is part of the economic system (for income redistribution) in organizational, regulatory, and equalization terms. The government uses tax transfers to make the economic system subject to other forces outside the market. In an open system, all of these subjects (and their

---

[1]In this chapter, we use the term autochthonous to refer to non-Chinese people (prevalently Italians, but also people coming from countries other than China or Italy).

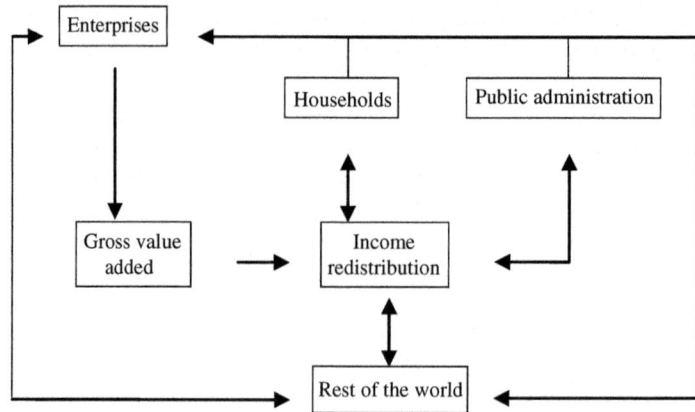

Fig. 1 Relationships among the institutional sectors of an economic system (authors' scheme)

relationships) interact with the rest of world (through exchanging goods, services, income, and transfers).

All of the flows in the economic circuit synthesized in Fig. 1 can be quantitatively described and inserted in the blocks of a SAM. We can modulate the level of detail as needed, depending on the availability of information and on the analytical objectives of the matrix.

When constructing the provincial SAM, we adopted a compact scheme that allows its use for different cognitive and simulation purposes. The economic agents included in the SAM are the local units of production located in the territory, regardless of the location of their headquarters. We often use the NACE ESA10 classifications to divide the units into production sectors. The other economic agents in the SAM are the institutional sectors, defined as decision-making centers and articulated in households, businesses, non-profit organizations, and public administrations situated in the province.

With the exception of their squareness, SAMs do not have a standard form. This leads to problems of uniformity, definition, and communication within the scientific community. However, it makes them extremely flexible instruments, adaptable to the study of particular contexts as a function of the amount of existing information and the ultimate purpose of their use. In the SAM built for Prato Province, we did not emphasize the distribution of income (as is the case with traditional SAMs). Instead, we highlighted the contribution made to the economic system by the migrant groups (particularly the Chinese) and the autochthonous groups compared with the other economic actors in the province.

As with any accounting matrix, Prato's SAM was estimated using indirect methods. The Regional Institute for Economic Planning of Tuscany (IRPET) annually estimates the accounting matrices at national, regional, and (for Tuscany) sub-regional levels. IRPET commonly adopts a system of cascade estimation, with matrices that start at the national level, progress through the regional level, and end at the provincial and local systems level. To construct the matrices, IRPET makes use of all of the available data, from Italy's national institute of statistics (ISTAT) accounts to the existing administrative statistics. IRPET make several assumptions of stability, for example, the technical coefficients of the inter-sectoral matrices, the import and taxation coefficients, and the structuring of the demand components. Using this information, IRPET estimates a matrix of initial values, also called an unbalanced matrix because the row and column sums are not equal. A balance is then executed (using a procedure devised by Stone et al. in 1942) that starts from the unbalanced initial data and their reliability values. The initial data are iteratively adjusted with an oscillation possibility that depends on the reliability assigned to each. Following the balancing procedure, the matrices obtained have equal row and column sums, and the aggregates are consistent with the data published by ISTAT.

Building a SAM combines the collection of available data from several sources with mathematical algorithms to find the coherence between all of the economic flows in one year and in one economic system (Pyatt and Round 1985). We made several assumptions for Prato's SAM, given the current data availability (from official and non-official sources) at a local scale. The assumptions relate to estimating the initial flows concerning businesses (production, value added, and exports) and families (income, direct taxes, and private consumption). This chapter does not describe the assumptions; it simply considers the use of the balanced SAM.[2]

The SAM produced by IRPET for the province of Prato consists of 67 rows and columns, organized according to the following classifications:

- We divide the production sectors into 28 branches that correspond to the sub-divisions of ISTAT's sectoral regional accounting. For some particular branches, we separate the Chinese businesses from the other businesses in the sector.
- We divide the institutional sectors (approximately six) into Chinese and non-Chinese households, Chinese and non-Chinese businesses (including family businesses, corporations, and quasi-corporations), private non-profit institutions serving households (NPISHs), and public administration.
- We divide the rest of world into three areas: the rest of Tuscany, the rest of Italy, and abroad. We adopt this distinction to estimate the flows of imports-exports, of tourism expenditure, and of current and capital accounts.

Table 1 summarizes the accounting matrix estimated for the province of Prato (without separating the blocks according to the different classifications).

We outline below what each of the titles associated with the SAM blocks represents.

Inter-sectoral exchanges: the trade of goods and services bought and sold among the production branches (disaggregated using the classifications in Table 5 that show the areas and the migrant and autochthonous groups).

---

[2]Previous works describe the SAM estimating procedure. These include IRPET (2014), Ministero dello Sviluppo Economico (2009), Casini Benvenuti and Paniccià (2003), and Targetti (2004).

Table 1 Block structure of Prato's SAM (estimates from Prato's 2010 provincial SAM)

	Branches	VA	Consumption	Balances	Paid transfers	Exports	Incoming tourism expenditure	Capital outflows	Incoming income flows
Production branches	Inter-sectorial exchanges	0.00	Domestic consumptions	0.00	0.00	Exports	0.00	Investments	0.00
VA and taxes	Domestic VA	0.00	0.00	0.00	0.00	0.00	0.00	0.00	Incoming VA
Domestic consumptions	0.00	0.00	0.00	0.00	Resident consumptions	0.00	Incoming tourism expenditure	0.00	0.00
Balances	0.00	0.00	0.00	0.00	0.00	0.00	0.00	Balance of sectors	0.00
Received transfers	0.00	Primary income	0.00	0.00	Inter-sectorial current transfers	0.00	0.00	0.00	Incoming current transfers
Imports	Imports	0.00	0.00	Balance of trade	0.00	0.00	0.00	0.00	0.00
Outgoing tourism expenditure	0.00	0.00	0.00	Tourism balance	Outgoing tourism expenditure	0.00	0.00	0.00	0.00
Savings + capital revenues	0.00	0.00	0.00	0.00	Savings	0.00	0.00	Inter-sectorial capital transfers	Incoming capital transfers
Outgoing income flows	0.00	Outgoing VA	0.00	Current account balance	Outgoing current transfers	0.00	0.00	Outgoing capital transfers	0.00

VA Value added

Domestic consumption: the expenditure on the purchase of goods and services by (Chinese and non-Chinese) households, private non-profit social institutions, and public administration.

Export: the sale of goods and services to other provinces of Tuscany, to other Italian regions, and abroad.

Investments: the purchases of property and capital equipment for production, plus the change in inventories and acquisition less the disposal of valuables. We separate the investments by the owning institutional sector and by purchased goods and services.

Domestic VA: the sector's value added generated by the province's production units, distinguished by sector.

Incoming VA: the value added coming from outside of Prato Province (the rest of Tuscany, the rest of Italy, and abroad).

Resident consumption: the purchase of goods and services by the resident households, divided between Chinese and non-Chinese households.

Primary income: the attribution of the valued added to the local institutional sectors (households, businesses, private non-profit social institutions, and public administration).

Current transfers: the current transfers between institutional sectors (mainly from social benefits, social contributions, and direct taxes).

Incoming current transfers: the current input from outside Prato (the rest of Tuscany, the rest of Italy, and abroad).

Outgoing current transfers: the current output to outside Prato (the rest of Tuscany, the rest of Italy, and abroad).

Incoming tourism expenditure: the inbound tourism expenditure by area of origin (the rest of Tuscany, the rest of Italy, and abroad).

Outgoing tourism expenditure: the outbound tourism expenditure by destination (the rest of Tuscany, the rest of Italy, and abroad).

Savings: the savings distinguished by the institutional sector.

Capital transfers: the capital transfers between the institutional sectors, including capital and inheritance taxes, tax amnesties, and direct investments between institutional sectors.

Incoming capital transfers: the money transfers from the outside for the purchase of capital goods. The transfers correspond to the usual foreign direct investments (FDIs), in this case calculated for the flows coming from Tuscany and from Italy. Additionally, this block records a number of European investment funds.

Outgoing capital transfers: the money transfers to the outside for the purchase of capital goods. The transfers correspond to the usual FDIs, in this case calculated for the flows going to Tuscany and to Italy. Mirroring the incoming capital transfer block, this block also records some capital taxes intended for European institutions.

4 Analyzing the Economic System and the Contribution of the Chinese Community Using the Provincial Accounts Extracted from the Social Accounting Matrix

The SAM consists of blocks with a precise economic meaning. The blocks retrace the entire economic circuit, starting from the final demand and accounting for the production and generation of value added, the distribution and redistribution of income, the consumption and savings, the capital transfers, and the net debt.

Prato's SAM estimated for migrants includes several account aggregates referring to the entire economic context, and distinguishes whether they are ascribable to the Chinese community or to the other residents in the area. This distinction concerns the production units and the households. Table 2 is an aggregate synthesis of the matrix, containing only the flows of final demand and production (as in a traditional input–output table).

The input–output matrix (Table 2) extracted from Prato's SAM describes the economic system and the linkages among the businesses and the households of both the Chinese migrants and the other communities (including the Italian) in the province. We denote with $T(i,j)$ the matrix blocks with row i and column j as coordinates, and discuss their significance.

Starting with the first row, block $T(1,1)$ represents the inter-sectoral exchanges among the production units; that is, the amount of goods and services exchanged between the branches. Moving to the right, block $T(1,2)$ gives the final consumption of the (Chinese and non-Chinese) households, block $T(1,3)$ gives the consumption of public administration and of private non-profit social institutions, block $T(1,4)$ gives the investments, and block $T(1,5)$ gives the exports.

In the second row, block $T(2,1)$ gives the value added generated by businesses (distinguished between Chinese and non-Chinese). The entire third row consists of

Table 2 Simplified input–output migrants/autochthons matrix (million €) (estimates from Prato's 2010 SAM)

	Chinese businesses	Non-Chinese businesses	Consumptions of Chinese household	Consumptions of non-Chinese household	PA and NPISH expenditure	Investments of Chinese households and businesses	Investments of rest of economy	Exports to rest of Italy	Exports to rest of world	Row total
	1		2		3	4		5		6
Chinese businesses 1	376	704	18	188	13	5	65	936	767	3,072
Non-Chinese businesses	1,072	4,571	139	2,613	1,319	115	1,346	2,802	1,378	15,355
VA 2	689	5,042								5,711
Net indirect taxes 3	15	116	16	352	3	5	63	0	18	588
Imports from rest of Italy 4	624	3,262								3,886
Imports from rest of world 5	315	1,660								1,975
Column total 6	3,072	15,355	173	3,153	1,335	125	1,475	3,738	2,163	

NPISH Private non-profit institutions serving households; *PA* Public administration; *VA* Value added

the net indirect taxes on products paid for by both the intermediate costs (column 1) and the components of final demand (columns 2–5). In the fourth row, block T(4,1) represents the imports from the rest of Italy. Finally, in the fifth row, block T(5,1) represents the imports from the rest of world.

It is possible to extract different types of economic aggregates from the SAM, distinguished both by sector (for production branches or institutional sectors) and by aggregate. This section briefly presents a series of aggregate tables extracted from Prato's SAM. The tables outline the provincial gross domestic product (GDP) and the main component account (Table 3); the GDP decomposition (Table 4); the production, value added data, intermediate costs, and indirect taxes by sector (Table 5); the sectoral composition of the value added by the Chinese businesses (Table 6); the share of the value added by the migrant/autochthonous groups (Table 7); and the exports to the rest of Italy and the rest of world (Tables 8 and 9).

The supply-and-use account shown in Table 3 is similar to a photograph of the economic system. It has two sections: the resource section comprises GDP, and indicates the amount of income generated by the system and by imports (that is, the amount of goods and services coming from the rest of world). The use section shows the components of final demand. This represents the quantities of goods and services asked by households and tourists, NPISH and public administration expenditures, investments (in this case including changes in inventories), and exports. In the estimated account, the amounts of resources and uses will correspond.

According to the estimates, in 2010 the provincial GDP amounted to €6.29 billion, with the GDP produced by Prato's Chinese businesses at €704.5 million (11.2% of the total). The total resident household consumption was €3.32 billion, with €172 million ascribable to Chinese households (5.2% of total domestic

Table 3 Main components of provincial gross domestic product separated by migrant/autochthonous group (million €) (estimates from Prato's 2010 SAM)

	Values	Shares
GDP (Chinese community)	704.65	11.2%
GDP (rest of economy)	5594.38	–
Imports from rest of Italy	3886.04	–
Imports from rest of world	1975.02	–
Total (resources)	12,160.08	–
Household expenditures (Chinese community)	172.73	5.2%
Household consumption (rest of economy)	3117.59	–
Tourism expenditure	35.31	–
PA expenditure	1313.26	–
NPISH expenditure	21.56	–
Gross investments (Chinese community)	124.56	7.8%
Gross investments (rest of economy)	1474.59	–
Export to rest of Italy	3737.66	–
Export to rest of world	2162.83	–
Total (uses)	12,160.08	–

GDP Gross domestic product; *NPISH* Private non-profit institutions serving households; *PA* Public administration

Table 4 GDP decomposition (€ million) (estimates from Prato's 2010 SAM)

	Allocation of GDP
Compensation of Employees (earned by Chinese households)	198
Compensation of Employees (earned by rest of households)	2470
Gross Operating Surplus allocated to Chinese businesses	514
Gross Operating Surplus allocated to other businesses	3585
Indirect taxes and Gross Operating Surplus allocated to Public Administration	725
Total	7492

GDP Gross domestic product

consumption). The gross fixed investments were €1.6 billion, with €124.56 ascribed to Chinese businesses and households (7.8% of the total).

The generated GDP is territorially distributed to households, businesses, and public administration through the compensation of employees, the gross operating surplus (GOS), and net indirect taxes. Two percent of GDP is allocated to Chinese households, 7% to Chinese businesses, 33% to non-Chinese households, and 48% to non-Chinese businesses (in terms of GOS). The remaining 10% is constituted by indirect taxes, and a small part of GOS is attributed to the government.

Table 5 Production and sectoral value added by migrant/autochthonous group, (million €) (estimates from Prato's 2010 SAM)

Production sectors	Production	VA	Intermediate costs	Indirect taxes
Agriculture, hunting and forestry	41	25	15	0
Fisheries, fish farming and related services	1	0	1	0
Extractive industry	6	4	2	0
Food, beverages and tobacco industries	96	16	80	0
Textiles, apparel and leather industries (Chinese community)	1730	483	1237	10
Textiles, apparel and leather industries (rest of economy)	1820	468	1341	11
Wood, paper and publishing industries	114	37	77	1
Coke industries, refineries, chemical and pharmaceutical industries	84	24	60	1
Manufacture of rubber, plastic and non-metallic mineral products	93	28	64	1
Metallurgy, except machinery and equipment	110	43	66	1
Electrical and electronic equipment, machinery (n.e.c.)	426	132	292	2
Manufacture of transport equipment	34	4	30	0
Manufacture of furniture; other manufactures; repairs (Chinese community)	39	13	25	0
Manufacture of furniture; other manufactures; repairs (rest of economy)	164	60	103	1
Electricity, gas, steam and air conditioning supply	263	137	123	2
Water supply; sewerage, waste management	188	90	96	2
Other industrial activities (Chinese community)	26	9	17	0
Construction (Chinese community)	4	2	2	0
Construction	869	295	568	6
Wholesale and retail trade; repair of motor vehicles and motorcycles (Chinese community)	207	94	110	3
Wholesale and retail trade; repair of motor vehicles and motorcycles (rest of economy)	1142	584	541	17
Transportation and storage	758	323	424	11

(continued)

Table 5 (continued)

Production sectors	Production	VA	Intermediate costs	Indirect taxes
Accommodation and food service activities (Chinese community)	27	15	13	0
Accommodation and food service activities	263	149	112	2
Information and communication services	329	179	148	2
Financial and insurance activities	361	195	156	10
Real estate activities (Chinese community)	40	24	16	0
Real estate activities	1176	1007	165	3
Professional, scientific and technical activities	488	262	220	5
Administrative and support service activities	369	164	201	4
Public Administration	380	261	108	12
Education	330	278	46	6
Human health and social work activities	285	129	144	12
Arts, entertainment and recreation	69	32	35	2
Other service activities (Chinese community)	21	15	6	0
Other service activities (rest of economy)	176	119	55	2
Other services (Chinese community)	38	15	23	1
Total	**12,566**	**5711**	**6723**	**131**
–Chinese community	2132	669	1448	15
–Rest of economy	10,433	5042	5275	116
Chinese community's percentage share on total value	17.0%	11.7%	21.5%	11.6%

ISTAT Branch classification of regional accounts (Aggregation of NACE REV.2 Classification)
VA Value added

Table 6 Sectoral composition of Chinese businesses (% share) (estimates from Prato's 2010 SAM)	Textile and clothing	81.1%
	Other manufactures	3.0%
	Construction	0.2%
	Trade	9.7%
	Accommodation and food service activities	1.3%
	Other services	4.6%

In addition to the snapshot of the economic system offered by the supply-and-use account, we can observe the amounts of production, value added, intermediate costs, and indirect taxes produced at the sectoral level. We can distinguish the

Table 7 Percentage share of sectoral production by migrant/autochthonous group (estimates from Prato's 2010 SAM)

Production sectors	Chinese community (%)	Rest of the economy (%)
Agriculture	0	100
–Textile and clothing	49	51
–Furniture and other manufactures	19	81
Other industries	1	99
Construction	0	100
–Trade	15	85
–Accommodation and food service activities	9	91
Other services	1	99

Table 8 Exports by sector and migrant/autochthonous group (million €) (estimates from Prato's 2010 SAM)

Production sectors	Export to rest of Italy	Export to rest of world
Agriculture, hunting and forestry	29.8	3.3
Fisheries, fish farming and related services	0.2	0.1
Extractive industry	1.9	0.9
Food, beverages and tobacco industries	76.9	12.9
Textiles, apparel and leather industries (Chinese community)	850.5	695.7
Textiles, apparel and leather industries (rest of economy)	897.6	739.7
Wood, paper and publishing industries	90.9	9.8
Coke industries, refineries, chemical and pharmaceutical industries	33.3	29.3
Manufacture of rubber, plastic and non-metallic mineral products	48.5	33.5
Metallurgy, except machinery and equipment	85.3	9.4
Electrical and electronic equipment, machinery (n.e.c.)	265.5	103.8
Manufacture of transport equipment	6.4	17.1
Manufacture of furniture; other manufactures; repairs (Chinese community)	16.7	18.9
Manufacture of furniture; other manufactures; repairs (rest of economy)	72.3	80.9
Electricity, gas, steam and air conditioning supply	1.8	0.0
Water supply; sewerage, waste management	35.4	0.0
Other industrial activities (Chinese community)	16.5	4.9
Construction (Chinese community)	0.0	0.0
Construction	4.7	1.6

(continued)

Table 8 (continued)

Production sectors	Export to rest of Italy	Export to rest of world
Wholesale and retail trade; repair of motor vehicles and motorcycles (Chinese community)	31.2	45.5
Wholesale and retail trade; repair of motor vehicles and motorcycles	150.4	232.5
Transportation and storage	309.2	27.4
Accommodation and food service activities (Chinese community)	4.9	0.1
Accommodation and food service activities	46.4	1.3
Information and communication services	103.3	10.8
Financial and insurance activities	65.1	2.3
Real estate activities (Chinese community)	6.3	0.5
Real estate activities	314.3	18.7
Professional, scientific and technical activities	32.9	19.0
Administrative and support service activities	59.0	18.9
Public Administration	0.2	0.1
Education	26.2	0.2
Human health and social work activities	0.7	0.0
Arts, entertainment and recreation	10.2	1.1
Other service activities (Chinese community)	4.6	0.4
Other service activities (rest of economy)	33.5	3.1
Other services (Chinese community)	5.3	0.8
Total	**4098.7**	**2314.2**
–Chinese community	935.9	766.8
–Rest of economy	3162.8	1547.5
Chinese community's percentage share on total value	22.8%	33.1%

ISTAT Branch classification of regional accounts (Aggregation of NACE REV.2 Classification)

Table 9 Percentage share of sectoral exports by migrant/autochthonous group with respect to the sectoral total (estimates from Prato's 2010 SAM)

Value of foreign exports	Chinese community (%)	Rest of economy (%)
Textile and clothing	48.5	52
Furniture and jewelry	19.0	81
Other manufacturing activities	0.5	100

Chinese sectors and production units from the other units operating in the context under scrutiny.

As shown in Table 5, the production value of the Chinese businesses in Prato is approximately €2.13 billion (17% of the total provincial production) and the value added is approximately €669 million (11.7% of the provincial total). The value added percentage share is lower than the production percentage share because Chinese businesses concentrate in low-value-added sectors.

Table 6 highlights the importance of the textile and clothing sector for Chinese businesses in Prato. Over 81% of the total Chinese production in the province is in the textile and clothing sector.

Table 7 shows the percentage of the total production (per macro-sector) generated by Chinese businesses. The table shows that Chinese firms produce 49% of Prato's total textile and clothing outputs, 19.17% of its furniture and fittings, 15.36% of its trade, and 9.45% of its housing and food services. Chinese businesses have a marginal impact in the other sectors in the province.

To verify the reasonableness of the estimates obtained, we look at the foreign exports of Chinese businesses. In 2010, Chinese businesses in Prato had exports of approximately €766.8 million (33.1% of the total exports from the province) (Table 8). These data are in line with the sectoral export coefficients for the rest of Tuscany. Chinese businesses export a high share of the total exports of goods for two reasons. First, because of the sectoral composition (Chinese businesses are concentrated in manufacturing sectors with high export rates). Second, because of the high degree of internationalization that characterizes these businesses. For example, Chinese firms export 48.5% of Prato's textile and clothing, and 19.0% of its furniture and jewelry (Table 9).

5   From the Matrix to the Economic Impact Model

Accounting matrices provide a partial or whole representation of the flows among the agents of an economic system for a particular year. The single blocks and the single cells in these matrices indicate the level of specific economic aggregates. Accordingly, the matrices provide a descriptive analysis of the economic systems, and are models that are capable of linking these aggregates.

IRPET constructs the accounting matrices annually, and continually enhances its analysis and the modelling tools drawn from accounting matrices. IRPET starts with elementary models and gradually incorporates increasingly complex models. The most traditional products of this modeling are Vassily Leontief's input–output models, also called Leontievian models. Their best-known reduced form is:

$$X = (I - A)^{-1}Y,$$

where X is the vector of sectoral production (the model's endogenous variable), Y is the vector of final demand (the model's exogenous variable), and $(I - A)^{-1}$ is Leontief's inverse matrix (also called Leontief's matrix), with A as the matrix of the technical coefficients of the symmetric input–output table. The dimension of the vectors and of the inverse matrix will match with the number of the production sectors classified in the inter-sectoral matrix.

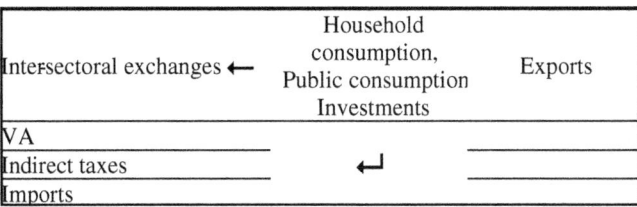

Fig. 2 One-year economic process using input–output matrices (authors' scheme). *VA* Value added

The Leontievian input–output equation is based on the most elementary assumptions made in the table. It supposes that the economy is closed to external trade (no imports or exports), and that there are no indirect taxes, trade margins, or induced effects on household consumption. As the matrices are gradually filled with additional information, the resulting inter-sectoral models are extended with improved specifications, more appropriate to describe the economic system in the short term.

The one-region input–output models produced by IRPET use symmetrical one-region input–output matrices and describe one part of the economic process. The part described starts from demand, and leads to the import of goods and services, their domestic production, and their income generation (Fig. 2).

This simulation allows the definition of the exogenous components (the final demand vectors of the symmetric matrices), and accordingly determines the endogenous components (production, value added, net indirect taxes, and imports). The exogenous variables used in the evaluation are precisely the demand vectors, with as many elements as the number of sectors in the model's input–output table. In the case of the Prato province, there are 28 branches, some of which distinguish between Chinese businesses and other businesses. The impact results can be presented in an aggregate form, or by sector, in terms of direct, indirect, and induced impact.

The tables in Sect. 4 descriptively illustrate the shares of production, value added, GDP, domestic final demand, and exports generated by the Chinese community compared with the total economy. When an input–output model accounts for the existing interrelationships between branches and institutional sectors, then we can infer the indirect and induced contributions to the economy of the Chinese households and businesses.

Table 10 shows the overall quantity of the entries in the supply-and-use account that are directly or indirectly attributable to Chinese businesses and households. If Prato's Chinese community did not exist, and if the demand addressed to its firms was not met by local producers, then the various entries in the supply-and-use

Table 10 Impact of the Chinese community's final demand (input–output model estimates)

Supply-and-use account	Entries of the supply-and-use account due to (million euro and total percentage share)					Total	Share of total economy (%)
	Consumptions of Chinese households	Investments of Chinese businesses and households	Regional exports of Chinese businesses	Foreign exports of Chinese businesses	Rest of demand met by Chinese businesses' production		
VA of Chinese community	5.5	1.4	292.3	238.5	131.3	669.0	100.0
VA of rest of economy	76.0	39.4	134.4	111.3	107.8	469.0	9.3
Total VA	**81.56**	**40.83**	**426.68**	**349.82**	**239.15**	**1138.0**	**19.9**
Net indirect taxes	16.99	5.26	9.31	120.58	141.78	293.9	33.2
GDP	**98.54**	**46.09**	**435.99**	**470.40**	**380.93**	**1432.0**	**21.7**
Inter-regional import	51.03	50.70	316.54	258.68	730.70	1,407.6	36.2
Foreign import	23.16	27.76	183.41	150.49	375.04	759.9	38.5
Resources	**172.73**	**124.56**	**935.94**	**879.57**	**1486.67**	**3599.5**	**28.9**
Intermediate demand	0.00	0.00	0.00	0.00	1189.40	1189.4	0.0
Household expenditure	172.73	0.00	0.00	0.00	211.22	384.0	11.5
PA and NPISH consumption	0.00	0.00	0.00	0.00	13.03	13.0	1.0
Gross investment	0.00	124.56	0.00	0.00	73.01	197.6	12.4

(continued)

Table 10 (continued)

Supply-and-use account	Entries of the supply-and-use account due to (million euro and total percentage share)						
	Consumptions of Chinese households	Investments of Chinese businesses and households	Regional exports of Chinese businesses	Foreign exports of Chinese businesses	Rest of demand met by Chinese businesses' production	Total	Share of total economy (%)
Inter-regional export	0.00	0.00	935.94	0.00	0.00	935.9	25.0
Foreign export	0.00	0.00	0.00	879.57	0.00	879.6	35.8
Uses	**172.73**	**124.56**	**935.94**	**879.57**	**1486.67**	**3599.5**	**28.9**

GDP Gross domestic product; *NPISH* Private non-profit institutions serving households; *PA* Public administration; *VA* Value added

Table 11 Share of provincial GDP activated by the Chinese community's final demand (input–output model estimates)

	Chinese businesses (%)	Businesses of other groups (%)
Consumption of Chinese households	0.1	1.3
Investments of Chinese businesses and households	0.0	0.7
Regional exports of Chinese businesses	5.1	2.4
Foreign exports of Chinese businesses	4.2	1.9
Rest of demand met by Chinese businesses' production	2.3	1.9

account would reduce. The final column in Table 10 represents the size of such a reduction for each item. If the Chinese community did not exist, then the GDP of Prato Province would be 21.7% lower, the valued added of non-Chinese firms would reduce by 9.3%, and regional and foreign imports would decrease by 36.2 and 38.5%, respectively.

The community's overall contribution corresponds to the sum of the single contributions for each component of demand whose presence is explained by the very existence of Prato's Chinese community. According to the results presented in Table 11, setting the total value added of the Prato province at 100, the portion of consumption by Chinese households represents 1.4%, where 0.1% is satisfied by the Chinese businesses and 1.3% is satisfied by other businesses. The investments of Chinese businesses and households produce 0.7% of GDP, all of which is achieved by non-Chinese businesses. The regional exports of Chinese businesses generate 7.5% of provincial value added (5.1% relates to the Chinese firms and 2.4% to the rest of economy). The foreign exports of Chinese businesses activate an overall value added of €349.8 million, which corresponds to 6.1% (4.2% generated by the Chinese firms and 1.9% by the rest of economy) of Prato's total. Finally, the rest of the (intermediate and final) demand[3] represents a share of 4.2% of provincial value added, where 2.3% is obtained by Chinese businesses and 1.9% by those of other groups. Table 12 gives the sectoral distribution of the direct and indirect contributions of the Chinese community.

The indigenous sectors that take the most advantage of the existence of Chinese businesses and households are, in order of importance: electricity supply, in which 23% of provincial value added is owing to the presence of the Chinese community; professional activities (16.8%); administrative activities (16.0%); financial and insurance activities (13.1%), and trade (10.1%).

---

[3]For this case, we assumed that if Chinese businesses did not exist, then this section of demand would not be met by the local production of indigenous businesses, and would thus vanish.

Table 12 Final demand related to the Chinese community (input–output model estimates)

VA	VA due to (million euro and total percentage share)						Total	Share of total economy (%)
	Consumptions of Chinese households	Investments of Chinese businesses and households	Regional exports of Chinese businesses	Foreign exports of Chinese businesses	Rest of demand met by Chinese businesses' production			
Agriculture, hunting and forestry	0.11	0.01	0.48	0.38	0.16		1.1	4.5
Fisheries, fish farming and related services	0.00	0.00	0.00	0.00	0.00		0.0	0.0
Extractive industry	0.02	0.02	0.14	0.11	0.07		0.4	8.2
Food, beverages and tobacco industries	0.04	0.00	0.04	0.03	0.02		0.1	0.9
Textiles, apparel and leather industries (Chinese community)	0.37	0.05	249.30	203.94	29.15		482.8	100.0
Textiles, apparel and leather industries (rest of economy)	0.14	0.04	10.51	8.60	2.28		21.6	4.6
Wood, paper and publishing industries	0.08	0.04	0.17	0.15	0.09		0.5	1.4
Coke industries, refineries, chemical and pharmaceutical industries	0.06	0.03	0.59	0.49	0.25		1.4	6.0
Manufacture of rubber, plastic and non-metallic mineral products	0.03	0.07	0.24	0.20	0.09		0.6	2.2
Metallurgy, except machinery and equipment	0.07	0.13	0.16	0.12	0.07		0.5	1.3
Electrical and electronic equipment, machinery (n.e.c.)	0.12	1.16	0.33	0.28	0.19		2.1	1.6

(continued)

Table 12 (continued)

VA	VA due to (million euro and total percentage share)					Total	Share of total economy (%)
	Consumptions of Chinese households	Investments of Chinese businesses and households	Regional exports of Chinese businesses	Foreign exports of Chinese businesses	Rest of demand met by Chinese businesses' production		
Manufacture of transport equipment	0.01	0.05	0.02	0.02	0.02	0.1	3.1
Manufacture of furniture; other manufactures; repairs (Chinese community)	0.02	0.03	5.83	6.59	1.00	13.5	100.0
Manufacture of furniture; other manufactures; repairs (rest of economy)	0.06	0.15	0.07	0.06	0.04	0.4	0.6
Electricity, gas, steam and air conditioning supply	0.93	0.42	13.82	11.41	5.97	32.6	23.7
Water supply; sewerage, waste management	1.34	0.22	5.65	4.61	2.31	14.1	15.8
Other industrial activities (Chinese community)	0.01	0.02	5.82	1.77	1.34	9.0	100.0
Construction (Chinese community)	0.00	0.07	0.01	0.01	1.65	1.7	100.0
Construction	0.38	14.88	1.60	1.32	1.08	19.3	6.5
Wholesale and retail trade; repair of motor vehicles and motorcycles (Chinese community)	2.12	0.83	18.01	23.81	49.35	94.1	100.0
Wholesale and retail trade; repair of motor vehicles and motorcycles	6.86	4.84	21.37	17.66	8.16	58.9	10.1

(continued)

Table 12 (continued)

VA	VA due to (million euro and total percentage share)						
	Consumptions of Chinese households	Investments of Chinese businesses and households	Regional exports of Chinese businesses	Foreign exports of Chinese businesses	Rest of demand met by Chinese businesses' production	Total	Share of total economy (%)
Transportation and storage	3.03	1.13	10.91	9.04	5.79	29.9	9.3
Accommodation and food service activities (Chinese community)	0.38	0.06	2.98	0.42	10.66	14.5	100.0
Accommodation and food service activities	2.61	0.57	4.01	3.33	2.77	13.3	8.9
Information and communication services	1.65	1.85	5.50	4.58	3.66	17.2	9.6
Financial and insurance activities	3.28	0.95	8.38	6.77	6.03	25.4	13.1
Real estate activities (Chinese community)	1.51	0.22	3.80	0.32	17.95	23.8	100.0
Real estate activities	44.58	10.32	17.78	15.14	12.86	100.7	10.0
Professional, scientific and technical activities	2.29	1.17	17.36	14.46	8.77	44.0	16.8
Administrative and support service activities	1.39	0.76	10.06	8.32	5.60	26.1	16.0
Public Administration	0.11	0.03	0.36	0.30	0.14	0.9	0.4
Education	2.08	0.14	1.72	1.43	0.97	6.3	2.3
Human health and social work activities	0.19	0.01	0.05	0.04	0.04	0.3	0.3
	0.42	0.09	1.17	0.96	0.64	3.3	10.3

(continued)

Table 12 (continued)

VA	VA due to (million euro and total percentage share)						
	Consumptions of Chinese households	Investments of Chinese businesses and households	Regional exports of Chinese businesses	Foreign exports of Chinese businesses	Rest of demand met by Chinese businesses' production	Total	Share of total economy (%)
Arts, entertainment and recreation							
Other service activities (Chinese community)	0.99	0.05	3.46	0.49	9.74	14.7	100.0
Other service activities (rest of economy)	4.15	0.37	1.90	1.55	0.79	8.8	7.4
Other services (Chinese community)	0.12	0.10	3.07	1.14	10.50	14.9	100.0
Total	81.56	40.83	426.68	349.82	239.15	1,138.0	19.9
–Chinese community	5.5	1.4	292.3	238.5	131.3	669.0	100.0
–Rest of economy	76.0	39.4	134.4	111.3	107.8	469.0	9.3
Chinese community's percentage share on total value	6.8%	3.5%	68.5%	68.2%	54.9%	58.8%	

VA Value added

6 Economic Evaluation of Provincial Policies

It is difficult to evaluate the economic development in the area reproduced by the accounting matrix, because there are several complex and interacting growth determinants. However, considering the development prospects of the area's predominant economic sector (textile and clothing) we can envisage a scenario with the following characteristics:

1. The technological and qualitative improvement of the entire fashion sector, entailing an increased quality (and price) of the products.
2. The reduction in the local production of semi-finished goods, resulting in an intensification of foreign imports (especially from China).
3. The growth in the demand for intermediate and sector-specific ancillary services, such as marketing and sales, and research and development services.

Table 13 Scenarios in the textile and clothing sector and changes in the SAM's exogenous variables (authors' assumptions)

1	Technological and qualitative improvement of the entire fashion sector, entailing an increased quality (and price) of products	The T&C sector's investments in machinery and equipment increase by 1% of current value
		The T&C sector's investments in research and development increase by 1% of current value
2	Reduction in the local production of semi-finished goods, resulting in an intensification of foreign import (especially from China)	The coefficient of imports (ratio between imports and total domestic demand) of products in the T&C sector increases by 1 percentage point
		The T&C sector's export prices increase by 1% of current price
3	Growth in the demand for intermediate and sector-specific, ancillary services, like marketing and sales, research and development services	The T&C sector's technical coefficient of business services (demand for business services on production) increases by 1 percentage point
		The T&C sector's share of VA (VA on production) increases by 1 percentage point, with a consequent reduction of technical coefficients
4	Increase in the exports to the EU and US	The exports of products in the T&C sector experience a real increase (net of prices) of 1%
5	Upgrade of Chinese firms to meet the quality and economic standards set by the Italian firms	The labour costs for the Chinese businesses in the T&C sector increase, taxation and insurance contributions align to the Italian standards, with a consequent negative impact on income and induced consumption

T&C Textile and clothing; *VA* Value added

4. The increase in the exports to the European Union (EU) and the United States (US).
5. The upgrade of Chinese businesses to meet the quality and economic standards set by Italian firms.

We can use the SAM as an economic evaluation tool for such scenarios, providing the assumptions are quantified in terms of (intermediate and final) demand. We use the SAM estimated for 2010 as the benchmark value of the provincial economy's annual flows. By modifying the level of some of the exogenous components of the SAM, we can consider the economic effect of these transformations in terms of the gap from the benchmark. Table 13 shows the equivalence between the above-illustrated scenarios and the percentage changes (compared with the benchmark value) in some of the demand components.

In scenarios 1–4, the considered variations are equal to one (as a percentage compared with the current value or a percentage point change in the corresponding coefficient). This is because it is impossible to accurately predict how the variables will evolve. By setting the variables equal to one, it is possible to calculate (using the simulation model based on the estimated SAM) their elasticity on GDP and on labor units. This corresponds to the percentage change the two variables will make, depending on the unit percentage change of each exogenous variable (modified as in Table 13). The fifth scenario differs from the others in that its corresponding assumption consists of the alignment of the contribution and tax burden to the

Table 14 Growth evaluation in association with the province's development prospects (SAM model estimates)

	Increase of GDP (million euro)	Increase of LUs (in units)	GDP percentage change (%)	LUs percentage change (%)
Investments in machinery and equipment (1% of current value)	0.03	0.33	0.00	0.00
Investments in research and development (1% of current value)	0.90	12.75	0.03	0.03
Increase of T&C's import coefficient (1 percentage point)	−2.28	−54.50	−0.05	−0.05
Increase of exports (1% of current value)	10.43	168.00	0.18	0.17
Increase of technical coefficient of business services (1 percentage point) and reduction of the other technical coefficients	10.33	380.00	0.18	0.39
Increase of the VA coefficient (1 percentage point) and reduction of technical coefficients	26.85	−141.83	0.47	−0.15
Real increase of exports (1% of current value)	10.43	168.00	0.17	0.17
Reduction of induced consumptions due to the actual increase of contribution and taxation (adjusted to the rest of economy)	−27.00	−215.00	−0.50	−0.20

GDP Gross domestic product; *LU* Labor unit; *T&C* Textile and clothing; *VA* Value added standard levels of the other businesses, which implies a reduction of job and fiscal irregularities. The results (in terms of elasticity) are presented in the last two columns of Table 14.

Table 14 indicates the absolute and relative variations of the province of Prato's GDP and employment rate, obtained by modifying the demand variables according to the scenarios assumed in Table 13. Once the percentage change of a specific exogenous variable is reliably known, we can estimate its effects on GDP and on labor units. We simply multiply the estimated variation by the elasticity figure contained in the last columns of Table 14. For example, assume that we know that textile exports will grow 20%. We then multiply 20 by the elasticity values 0.18 and 0.17 (fourth row in Table 14) to respectively get the GDP and labor unit growth estimates resulting from this increase of exports (3.6 and 2.4%, respectively). We can apply the same calculation to any other hypothesized exogenous variable.

7   Conclusions

The SAM employed in this chapter provides an accurate picture of the province's current economic structure and an ex-ante measure of the possible economic effects of integration. However, this tool gives only a partial impact evaluation of an immigrant community's integration. This is because the social aspects of integration cannot be measured simply by generated GDP. From a political and social viewpoint, there are considerably more influential non-economic dimensions in modern societies, such as social cohesion, the environment, and the landscape. A further reason for the partial impact evaluation by the SAM is that—even if we restrict the analysis to the economic impact alone—the long-term random, non-linear effects might generate in the future larger economic advantages than the immediate effects convey. For example, consider the huge socio-economic potential of the children from other communities who follow the same education path. Further, consider the growing use of local public services by immigrants (who can partly access health and welfare services, follow building procedures, or enroll their siblings in primary and secondary schools) until some of them enter local politics. Such occurrences could lead to new forms of collaboration, union agreements, and organizations, with unpredictable dynamics and indirect effects on the province's economy.

Clearly, the integration between old and new residents is a long-term process, and foreign immigration to Italy is a relatively recent phenomenon, dating from the 1990s. Currently, the integration is insufficiently mature; however, it might reach maturity if the actors in the provincial economic system are willing to move in that direction.

The Prato district is currently in a vulnerable period of development. It contains both critical elements (precarious—if not illegal—working conditions, exacerbated by the high level of price competition and the conflicts between the two local communities) and exploitable potentials (the Chinese community's strong industriousness, work ethic, and motivation, and international relationships that are not limited to the sale of final products). Public policies should seek to enhance these potentials, and to recreate the combination of cooperation and competition that previously drove the economic development and the social integration of the Prato district.

The scenarios, based on the assumption of integration, presuppose overcoming the local liabilities through a synergy between the Chinese and the autochthonous communities. The Chinese community would increase its relationships with local companies, institutions, and families (with increases in its product retail). The autochthonous community would increase its foreign market share through the intermediation by Chinese companies.

Contrastingly, if conflict prevailed, then social unrest would undoubtedly increase in both communities, and the Prato economy would not adapt to the changed international competition scenario. Clearly, the integration of such a substantial part of the population, which has steadily immigrated into the province, is necessary for social cohesion. However, it is also necessary for the economic competitiveness of the district, and therefore the future development of the area.

References

Berti F, Pedone V, Valzania A (eds) (2013) Vendere e comprare. Processi di mobilita sociale dei cinesi a Prato. Pacini Editore, Pisa

Casini Benvenuti S, Paniccià R (2003) A multi-regional input-output model for Italy. IRPET, Firenze

Colombi A (ed) (2002) L'imprenditoria cinese nel distretto industriale di Prato. Leo S. Olschki Editore, Firenze

Dei Ottati G (2014) A transnational fast fashion industrial district: an analysis of the Chinese businesses in Prato. Camb J Econ 38(5):1247–1274

IRPET, Provincia di Prato, ASEL (2014) Prato: il ruolo economico della comunità cinese. IRPET, Firenze

Ministero dello Sviluppo Economico (2009) La matrice di contabilità sociale: uno strumento per la valutazione. IPI, Roma

Pyatt G, Round J (1985) Social accounting matrices: a basis for planning. The World Bank

Scandizzo PL (1994) I modelli di equilibrio economico generale e la valutazione dei progetti d'investimento. ISPE, Roma

Stone JRN, Champernowne DG, Meade JE (1942) The precision of national income estimates. Rev Econ Stud 9:111–125

Targetti R (ed) (2004) Matrici regionali di contabilità sociale & analisi di politiche economiche: il caso della Liguria, Toscana e Marche. F. Angeli, Milano

Ethnography of the Fast Fashion Community: Chinese Entrepreneurs in Prato

Stefano Becucci

Abstract The city of Prato is now a social microcosm, emblematic of Italy's main immigration problems and of market globalization. This chapter investigates the organization of the Chinese fast fashion sector, and the factors contributing to its growth. I also investigate whether the presence of Chinese entrepreneurs causes a disadvantage for the local textile entrepreneurs and workers. Alternatively, did the Chinese fast fashion sector grow as a parallel district that shares few relationships with textile production? I address these issues through ethnographic tools such as open interviews with key informants and field research in the Macrolotto 1 industrial district (an industrial area in Prato occupied chiefly by Chinese fast fashion firms). The first part of the chapter analyzes the local Chinese entrepreneurs involved in fast fashion. The second part focuses on the connections between the Chinese entrepreneurs and the local economic players. Finally, the third part of the chapter examines the reactions of the local population toward the presence of Chinese immigrants (and particularly their businesses).

Keywords Fast fashion · Chinese entrepreneurs · Textile district · Ethnographic research

1 Introduction

The city of Prato is now a social microcosm, emblematic of Italy's main immigration problems and of market globalization. Demographically, Prato's population of immigrant residents has significantly increased—from 12,015 in 2002 to 34,171 in 2014 (corresponding to 18% of its total inhabitants). Among the foreigners in Prato, Chinese immigrants are the most plentiful. In 2014, there were 15,957 Chinese immigrants in Prato, equivalent to 47% of all of the foreign residents in the city (Municipality of Prato 2003, 2015). Economically, Prato's industrial district,

S. Becucci (✉)
Department of Social and Political Sciences, University of Florence, Florence, Italy
e-mail: stefano.becucci@unifi.it

which is the true historical source of the city's wealth, has changed significantly. Once one of the top national players in Italy's industrial textile production, over the past decade Prato has progressively decreased this manufacturing sector. As local entrepreneurs closed their businesses and left the textile sector, foreign firms have grown, particularly those managed by Chinese people. The Chinese are the most dynamic segment of all of the foreign entrepreneurs in Prato, and in 2013 accounted for 63% of all foreign firms in the province of Prato (Prato Chamber of Commerce 2014).

The decline in local firms, together with the increase in Chinese businesses, contributes to the contrasting reactions toward these immigrants from the local population. One view is that the Chinese community seems to represent the natural scapegoat for the social tensions connected with the declining textile sector and the ensuing increase in poverty in the city. Another view is that the (*troubling*) hard-working Chinese way of life fuels the accusations against these immigrants of unfair competition (not without evidence) (Girard 1987).[1] These aspects encompass some of the social and economic dynamics needed to analyze the Chinese community involved in *fast-fashion*[2] production in Prato.

This chapter is divided into three parts. The first part analyzes the local Chinese entrepreneurs involved in fast fashion. The second part focuses on the connections between the Chinese entrepreneurs and the local economic players. The final part examines the reactions of the local population toward the presence of Chinese immigrants (and particularly their businesses).

2 Research Questions and Methods

The first issue underlying the research regards how the Chinese fast fashion sector is organized. The second issue concerns the factors that caused the huge growth of Chinese fast fashion in Prato city. Is it true that, as some of the people interviewed during the field research stated, fast fashion production developed to the detriment of local entrepreneurs? Conversely, could Chinese fast fashion be considered a *parallel district* that is increasingly flanking the area's historic textile production?[3]

---

[1]Between 2000 and 2009, Prato's inhabitants employed in the *industrial and artisan* sector decreased from 41,080 to 34,049. The largest decrease involved the textile sector that declined from 25,304 employees in 2000 to 13,683 in 2009 (Prato Industrial Entrepreneurs Study Centre 2012).

[2]By *fast fashion*, I mean a garment sector characterized by very rapid production and sales, where the time gap between producing the clothes and their consumption by the market is very short (Guercini 2001, pp. 69–79).

[3]I use the term *parallel district* descriptively here, as a form of production that shows certain aspects encompassed in the wider local industrial district. Some other commentators use the term to refer to Chinese entrepreneurs as *foreign bodies* with respect to the local economic fabric, similar to the way the city population tends to view immigrants (Pieraccini 2008, 2010).

In response, this article addresses the current relationships between the local and the Chinese entrepreneurs. Additionally, based on the interview results and statistical data, the analysis focuses on the decline of the local textile production and the parallel increase of the Chinese fast fashion firms. The development of Chinese firms and the decline of local entrepreneurs have engendered resentment among political institutions, economic associations, and the population as a whole, leading to intolerance toward Chinese immigrants. As I show, this intolerance is fueled by certain misunderstandings, and by real problems requiring a solution.

The research is based on ethnographic methods, including open interviews with key informants, and field research in the Macrolotto 1 industrial district on the city's outskirts (occupied chiefly by Chinese fast-fashion firms). Between January 2012 and September 2013, I conducted 32 investigations in the Macrolotto 1 area. I visited approximately 40 Chinese firms several times, and questioned the owners and the workers about their production organization, costs, prices, and clients. Additionally, between January 2012 and April 2014, I interviewed 19 professional and informed individuals including local economic association personnel, law-enforcement officers, political administrators, several Italian entrepreneurs, and a Chinese entrepreneur.[4] Selected mainly by their institutional role, I questioned these key informants to analyze the current situation of the textile district, the organization of Chinese fast fashion, and the possible relationships between the two. Moreover, I asked the Italian interviewees to evaluate Chinese immigration in the city, with particular reference to Chinese entrepreneurs.

3 Fast Fashion in Macrolotto 1

Planned in the late 1970s, the Macrolotto 1 industrial district extends to 150 hectares. Bordering with the bigger Macrolotto 2, both areas have a building typology based on workshops without residential housing on the upper floors. When Macrolotto 1 was first built, it was occupied by Italian entrepreneurs; however, it is now the main hub for Chinese firms involved in fast fashion. According to a 2012 Chinese/Italian telephone book that contains advertisements by Chinese firms, the province of Prato had 823 businesses with Chinese owners, 580 of those in the clothing sector.[5] Within those advertisements were one dyer, two cloth printers, three designers, 12 clothing import/export companies and three textile import/export companies. Analyzing the advertisements, I established that 494 out of the 580 Chinese clothing firms are based in Macrolotto 1, corresponding to 85%.

---

[4]The list of interviewees is included as an appendix to this chapter.

[5]This is a rough figure. I base it only on the advertisements that identify the type of firm directly or indirectly connected with the garment industry.

In the field research, I was helped by an Italian individual (henceforth referred to as G, the guide), who liaises daily with approximately 100 Chinese entrepreneurs. G works for a Pakistani trader living in Germany. The trader visits Macrolotto 1 each week, to select sample collections for testing in 20 German shops. If the trial order is successful with his customers, then the trader orders large quantities of clothes from the Chinese firms in Macrolotto 1. The garments are sent weekly via medium-sized vans (in other cases, monthly via truck) to German cities such as Stuttgart and Dusseldorf, where the trader's shops are located. The trader also acts as a broker for several German clothing brands (comparable to the OVS retail chain in Italy). For every purchase of the brands made in Prato, the Pakistani trader receives a percentage. G supervises the entire trading process, from the order, to shipping the clothes to Germany. G deals with 10,000–20,000 clothing items per month, peaking in the summer months at 60,000–80,000. The Pakistani trader manages the financial transactions; however, G reports that approximately 40% of the orders are invoiced, while the remainder are paid in cash (euros) when the trader comes to Prato.

The first time I accompanied G in visiting the Chinese workshops, the entrepreneurs and the workers were cautious, probably because I was unfamiliar. G recalls facing the same suspicion when first visiting Macrolotto 1 as an employee of the Pakistani owner: "*I knocked on the door of the workshop many times, but it remained closed because they did not know me.*" It was subsequently relatively easy to visit the Chinese workshops to question the owners and employees.

I first describe the workspaces, of which there are (broadly) two workshop types. The first type of workshop is 500–700 m^2 in size (often a subdivision of an originally larger space). Most of the available space acts as a showroom. On one side, there is generally a staircase leading to an upper floor used for storage. According to G (who visits the workshops daily), the upper floor is also used as a dormitory, "*in the morning I see clothing hanging out to dry*". In the showroom area, there may be workers affixing labels to clothes for boxing and shipping to the customer's destination. G does not speak Chinese, and communicates with the Chinese entrepreneurs in Italian. Therefore, during G's visits, there may be young second-generation Chinese people in the workshop for the specific purpose of talking to and planning with G. The final part of the workshop, representing approximately 10% of the space, always contains a machine for cutting fabric. Further, it tends to contain several rolls of fabric along the walls and occasionally some sewing machines. The second type of workshop is smaller, approximately 200–300 m^2, and does not have a showroom space. Those workshops always have a machine for cutting fabric and several sewing machines (between 5 and 10). Such workshops only produce garments on demand.

On several occasions, I asked about the origin of the fabrics in the workshops. The Chinese owners responded by saying they were produced by local Italian firms. However, several times, I noted fabric rolls with labels from foreign countries such as South Korea. My observation corresponds to information obtained from the interviews with the law enforcement officers. The officers claim that the fabric used to produce garments comes from foreign countries such as China, India, and South

Korea.[6] It is rough fabric, largely consisting of synthetic fibers such as polyester or wool blends, and is undyed. During the study, the law enforcement officers showed me some footage of police inspections of Chinese firms.

When the garment design is chosen and the fabric cut, the ensuing production stages tend to occur outside the Macrolotto 1 district. Based on my conversations with G and my interviews with the law enforcement officers, I ascertained that the fabric is sent to sewing shops established in the central area of Prato city—the borough of San Paolo, where most Chinese immigrants live.[7] These sewing shops are the full-fledged workshops: usually apartments, basements, and garages in which there are 20–40 sewing machines. These sewing shops can also be used as dormitories, with the workers adapting to the small spaces as much as possible. Once assembled, the garments are ironed (Chinese ironing teams move from one part of the city to another on demand) and the clothing is then returned to Macrolotto 1. Finally, workers attach labels saying *Made in Italy* to the clothes. Legally, the labels legitimately draw the attention of Italian (and foreign) customers to local artisanal traditions. In reality, only a small part of these labels represent the real production process. On the back, in Italian and English, the labels claim:

> Like the work that goes into the production of this garment, the materials are made in Italy. This guarantees the value and quality that can be obtained only through Italian experience in this sector.

For most women's wear (dresses, skirts, shirts, trousers, coats, and jackets), the 2012 wholesale prices were €3–€30 (€3 for polyester shirts and skirts, €14 for jackets, and €30 for coats). In the ensuing field investigations conducted in 2013, the low-end prices had increased by up to €5, while the jacket and coat prices had not changed. Notably, such prices are possible only for large quantities, as ordered by G's Pakistani employer. He sells garments in Germany for three to four times the price that he paid. A skirt or shirt sells for €12–€20; prices attractive to the customers, who believe that they are buying clothing *made in Italy*.

To explain why the Chinese Macrolotto 1 workshops can offer these prices, the interviewees offer some hypotheses.[8] One issue is the fabric prices in Macrolotto 1. Polyester costs €1.80–€2.80 m^{-2} (approximately the quantity necessary to produce a garment). Such low prices are generally only possible if the fabric is imported from countries such as China. The low prices lead to low production costs. In September 2013, during one of my last visits to the workshops, I asked about the origin of the fabric for a women's jacket selling for €13. The Chinese seller answered, "*It is Chinese and, considering these prices, it can be no other way.*"

---

[6]Interview in Prato, October 2012.

[7]This area, the so-called Macrolotto 0, was once occupied by local small firms producing wool garments (Bressan and Tosi Cambini 2011).

[8]Interviews with a representative of the National Federation of Artisans (CNA), a representative of Confartigianato, and the President of Confindustria (the national industrial entrepreneur association), Naples (Prato and Naples, September–October 2012).

Some interviewees pointed out that the lack of quality controls on the fabric and the very low wages paid to the workforce in its country of origin reduce the selling prices by at least 60% compared with the Italian textile businesses.[9] According to the interviewees, an article of clothing made in a Chinese workshop costs as little as €1.80 for the raw material (the minimum value) plus a workforce cost of 50–70 cents. With the exception of the design and cutting processes (bespoke to each design), the production does not require specific expertise (for example, the garment seams are wide mesh and crudely finished). Additionally, the workforce does not generally receive legal wages; they are paid per job. Being paid per job is also a common practice in businesses that formally respect the law. In these cases, the costs related to wages, social security, and insurance are charged to the employee.[10] Similarly, the Chinese entrepreneur who was interviewed, reports that employing his fellow countrymen as workers significantly reduces production costs.[11]

Chinese entrepreneurs make a very low profit per article of clothing sold for €3, while the margin is higher on those sold for €5. However, overall, the profits are still very low. According to those interviewed, the profit on each garment is less than one euro and is sometimes only a few dozen cents. Hence, a Chinese entrepreneur must sell several thousands of pieces per day (in the best-case scenario) to get a significant profit. Two basic conditions allow the Chinese entrepreneurs to sell fast fashion at very low prices. The very low costs, owing to a workforce available at extremely low wages, and the production of large volumes of garments.

During the field investigation, I frequently encountered small groups of buyers coming from Northern Italy and from several other European countries such as France and Poland. Like G's Pakistani trader, they regularly come to Macrolotto 1 to purchase large quantities of clothing at wholesale prices. I interviewed one Italian clothes trader who runs stalls at some of the larger open markets in Florence, such as Cascine and Piazza delle Cure. For the last number of years, he regularly visits Macrolotto 1 to purchase clothes. He reports, "*All of my colleagues working at open markets here do the same.*" Annually, he buys approximately 10,000 articles of clothing from five Chinese workshops for €5–€20 per garment (the latter amount for a mixed wool/polyester coat). From an economic standpoint, he points out:

> I cannot sell a coat for €150–€200. My customers who live on a monthly salary of €1,200 would never buy it, especially in today's economic crisis, where people pay attention even to €5. So, I need to offer my merchandise for a maximum of €50–€60. By purchasing a coat for €20, I can sell it for around €60, which is more or less twice what I bought it for... All the jeans we sell for €50–€60 come from abroad, and this includes those sold in the shops

---

[9]Interviews with a law enforcement representative.

[10]Interview with a trade union representative (Prato, September 2013).

[11]This Chinese entrepreneur established a new firm several years ago, employing both Italian and Chinese people. He recalls that his fellow countrymen tend not to employ Italians, because "*with Italians, you know that you need to respect the law, there are trade unions, holidays to be paid and so on. When you hire a Chinese worker these problems do not exist, so [the workforce] costs less, much less*" (Prato, June 2013).

for €80. I get them from a Chinese trader in the Esquilino borough [an area near Rome's central railway station, centered around Piazza Vittorio] who imports the jeans from China. The cleaning process alone for jeans costs €10. If the jeans were produced in Italy, they would retail for €150–€200.

Interview conducted in Campi Bisenzio (Province of Florence, February 2012).

In Macrolotto 1, there is a particularly large demand for low-cost goods on Tuesdays and Fridays, the days usually devoted to merchandise forwarding. In the field investigations conducted between 19.00 h and midnight, I observed a constant flow of medium-large vans entering and exiting the Macrolotto 1 workshops. This frenetic movement of people and vehicles contrasted starkly with the lack of activity in the nearby Macrolotto 2 area. That area was quiet, with the closed units barely illuminated by the emergency lights outside the factory doors, a situation common in most industrial districts. In comparison, despite Macrolotto 1 lacking a good public lighting system, the entire district was illuminated by neon signs, by light coming from doorways, and by the headlights of the vehicles driving around.

Other elements also recount the busy activities within the Macrolotto area. The district has two cafés, eight Chinese restaurants open until after midnight, gazebos cooking fast food, and a Chinese seller of typical Italian food. Even during the day, this industrial area presents itself as a dynamic (and informal) economic microcosm. For example, a Neapolitan seller drives around in his van, using his poor Chinese to offer fruit and vegetables to the workers, and several enterprising Chinese men travel around offering fast food to the employees.

The costs of renting the workshops also show the economic importance of this industrial area. Although I could not officially establish the rents, according to G, a building of 1000 m^2 costs up to €10,000 a month. This probably corresponds to the highest rent for specific areas in Macrolotto 1, where I noted the greatest movement of vehicles and people at night. Regardless, the workspaces are particularly sought by Chinese entrepreneurs. Several (Chinese) people are specifically tasked with searching for newly available spaces and with relaying this information to the Chinese entrepreneurs who want to locate in the Macrolotto 1 area.

Notably, the owners in this industrial area are almost all Italian entrepreneurs or former entrepreneurs. According to the Macrolotto 1 manager (responsible for liaising between the owners and the tenants), of the 230 owners only three are Chinese. The 2011 internal census in Macrolotto 1 counted approximately 400 firms: 150 Italian and 250 Chinese.[12] However, my investigations indicate that are actually many more Chinese firms (from my travels in the area, from reports by G, and based on the data from the Italian/Chinese telephone books). The district's manager did not provide actual figures for the rent prices. However, he admitted that after the arrival of the Chinese entrepreneurs:

Italian owners got much more money. Among us, we ironically refer to one of these owners as 'Paperon de Paperoni' [the Italian version of Scrooge] because he has seven or eight large industrial buildings for a total of 7,000–8,000 square meters. Rumor has it that he asks

---

[12]Interview conducted in Macrolotto 1 (Prato, February 2012).

for annual rent of up to €100 per square meter, and certainly not all of this money is legally declared. When an industrial building is put up for sale, he is the first to make an offer to buy it... The Chinese are really good businesspeople: they pay regularly and do not cause trouble. If someone fails to pay a bill, we call him and he immediately comes and settles up in cash.[13]

Interview conducted in Macrolotto 1 (Prato, February 2012).

I saw no evident problems between the Italian and the Chinese entrepreneurs; however, there are signs indicating how the former view their Asian colleagues. For example, a carpentry shop in Macrolotto 1 displays an uncommonly large Italian flag, as if the owner wants to demonstrate that he is part of an Italian territory in which he perceives himself as a foreigner in his own home. The Macrolotto 1 manager reports that, among the owners, there are conflicts between the so-called *dry* and *wet* producers (referring to the use of water to produce fabric, the former having divested their business while the latter have continued in business). The wet owners are very worried about the presence of the Chinese entrepreneurs, while the dry owners are reaping huge economic benefits by leasing their properties.

4   Connections Between Chinese Fast-Fashion Businesses and the Local Textile District

To look for possible relationships between local textile businesses and Chinese fast-fashion firms, I consider two phases of the production process: the dyeing (and printing) of the garments, and the garment design.

Regarding the dyeing process, I contacted ten Italian entrepreneurs with firms in Macrolotto 1. Of these, eight say that they do not have any relationships with the Chinese entrepreneurs, while two maintain indirect connections with them (they work for local textile producers who, in turn, sell fabric to the Chinese entrepreneurs). Despite encountering suspicion and distrust from the Italian entrepreneurs, one agreed to talk about the research topic. He says that the Italian dyers are not particularly involved with the Chinese fast fashion firms, because the Chinese entrepreneurs dye the garment rather than the fabric. The Chinese entrepreneurs buy partially manufactured fabric, generally white or cream in color, and make the clothing using that fabric. They then observe the market trends, and dye the finished garment appropriately. This process does not require as much capital or professional knowhow as dyeing the fabric directly. To explain his point, this Italian

---

[13]A former Italian entrepreneur confirmed the figures reported by G and by the Macrolotto 1 manager. He was one of the first local entrepreneurs to rent his industrial building to Chinese entrepreneurs in 1996, because "*they paid double the rent of the Italians*" (Prato, April 2014).

entrepreneur compared his firm with that of a Chinese competitor. He has a working space of 2300 m^2 and several huge dyeing machines that now work at no more than 40% of their full capacity, because his firm does not receive sufficient orders. In contrast, the garment-dyeing process simply uses big washing machines. Additionally, if the Chinese producer were to dye fabric, "*after dyeing 1000 m, he could use only half, so what happens to the remainder?*"[14] By deferring the dyeing process to the end, the Chinese entrepreneur chooses the best color to tap into the current fashion trends.[15]

For dyeing, the Chinese entrepreneurs tend to use Chinese dyers; even if the latter generally do not have the specialized knowledge needed for the dyeing machinery and must thus employ Italian technicians.[16] Although the Italian dyers are involved in this process (as in some cases I discovered by talking to them), they do not benefit sufficiently to emerge from the economic crisis they face. Italian fabric printers do work with the Chinese fast-fashion firms. As the Italian dyer reports:

> I have three colleagues working regularly for the Chinese. They print the fabric on a white background and later add the chosen color to the garment based on market trends. This was particularly true this past year when camouflage-type garments became popular.
>
> Interview conducted in Macrolotto 1 (Prato, September 2013).

In regard to garment design, my interviewees reported that the designers are both Italian and Chinese. Additionally, both a trade union representative and G pointed out that the fastest way to get new designs is to buy fashionable garments in city shops, and then disassemble them and reproduce them with the help of designers. According to the interviewed Chinese entrepreneurs (and as demonstrated by contacts with Italian dyers), increasingly:

> Chinese firms employ Italians as bookkeepers, secretaries, and designers, but there are also Chinese entrepreneurs purchasing fabric from local producers.
>
> Interview (Prato, June 2013).

---

[14]Macrolotto 1 (Prato, September 2013).

[15]Benetton, one of Italy's largest clothing firms since the early 1990s, anticipated this new system of production. As one researcher points out (translated from Italian):

> the revolution of garment-dyeing allowed [this brand] to make products that were only dyed when they were finished, thus exploiting the sales data coming from its retail shops and adapting its supply to the current market trends.
>
> (Cietta 2008, p. 3).

[16]Interview with a trade-union representative (Prato, September 2013).

5   Local Society Concerns Regarding Chinese Entrepreneurs: Misunderstandings and Real Problems

Owing to the entry of the Chinese entrepreneurs who satisfied a huge demand for low-cost goods, the Macrolotto 1 industrial district did not decline, as other Italian industrialized areas did when the Italian entrepreneurs left their businesses. However, possibly because of this, the local public is worried about the Chinese immigrants. As an Italian woman, who speaks Chinese and works as a translator for the local court, reports:

> In Prato there is no relationship between the local population and the Chinese immigrants. On the contrary, there is reciprocal incommunicability. People consider the Chinese immigrants to be usurpers because their involvement in fast fashion is associated with the closure of the local textile producers. My own father owned a small wool garment firm that worked for a larger firm. He closed his business because he retired, but he would have had to close it anyway because of the lack of new orders.[17]

> Interview (Prato, July 2011).

The distrust toward the Chinese immigrants is at least partially fueled by a misunderstanding: the perception that there is a specific link between the shutdown of the local textile businesses and the growing number of Chinese fast fashion firms. Initially, the statistics concerning this manufacturing sector appear to confirm that sentiment. In 2002, the non-Chinese local textile/clothing firms in Prato Province amounted to 5201, while in 2013 there were 2644, reflecting a 51% decrease.[18] During the same period, the number of Chinese firms grew from 1263 to

---

[17] An earlier study found that in Prato the Chinese entrepreneurs are seen as having stolen work from the local population (Chen 2011). A similar perception—in this case related to the fear of crime—emerged from one of my interviews. A magistrate who worked for years at Prato's city court (and now works in the court of Florence) reported:

> Around a year before the 2009 local political election [which gave city government to center-right political parties] I predicted the winner. I was invited to talk at a public debate on security and crime in a city borough that has historically been left wing. When I said that it is not possible to fight Chinese immigrants only from a judiciary standpoint, I immediately sensed that the audience stepped back. Later a young man in the audience said that every time he takes the train at the Porta Serraglio railway station [close to the Chinese settlement in the city] he is afraid that he will be the victim of crime. I replied that the perception of insecurity is not connected to Chinese criminality. However, the people present were astonished that I, of all people, would make such a statement. It was as if these people were saying to me: '*You cannot understand us because you do not know anything about these things... we really feel in danger.*' When I subsequently started to talk about what we do as public magistrates to fight Chinese criminality in the city, then people's opinion changed.

> Interview (Florence, July 2011).

[18] The comparison is between non-Chinese textile/clothes firms and Chinese firms present in the same textile/clothing sector. I use the expression non-Chinese firms, because the available data can be divided between all firms and Chinese firms. Clearly, the non-Chinese category includes a great majority of Italian firms and a very small number of other foreign firms.

3575, marking an increase of 283% (Prato Chamber of Commerce 2003, 2014). However, these data may be misleading if taken as a representative picture of this sector. To better evaluate the changes that occurred over the last decade, it is important to differentiate between the textile and the clothing firms. First, consider the textile firms. In 2002, there were 4554 textile firms in the province of Prato; while in 2013, there were 2256 (50% decrease). In the same period, the number of Chinese textile firms increased from 43 (1%) to 320 (14%). Next, consider the garment firms. In 2002, there were 1910 garment firms in Prato province; while in 2013, there were 3963 (roughly a 100% increase). Of those, the Chinese firms increased from 1210 (63% in 2002) to 3255 (82% in 2013). Hence, the numbers of Chinese firms are increasing in both the textile and the garment sectors; however, those in the garment segment have very significantly increased.

In the garment sector, there is no competition with local firms, as might be supposed initially. However, competition certainly exists in the textile sector that— as opposed to the clothing sector—presents significant barriers to entry in terms of capital and qualified workers. Historically, competition existed in the garment sector. Then, in the 1990s (when Chinese firms worked primarily in wool production), the Chinese entrepreneurs competed with the local Italian firms involved in sub-supply to larger Italian businesses. In the mid-2000s, the Chinese entrepreneurs started a new large-scale fast fashion production, prominently consisting of artificial fibers such as polyester as well as wool blends. Essentially, this fast fashion niche did not previously exist in the local economic context, in terms of the type of material used (polyester instead of carded wool) and of the fast production times (Dei Ottati 2013). Indeed, fast fashion production was never a prominent activity in the history of Prato's textile industry.

The manufacturing district was (and is) characterized by the production of fabric and only partially by the production of garments. Historically, the garments were only made of wool, and were divided into two types: planned and fast fashion wool clothes knitted by small local firms.[19] This type of production began to decline in the early 1980s—long before the arrival of Chinese entrepreneurs[20]—because of changing market trends, with preferences emerged for clothes made of fabrics other than the traditional wool (Dei Ottati 2004; Ferrucci 1996; Bracci 2008; Fabbri 2011). This is part of a gradually declining trend in the overall demand for wool as a basic component. The percentage of wool products in the entire local textile production decreased from 95% after World War II, to 75% in the 1970s, 55% in the 1980s, and 35% in the early 2000s (Marigolli 2004).

---

[19]Consider the figures for 1976, when Prato's textile industry was at its peak. In that year, Prato city was home to 4914 firms involved in textile production and to 730 firms in the garment industry. Moreover, in 1991, Prato province had 34,956 workers in the textile sector and 2739 in the clothing sector (Cerreta 1999).

[20]The new-wave of Chinese immigrants to Prato started in the early 1990s. At the time, their presence was on a small scale, as evidenced by the 212 Chinese firms existing in Prato in 1993 (Ceccagno 2003).

In regard to Chinese fast fashion, on several occasions I asked representatives of the local economic associations why the Italian entrepreneurs did not diversify their businesses to cover the entire production chain from producing fabric to making garments. They responding by saying:

> We are talking about two different professions: one is textile production, entailing greater expertise in this process, and the other is making and trading clothes. These activities require significantly different knowhow, mindsets, and relationships.
>
> Interviews with three representatives of artisan and industrial associations.
>
> (CNA, Confartigianato, and Unione Industriale) (Prato, July–October 2012).

With the exception of a few local brands that manage to operate on an international level covering the entire production chain, Prato's entrepreneurs place themselves at the upper end of the chain (textile production) rather than at the lower end (production of clothing).

As voiced in several of the interviews, the local industrial fabric crisis originated some time ago, with the arrival on the international market of countries such as China and India. These new market entrants were able to offer their goods at very competitive prices. A further factor in the textile sector crisis is the lack of a generational change within the local firms. The children of the Italian entrepreneurs who drove the great development of the local industrial firms, did not follow their parents' lead. As stated by the trade union representative:

> My father was a small wool entrepreneur, and in my family I grew up with 'bread and cannelli' [types of cylinders put on the spindle to spin the wool]. However, neither I nor my two brothers followed in our father's footsteps, and my own two sons did the same.
>
> Interview (Prato, September 2013).

Similarly, the director of the Industrial Association Study Centre points out:

> Last year the city's technical secondary schools barely enrolled enough students to constitute a first-year class. This is a problem, because this professional expertise would be very important for a textile district.
>
> Interview (Prato, October 2012).

A further notable aspect is the significant change in market trends. Several decades ago, producers made garments (and fabrics) knowing that they would last for years. From this standpoint, the market has completely changed. Entrepreneurs in the garment industry know that the current styles will change the following season. The fashion industry dictates that there is no demand for last-season's stock; hence, the entrepreneurs need to take *real-time* opportunities coming from the fluctuations in demand (Marazzi 1999). The current changeable demand for clothes (as well as for other goods in broader terms) has contributed to developing a huge fast fashion production. Effectively, this manufacturing sector is specifically prepared to identify new market trends and to rapidly translate them into goods to offer consumers.

The second misunderstanding that feeds negative feelings toward Chinese entrepreneurs is based on the assumption that they copy designs, giving them an unfair competitive advantage over their Italians colleagues. Several interviewees reported this unfair behavior; however, it is worth quoting an Italian dyer:

> Today everybody copies. Once it was very difficult to obtain the professional secrets of other entrepreneurs, because only agents managed the sample collections. Now, thanks to new technologies, anyone can take a picture of the new designs on the market and then reproduce them. Although all entrepreneurs can copy, this operation can be done in various ways. What really makes a difference is whether or not one adopts the expertise offered by the professional backgrounds present in certain territories.
>
> Interview conducted in Macrolotto 1 (Prato, September 2013).

Similarly, an Italian trader who buys clothes from Chinese fast fashion businesses notes (translated from Italian):

> Often we give Chinese entrepreneurs designs and perhaps they copy them; but in any case it is a chain repeating itself because we too copy from someone else.
>
> Pieraccini (2010, p. 31).

In reality, copying is not enough to appeal to customers, rather it is essential to take advantage of the extensive professional background present in the local district. For example, this means employing Italian designers, technicians, and other personnel supplying business services. All of these elements emerged during the field research as well as in other studies (Marsden and Caserta 2010; Dei Ottati et al. 2015). These advantages increase for Chinese entrepreneurs insofar as they establish connections with the local economic context.

Finally, some Chinese firms trade illegally in several ways; including tax evasion and the infringement of employment laws and workplace safety regulations. These infringements feed the local criticism regarding unfair competition. On December 1 2013, violations of workplace safety regulations caused a fire in an industrial building in Tavola (close to Macrolotto 1), and seven Chinese workers died.[21] Overall, these transgressions permit Chinese entrepreneurs to overcome the natural legal barriers to market entry. Prato's local administration tries to eliminate these illegalities by subjecting Chinese firms to systematic inspections.[22] However, the 340 inspections per year (2010–2012) mean that undertaking a complete check would take several years, given the large number of firms to be inspected. The main way to make Chinese entrepreneurs respect workplace laws is by establishing communications between the local institutions and the Chinese community's points

---

[21]L. Montanari, "Condannati per i morti nel rogo di Prato," in *La Repubblica*, January 13, 2015.

[22]According to data provided by the municipal administration of Prato, 319 Chinese firms were checked in 2010, leading to the seizure of 145 industrial buildings and 6259 machines. In 2011, there were 365 inspections, with the seizure of 179 industrial buildings and 5254 machines. In 2012, there were 338 inspections, with the seizure of 127 industrial buildings and 5508 machines.

of reference. Without this conduit, there is a risk that the Chinese immigrants will understand the repressive policies grounded on penal laws as discrimination against them.[23]

Concerning legalities, a growing number of small Italian businesses became involved in workplace violations and tax evasion during the 1970s (Becattini 1997). That phenomenon still affects Italy, which currently faces approximately €200 billion in tax evasion every year (Chiarini et al. 2009). Indeed, the interviewed Prato municipal councilor acknowledged that some local Italian firms were involved in tax evasion in the past. However, regarding the tax evasion among Chinese entrepreneurs, he says that the wealth earned *"ends up getting sent to China, whereas wealth once remained in the city."* Although this statement raises contrasting interpretations (during the 1970s, Italian entrepreneurs also transferred money abroad to avoid taxes), recent judiciary investigations conducted in Prato and in other Italian cities discovered huge sums of money transferred from Italy to China (Court of Florence 2010; Cnel 2011).

6   Conclusions

The qualitative method used here means that it is impossible to apply the research results to all of the Chinese entrepreneurs involved in fast fashion production on a generalized level; however, the results are indicative of patterns (Montesperelli 1998). The field research on fast fashion confirms some elements that emerged in other studies conducted on a local level (Pieraccini 2010; Chen 2011). Particularly, that Chinese fast fashion is based on very low prices, on low profits for any sold clothing, and on very intensive forms of exploitation, including self-exploitation.

Certain typical aspects characterizing the economy of industrial districts are reproduced among Chinese entrepreneurs, and facilitate development. Notably, these include: (1) family businesses combining social and economic resources. This component was distinctive in the origin of Italian industrial districts in the last century. (2) Settlement in an area with a well-established professional background. This gave the Chinese entrepreneurs an advantage in terms of access to qualified personnel and machinery. (3) The opportunity to construct a transnational business network. Through these networks, the Chinese entrepreneurs were able to import fabric at low rates directly from China and from other emerging countries (Becattini 1998; Bagnasco 1977; Trigilia 2004; Dei Ottati 2009; Fabbri 2011).

The information gathered during the field research does not confirm the assumption that the development of Chinese fast fashion in Prato drained the resources and the work from the local population. As confirmed by the

---

[23]On interviewing several Chinese entrepreneurs in Prato several years ago, Chen (2011) points out, *"Chinese migrants feel Italian officials are targeting and taking advantage of their vulnerabilities simply because of who they are"* (Chen 2011: 28).

interviewees, the garment sector was never the core business of local Prato entrepreneurs. The majority of the locals are involved in the production and export of textiles. Chinese fast fashion represents a new type of production that arose autonomously in the broader local district. However, certain relationships are emerging between the Italian and the Chinese entrepreneurs regarding the use of local designers, technicians, fabric printers, and dyers. Thus far, these relationships do not refute the existence of a parallel district in the wider urban economic context. Contrary to certain negative considerations regarding Chinese entrepreneurs, the relationships they have established within the economic context represent an advantage for some Italian entrepreneurs and for the city as a whole.[24]

The presence of Chinese immigrants has elicited contrasting reactions in the city. Some of the population exhibit incommunicability and discontent toward Chinese immigrants. The local population's current perception of Chinese immigrants seems to come from rejection as well as subordinated inclusion (Cotesta 1992). The Chinese entrepreneurs are considered a *foreign body* with respect to the local context. Nevertheless, a closer inspection shows that the Chinese immigrants share a number of distinctive behavioral aspects with the local population that support the local industrial district. These behavioral aspects are hard work and personal sacrifice, both of which orient toward economic success. Accordingly, perhaps the local negative reactions toward the Chinese immigrants mainly relate to their being foreigners, people outside the history of the city (Simmel 1989). Not coincidentally, the interviewed trade-union representative remembers that, in the past:

> "All of us belonged to the same culture, to left-wing political parties, and the same meeting halls such as the Case del Popolo." (Case del Popolo was a network of meeting places that arose in Italy after World War II within the Socialist and Communist parties, where people met both for political engagement and to spend their leisure time).

Today, the social and political context is very different. On the one hand, the cultural composition of the local population has changed irreversibly. On the other hand, the crises in Italy's political parties means that they no longer play a key role in socialization and in building an identity within a set of shared values. The population perceives itself as a community—what Giacomo Becattini refers to as a social factor that contributed to the development of the local industrial district—that appears to be facing a profound crisis (Becattini et al. 1997).

Even if several aspects of the Chinese immigration are disturbing and difficult to resolve, it is only by starting from an inclusive citywide perspective that we can hope to establish the basic conditions to combine both economic development and respect for the law.

---

[24]According to a recent report by the Regional Institute for Economic Planning of Tuscany (IRPET), the economic contribution provided by the Chinese community in the province of Prato amounts to €705 million, corresponding to 11% of the province's entire gross domestic product (IRPET 2015).

Appendix 1

List of persons interviewed between January 2012 and April 2014 (Prato, Florence, and Naples).

- Councilor of the Municipality of Prato
- Representative of Confederazione Nazionale Artigiani (CNA)
- Representative of Confartigianato
- Representative of the Entrepreneurs Industrial Association Study Center
- President of Naples Entrepreneurs Industrial Association (Confindustria)
- Representative of the police force
- Representative of the police force
- Representative of the customs office
- Chinese garment entrepreneur
- Italian garment entrepreneur
- Italian former-entrepreneur
- Trade union representative (CISL)
- Trade union representative (CGIL)
- Trade union representative (CGIL Florence)
- Italian trader of clothes (Campi Bisenzio, Florence)
- Italian dyer entrepreneur
- Manager of Macrolotto 1
- Italian translator from Italian to Chinese
- Prosecutor for the Court of Florence.

References

Bagnasco A (1977) Tre Italie. La problematica territoriale dello sviluppo italiano. Il Mulino, Bologna

Becattini G (1997) Prato nel mondo che cambia (1954–1993). In: Becattini G (ed) Prato storia di una città. Il distretto industriale (1943-1993), vol IV. Comune di Prato—Le Monnier, Firenze, pp 465–600

Becattini G (1998) Distretti industriali e Made in Italy. Le basi socioculturali del nostro sviluppo economico. Bollati Boringhieri, Torino

Becattini G, Absalom R, Dei Ottati G, Giovannini P (1997) Il bruco e la farfalla. Ragionamenti su di un decennio di vita pratese (1943–1953). In: Becattini G (ed) Prato storia di una città. Il distretto industriale (1943–1993), vol IV. Comune di Prato—Le Monnier, Firenze, pp 369–464

Bracci F (2008) Migranti cinesi e contesto locale: il distretto pratese e la transizione fredda. Sviluppo Locale 31(XIII):91–111

Bressan M, Tosi Cambini S (eds) (2011) Zone di transizione. Etnografia urbana nei quartieri e nello spazio pubblico. Il Mulino, Bologna

Ceccagno A (2003) Le migrazioni dalla Cina verso l'Italia e l'Europa nell'epoca della globalizzazione. In: Ceccagno A (ed) Migranti a Prato. Il distretto tessile multietnico. Franco Angeli, Milano, pp 25–68

Cerreta MG (1999) La presenza artigiana e la sua evoluzione all'interno delle attività economiche del distretto industriale pratese. In: Colombi M (ed) Caratteristiche del comparto artigiano nell'area pratese. Quaderni IRIS, pp 1–27

Chen C (2011) Made in Italy (by the Chinese): economic restructuring and the politics of migration. Inter Asia Papers 20:1–34

Chiarini B, Marzano E, Schneider F (2009) Pressione fiscale e evasione fiscale: un'analisi degli aspetti strutturali e delle caratteristiche di lungo periodo. In: Longobardi E, Petretto A (eds) Saggi di economia della tassazione. Franco Angeli, Milano, pp 119–140

Cietta E (2008) La rivoluzione del fast fashion. Strategie e modelli organizzativi per competere nelle industrie ibride. Franco Angeli, Milano

Cnel (2011) Consiglio Nazionale dell'Economia e del Lavoro. La criminalità organizzata cinese in Italia. Caratteristiche e linee evolutive (www.cnel.it, downloaded 30 June 2011)

Cotesta V (1992) La cittadella assediata. Immigrazione e conflitti etnici in Italia. Editori riuniti, Roma

Court of Florence (2010) Ufficio del Giudice per le indagini preliminari presso il Tribunale di Firenze. Ordinanza applicativa di misure cautelari personali e reali, N. 9667/09 RGGIP, June 16

Dei Ottati G (2004) Uscita, voce, e l'evoluzione del distretto industriale: il caso dello sviluppo post-bellico di Prato. In: Bellanca N, Dardi N, Raffaelli T (eds) Economia senza gabbie. Studi in onore di Giacomo Becattini. Il Mulino, Bologna, pp 185–217

Dei Ottati G (2009) Distretti industriali e doppia sfida cinese. QA – Rivista dell'associazione Rossi-Doria 1:123–142

Dei Ottati G (2013) Imprese di immigrati e distretto industriale: un'interpretazione dello sviluppo delle imprese cinesi di Prato. Stato e Mercato 98:171–202

Dei Ottati G, Acocella I, Manzo C (2015) La recente evoluzione delle imprese cinesi di Prato: diversificazione e relazioni transnazionali e miste. In: Istituto Regionale Programmazione Economia della Toscana (Irpet) Relazioni locali e transnazionali delle imprese cinesi di Prato e loro contributo all'economia della Provincia. Firenze, pp 21–41 (www.irpet.it, downloaded on 15 July 2015)

Fabbri M (2011) Imprenditori cinesi nel settore delle confezioni e dell'abbigliamento. In: A Chiesi (ed) Il profilo nazionale degli immigrati imprenditori in Italia. Consiglio Nazionale dell'Economia e del Lavoro (Cnel), pp 114–136 (www.cnel.it, downloaded on April 3, 2014)

Ferrucci L (1996) I processi evolutivi nei sistemi di piccole imprese. Il distretto tessile pratese. Angelo Guerini e Associati, Milano

Girard R (1987 [1982]) Il capro espiatorio. Adelphi Edizioni, Milano

Guercini S (2001) Relation between branding and growth of the firm in new quick fashion formulas: Analysis of an Italian case. J Fashion Mark Manage 5(1):69–79

Istituto Regionale Programmazione Economia della Toscana (Irpet) Relazioni locali e transnazionali delle imprese cinesi di Prato e loro contributo all'economia della Provincia. Firenze (www.irpet.it, downloaded on 15 July 2015)

Marazzi C (1999) Il posto dei calzini. La svolta linguistica dell'economia e i suoi effetti sulla politica. Bollati Boringhieri, Torino

Marigolli M (2004) Il distretto, il futuro. In: Acerbi S, Brenna S, Dei Ottati G, Epifani G, Fedeli V, Giovagnoli F, Gregori G, Marigolli M, Maselli M, Mattei F, Rinfreschi L, Silvestri L (eds) Prato. Il distretto, la città, il futuro. Pentalinea, Prato, pp 13–26

Marsden A, Caserta D (2010) Storie e progetti imprenditoriali dei cinesi a Prato. Camera di Commercio, Prato

Montesperelli P (1998) L'intervista ermeneutica. Franco Angeli, Milano

Municipality of Prato (2003) (http://statistica.comune.prato.it, downloaded on 3 Sept 2013)

Municipality of Prato (2015) (http://statistica.comune.prato.it, downloaded on 28 June 2015)

Pieraccini S (2008) L'assedio cinese. Il distretto "parallelo" del pronto moda a Prato. Il Sole 24 Ore, Milano

Pieraccini S (2010) L'assedio cinese. Il distretto senza regole degli abiti low cost di Prato. Il Sole 24 Ore, Milano

Prato Chamber of Commerce (2003) Rapporto sull'imprenditoria straniera in provincia di Prato, December

Prato Chamber of Commerce (2014) Rapporto sull'imprenditoria straniera in provincia di Prato, December

Simmel G (1989 [1908]) Sociologia. Edizioni di Comunità, Torino

Trigilia C (2004) Distretti industriali e distretti high tech. In: Bellanca N, Dardi M, Raffaelli T (eds) Economia senza gabbie. Studi in onore di Giacomo Becattini. Il Mulino, Bologna, pp 27–47

Italian-Schooled Chinese Migrant Youth in Prato: The Liability of Outsidership and Social Identity Formation

Adua Paciocco and Loretta Baldassar

Abstract Chinese migrant youth in Prato are characterized by heterogeneity. This chapter reports on a select group—Italian-schooled Chinese migrant youth—and their complex social identities. Their parents are Chinese migrant business operators or workers who are arguably defined by a liability of outsidership, because they are external to mainstream business networks. On finishing their education, these young people claim they will most likely work in Chinese-run businesses in Prato. Data for this chapter are drawn from semi-structured interviews where the group self-identify, discuss their relationships with non-Italian-schooled Chinese peers, their friendship group preferences, their sense of belonging, and their language repertoires. The interview data suggest that these young people have locally produced, translocal Chinese-Italian social identities. Their sense of Chinese identity develops in the context of strong nation-state and local discourses of *othering*, and because their parents are external to local Italian social and business networks. The young peoples' sense of Italian identity develops through their participation in Italian social life; however, it is limited to muted self-ascription. We argue that this identity position provides the Italian-schooled youth with both cultural and social capital. This capital can help to develop weak ties with the Italian business community, and could potentially break down the liability of outsidership that characterizes their parents' Chinese businesses in Prato. The social identities of these young people are characterised as translocal because they are shaped in Chinese and Italian cultural spaces in Prato, which hold the promise for improved integration for future generations.

Keywords Chinese migration · Italian immigration · Chinese youth · Second generation · Social identity

A. Paciocco (✉)
Pescara, Italy
e-mail: aduapaciocco@gmail.com

L. Baldassar
University of Western Australia, Perth, Australia
e-mail: loretta.baldassar@uwa.edu.au

© Springer International Publishing Switzerland 2017
S. Guercini et al. (eds.), *Native and Immigrant Entrepreneurship*,
DOI 10.1007/978-3-319-44111-5_6

97

1 Introduction

This chapter examines the hybrid and translocal Chinese-Italian social identities of a select group of Italian-schooled Chinese migrants (aged 18–20) in Prato. We argue that their social identities develop out of the sociocultural context in which they are situated. The group comprises children of Chinese migrants who live in a nation-state with an exclusionist propensity toward non-EU migrants (Ambrosini 2012; Baldassar et al. 2015; Marsden 2014), which is particularly evident in the experiences of the Chinese migrants in Prato (Bracci 2015; Latham 2015; Raffaetà et al. 2015). Their parents are either Chinese migrant business operators (mainly involved in the garment and textile trade), or are workers in these businesses.

The exclusionist discourse toward non-European Union (EU) migrants makes it particularly difficult for Chinese migrants to become Italian citizens. This means that they do not have access to a public voice or to political representation. In Italy, national (state) and local (regional and municipal) legislation monitors non-EU migrants, making all Chinese migrants appear undesirable. Negative discourse toward Chinese migrants in Prato is particularly intense. This negativity is fueled by the popular belief that the migrants displaced the Italian-run textile and garment production businesses, which were the exclusive domain of the local (Italian) dominant group before Chinese migrants arrived (Colombi et al. 2002; Dei Ottati 2009).

Chinese migrants arrived in Prato to work in the local garment production industry at a time when Italian-run businesses were experiencing a shortage of labor. Thus, the Italian-run businesses outsourced their production to the Chinese migrants. This proved advantageous for the Italian-run businesses because Chinese labor costs were lower than Italian labor costs. Within 10–15 years, the Chinese migrants became highly efficient, independent operators in the garment industry, relying on peer social network ties to staff their businesses. They did not follow the local business practice, instead they developed their own *fast-fashion* production model. This model directly supplies the buyers and avoids the middlemen, which reduces costs and results in savings for buyers, and eventually consumers (Pieracini 2008).

As argued elsewhere in the book (particularly see the first two chapters and the chapter authored by Guercini and Milanesi), these Chinese-run businesses face a liability of outsidership because they are external to the reference network, which impedes effective internationalization. In addition, the Chinese-run garment and textile businesses in Prato are often referred to as a parallel industry to the similar Italian-run businesses (Bracci 2015; Pieracini 2008). This chapter considers the potential role that young Italian-schooled Chinese migrants may play in tempering the outsider liability of the Chinese garment and textile businesses of their first-generation migrant parents.

2 Method and Approach

We studied a group of young Chinese migrants attending some of the senior secondary schools in Prato. Data collection comprised questionnaires and semi-structured interviews. We used a grounded theory approach and content analysis to analyze the data. We found that these Italian-schooled Chinese migrant youth in Prato talk about themselves in ways that suggest they embody hybrid Chinese-Pratese and translocal Chinese-Italian social identities. We analyzed the students' discursive constructions of self, based on the sociocultural linguistic framework for identity analysis (Bucholtz and Hall 2005), which holds that an individual's social subject position is defined through language and in relation to the context in which they are situated. We also studied the participants' linguistic repertoire to analyze the symbolic value they ascribed to languages that feature in their language use (Bourdieu 1977, 1991; Bucholtz and Hall 2005). Our findings draw on Barth's theory of ethnic group formation (1969), Bourdieu's (1990) concepts of habitus and social identification, and Greiner and Sakdopolak's concept of translocality (2013).

Bucholtz and Hall's sociocultural linguistic framework defines identity as:

> [A] relational and sociocultural phenomenon that emerges and circulates in local discourse contexts of interaction rather than as a stable structure located primarily in the individual psyche or in fixed category positions.
>
> Bucholtz and Hall (2005, pp. 585–586).

Their framework *"focuses on both the details of language and the workings of culture and society"* (2005, p. 586) and contains five principles: emergence, positionality, indexicality, relationality, and partialness. Our analysis uses their emergence, indexicality, and relationality principles.

The *emergence* principle highlights how identities are jointly negotiated, and are discursively constructed in interaction with others. The *indexicality* principle maintains that linguistic form and a speaker's language practice both provide insight into an individual's social identity. A speaker's language practice includes the languages they speak that feature in their linguistic repertoire (among other variables not included in our analysis). We analyze the students' linguistic form in their discursive constructions of self. We also examine their attitude to, and consideration of, the languages that feature in their linguistic repertoire. Linguistic form refers to the parts of speech that speakers use to claim identities, such as nouns and pronouns. We particularly focus on the students' attitudes to specific language systems—that is, the symbolic value that they award to them. Languages have symbolic value and inherent social meaning, because they are embedded in a situationally defined linguistic market economy that is regulated by social subjects within its power hierarchy (Bourdieu 1977, 1991). The *relationality* principle maintains that social identity is *"discursively constructed"* in relation to other social subjects through *"the workings of culture and society"* (Bucholtz and Hall 2005, p. 586). Applying this principle helps us to take account of the impact that exclusionist nation-state and local anti-immigrant discourse has on the identity formation of the students, which we refer to as *othering*.

Barth (1969) bases his theory of social group formation on his observation of ethnic groups, particularly the movement of individuals across groups and their sense of belonging to various groups. Barth considers that social identity formation is defined at the group boundary level. He understands that individual identity formations are not homogenous: they are actually heterogeneous. This heterogeneity means that individuals can feel a sense of belonging to various social groups and often exhibit (some of) their cultural traits. Barth's understanding that individual identity formation is characterized by heterogeneity explains why individuals have complex, multifaceted identities. Such is the case of the students in our study who define themselves as having Chinese-Italian identities, which we claim are also translocal.

In contrast to Barth, Bourdieu (1990) focuses on the individual rather than on group identity formation. He posits that each individual possesses a habitus that contributes to the definition of his or her social identity. Bourdieu considers that habitus is the knowledge an individual has acquired through experiential learning in the past. This knowledge is independent of the present, but its enactment in the present will influence the individual's future. Notably, habitus initially forms in early social life in familial domains; however, it changes continually over the course of an individual's social life as a result of their socialization. Essentially, Bourdieu claims that past socialization shapes the trajectories of an individual's life, including the formation of their social identities.

Further, Bourdieu (1990) posits that social identity is defined by the position that individuals occupy in their situated social field. That is, the social groups to which they ascribe and the categories that others (individuals, groups, institutions) in the field ascribe to them. He maintains that an individual's position in the social field is determined by their habitus interacting with the hierarchically ordered social subjects (institutions, groups, and/or individuals) that characterize the field. That is, the power differentials that characterize an individual's social field determine their social identity. Therefore, the field becomes a site of metaphorical struggle for the individual in their quest to gain a position within it. Notably, Bourdieu's understanding of how social identities are defined is criticized for undervaluing the fact that agentive choice has the potential to influence identity formation (Ortner 1984). Moreover, it does not consider that endogenous and exogenous change can influence the hierarchical ordering of a social field (Wimmer 2008), thus affecting the identity of social groups.

The translocality concept features in a number of disciplines including geography, architecture, and migrant studies, particularly in research that foregrounds the relationships between individuals/social subjects and the space(s) they occupy. We apply Greiner and Sakdapolrak's (2013) concept of translocality in studying the social identity of the Chinese-Pratese students. Greiner and Sakdapolrak consider that translocality refers to the sociospatial dynamics and processes of simultaneity and identity formation that transcend boundaries—including, but not limited to, those of nation-states.

3   Study Participants, Setting, and Data Collection

Nineteen students (a mix of second-generation, 1.5-generation and 1.75-generation Chinese migrants) over the age of 18 (seven males and 12 females) participated in this study. The students were enrolled in lyceums and vocational schools in the town of Prato. Children in Italy start school at 6 years old and progress through three schooling levels, primary (for 5 years), middle (for 3 years), and senior secondary (for 5 years). Most of the students in our study were in their final year of senior secondary school. Several of the students were older than their classmates, because they had failed their exams in previous years and were held back a year. Some of the 1.5-generation students were older than their classmates because on their initial arrival in Italy they were assigned to lower year levels because of their limited Italian language skills. This is a common local practice for migrant students who arrive in Italy with low Italian language skills. One of the student's parents were wholesalers of hairdressing supplies. The others were children of Chinese-Pratese business operators and workers in the garment production industry.

We classified the participating students as second-generation, 1.75-generation, and 1.5-generation migrants, based on their socialization history (Rumbaut 2004). The second-generation students were born in Prato or elsewhere in Italy. The 1.75-generation students were entirely educated in Italy, having been born in China and having relocated to Prato before reaching school age. The 1.5-generation students started their schooling in China and relocated to Prato before entering their teens. Some of the students had intermittent schooling, being partly schooled in China and partly schooled in Italy, and frequently relocating between both countries. We could not classify these students using our adopted schema. However, we considered them as 1.5-generation because, like the other 1.5-generation migrants, they were educated in both China and Italy. One student's parents were from China's Fujian Province. The others are the children of migrants from Wenzhou, in the Zhejiang Province of mainland China, or from other locations in Zhejiang.

All of the participating students were enrolled in public, government schools. Four of the students attended one of the most prestigious lyceums in Prato. That lyceum is attended by Italian children who mostly come from an upwardly mobile socioeconomic background and is located in an elite residential (mainly Italian) area of Prato. Five of the students attended a lyceum situated in Prato's Chinatown. It is likely that this lyceum attracts Italian students from a lower socioeconomic background than the first lyceum. The remaining 10 students were enrolled in three different vocational schools, all located on the outskirts of Prato. We deliberately do not include the names of the schools, and we use pseudonyms to protect the identity of the participants.

Italian lyceums typically prepare students to undertake further study in institutions of higher education. Their students generally intend to qualify as professionals or semi-professionals. The vocational schools generally prepare students to undertake blue- and white-collar occupations. However, vocational school students are not necessarily precluded from entering higher education and becoming professionals or semi-professionals.

The young Chinese migrants who participated in this study are a select group who are not representative of all of the young Chinese migrants living in Prato. Prato's young Chinese migrants are socially stratified and heterogeneous, comprising a cross-section of social groups. The members of one sizeable group have never attended school in Italy, are illiterate in Italian, and consequently relatively highly excluded from participation in Italian social life (Paciocco 2015).

Our data were collected in the 2011–2012 school year. Statistics issued by the local education department office for that year confirm that the Chinese migrant students who participated in this study constitute a select group (Provincia di Prato 2011). That office reports that there were only 460 Chinese migrant students enrolled in senior secondary school in the 2011–2012 school year in Prato. In total, there were only 1750 Chinese migrant students enrolled in Prato's entire school system (pre-school, primary, middle, and senior secondary school) that year.[1] This highlights the very low school attendance rate for young Chinese migrants in Prato considering that at the time the research was conducted there were over 13,000 resident Chinese migrants in Prato.

We collected the data from completed questionnaires and from researcher conducted semi-structured interviews. The questionnaires had two sections. The first contained biographical questions (date and place of birth, parents' place of birth, migration history, level of education, and information on siblings). The second section contained questions on languages spoken, attitude to mainland China and to Prato, important events and people in the students' lives, and plans for the future. The semi-structured interviews focused on the languages spoken by the students, and their language practices with their parents, siblings, and peers. The semi-structured interviews also invited the students to self-identify, to talk about

---

[1]The fact that only 460 Chinese migrants out of 15,029 documented Chinese migrants resident in Prato in 2011 (Comune di Prato 2014) were attending senior secondary school in 2011–2012 indicates that the study participants are indeed a select group. The number seems to be very low, considering that it is unlikely that the Chinese-Pratese population is an elderly, ageing one. At the time of the data collection, Prato's population was approximately 200,000, with 5.4% being documented Chinese migrants (Cinesi 2013).

their attachment to their parents' place of birth and/or to mainland China. We conducted the semi-structured interviews in Italian because all of the students were competent Italian-speakers.

The interviews were audio-recorded (not video-recorded) to protect the students' identity. We analyzed the data for content using a grounded theory and a content analysis approach. We compared the questionnaire data and semi-structured interviews to validate the findings. We analyzed the data by the migrant generation group of the students and by the school they attended. We considered the migrant generation, because life stage variables can influence the trajectories of migrant's lives (Rumbaut 2004). Further, education being an indicator of social class (Vandrick 2014), we also considered the school attended by the students because the schools are ranked according to the symbolic value they have in the situated social field. The prestigious lyceum has the highest symbolic value, followed by the lyceum located in Prato's Chinatown, and then the vocational schools.

4 Data Analysis and Discussion

The students' translocal Chinese-Italian identity clearly emerges (Bucholtz and Hall 2005) from data in which they self-identify and self-represent. This includes talking about their attitude toward mainland China, talking about their language practice and the symbolic value they attribute to language, and talking about their parents' place of birth, mainland China, and Prato.

This section explains how this identity position is constructed. First, we show how the students claim Chinese identity and theorize why they do so. Second, we report on the students' Italian identity position. We consider how their position can potentially assist in breaking down the liability of outsidership that characterizes the Chinese-run businesses in Prato at the local level, since most of the students indicated that they would probably work in Chinese businesses in Prato. We then examine how the students' Chinese-Italian identity can be defined as translocal. We argue that the Italian identity positions of the young people in our study arise because they are made to feel other. We also argue that the liability of outsidership that characterizes their situated social field may have contributed to the development of their Chinese social identity position.

The participating students self-identified as Chinese, claiming their Chinese social identity through their Chinese cultural heritage, as is evident in the following representative examples:

> For better or worse, it [China][2] is where you come from. (Linli, female, second-generation, vocational school).
> …in any case, being Chinese… (Kexia, female, second-generation, vocational school).
> Well, all told, I am Chinese. (Laixia, female, 1.75-generation, lyceum).

---

[2]The information provided in square brackets is intended to clarify the content of the data.

These excerpts from the semi-structured interviews indicate that the students claim Chinese identity as an essentialist fact. However, we posit that they claim this identity position because they are considered other in their situated sociocultural context. This otherness clearly emerges when talking about the prejudice and racism they experience, or have experienced, in Prato:

> The people who I like best are those who are not prejudiced toward foreigners. They must be well mannered, and above all they must be interested in the many cultures that are present in Prato. (Panxia, female, 1.75-generation).

The fact that non-EU migrants, and specifically Chinese migrants in Prato, are subject to discourses of othering is documented in research on non-EU migration to Italy, and corroborates our findings (Ambrosini 2012; Baldassar et al. 2015; Bracci 2015; Latham 2015; Marsden 2014; Raffaetà et al. 2015). Italian immigration legislation regarding non-EU migrants—specifically citizenship law for non-EU migrants, security pact legislation, and restrictive local laws that were implemented to "safeguard" Italy from non-EU migrants—clearly indicates that the nation-state is exclusionist toward them (Baldassar et al. 2015; Marsden 2014; Raffaetà et al. 2015).

First-generation non-EU citizens must be residents in Italy for a 10-year period to qualify for Italian citizenship. However, residency is dependent on a permit of stay, which non-EU citizens are only entitled to if they have a legal work contract for 2 consecutive years. Notably, 2-year work contracts in the private sector (the sector in which most Chinese migrants in Prato are employed) are not particularly common.[3] There are a number of reasons for this: the Chinese-run businesses may not observe Italian working standards and practices,[4] Italy has been in an economic crisis since 2008, and the Italian economy has been in and out of recession since 2008. Regardless, the children of all non-EU migrants born in Italy can apply for Italian citizenship at age 18. However, if the children of Chinese migrants are awarded Italian citizenship, then they must relinquish their Chinese citizenship (to which they are entitled through *ius sanguinis* or lineage). This is because the Chinese government does not allow its nationals to have dual citizenship (Pedone 2013b). The children of Chinese migrants could thus face a dilemma when confronted with this choice.

It is also useful to distinguish between formal and substantive forms of citizenship. In their study of the social identity of Chinese migrant youth in Prato, Raffaetà et al. (2015) explain that some feel a substantive sense of belonging to

---

[3]The migrants from countries such as the United States, Canada, and Australia might access Italian citizenship more readily, although they are also non-EU citizens. Unlike the typical Chinese migrants to Italy, they are generally skilled workers with cultural capital (Bourdieu 1986) that puts them in an advantageous position to find safe and secure employment. In contrast, the Chinese migrants to Italy are generally, but not always, unskilled workers, or people prepared to venture into new lines of work for socioeconomic improvement (Pedone 2013a).

[4]There are many media reports on the work practices of Chinese-run businesses in Prato that do not conform to Italian standards. Such reports point out that Chinese employees work for excessively long hours in deplorable physical environments (Alfieri 2012).

Prato, although they may not be entitled to formal citizenship. That is, these young people nurture a feeling of belonging to the social space in which they are situated in Prato, despite not legally belonging to the Italian state (see also Baldassar and Raffaeta` 2017). We support this claim in our analysis by considering the way that the Italian-schooled students talk about their sense of belonging to their parents' place of birth, to mainland China, and to Prato.

Returning to nation-state legislation on non-EU migrants, Italy introduced its security pact legislation in 2009. This legislation allows the introduction of local or regional monitoring agreements. Such agreements are undertaken and signed by state and local governments, and by Italy's police forces, with all of the signing parties committing to monitoring migrants. These agreements are typically undertaken in locations that have high migrant populations; they are not targeted at specific individuals or groups, but at collective migrants. One such agreement was signed in 2013 for Prato. It was signed by the Tuscan regional government (where Prato is situated), the governing entity of the township of Prato (formerly the province of Prato), and local Pratese police forces (Comune di Prato 2013). Additionally, 445 by-laws were enacted in the period 2008–2010. These by-laws were overtly directed at "poorer" and "disorderly" migrants, and were issued in certain regions, such as Emilia-Romagna, Friuli, Lombardy, and Veneto (Ambrosini 2012, p. 142). Legislation of this type could set a precedent for similar ad hoc legislation in Prato.

Bracci (2015) and Latham (2015) explain how the local popular discourse also constructs the Chinese migrants as other. Bracci reports that Chinese migrants in Prato are depicted as "deviant" and "the enemy" in local media, and that they are portrayed as an incurable ill inflicting society. This discourse was explicitly used by the right-wing political parties during the 2009 local municipal elections to garner local support. Latham comments that when the Chinese migrants are represented in the Italian media, it is only in a negative context and never, for example, in entertainment media.

As this book makes clear, the Chinese business operators and workers are considered external to the networks of parallel Italian-run businesses. This enduring liability of outsidership constitutes another type of othering that the Chinese in Prato are subject to, in addition to the exclusionist nation-state and negative local discourse toward them.

The young Italian-schooled group who participated in this study grew up in a hostile social and political environment. They face exclusionist nation-state discourse about non-EU migrants and local discourse about Chinese migrants in Prato that defines them as other. Therefore, they have no alternative but to claim Chinese identity. The dominant exclusionist nation state discourses, powered by the media, effectively deny these young people an Italian identity position, despite their own sense of belonging and their participation in public Italian social spaces through their schooling. Hence, their Chinese identity has been intersubjectively defined in relation to the other social subjects in their social field—the Italian nation state and the media. Notably, those who participated in our study claim Chinese identity through agentive choice, although they were theoretically Italian social subjects (relationality principle, Bucholtz and Hall 2005). They also overtly mark their Chinese social identity through their use of subject pronouns (for example, *it* and *you* when Linli states "*it [China] is where you come from*") and in expressions such as *being Chinese* in the self-identification data reported above (indexicality principle, Bucholtz and Hall 2005). These young people claim Chinese identity by making salient a highly visible marker of identity—their phenotype—in relation to the typically local white Caucasian/Western phenotypes of the dominant social group in their situated social field (relationality principle). This is clear in statements such as "*Well, by just looking at me you can see that I am Chinese*" (Songli, male, second-generation, lyceum). Additionally, the students also claim Chinese identity through their knowledge of different Chinese dialects, or their perception of the knowledge of Chinese dialects they should have, for example:

> It is my language and I should know it [Chinese dialects]. (Zhiyuan, male, 1.5-generation, prestige lyceum).

It has also been argued that the students claim a Chinese diasporic identity through varieties of Chinese, more specifically Mandarin, to mark their identity (Paciocco, forthcoming). It is also inevitable that the students claim Chinese identity because they are children of first-generation Chinese migrants belonging to a macro-demographic group making a significant impact in Prato, and whose habitus has been shaped in the Chinese social spaces in Prato. Our results show that such social spaces are familial spaces for our participants. However, there are other Chinese private domains where young Chinese people gather in Prato, including afterhours Chinese and culture schools, Chinese pubs, Chinese church groups, and the homes of peers. Further, there are public spaces that are not the exclusive domain of Chinese migrants, such as shopping centers, where young Chinese people gather in groups (Paciocco 2015).

The participating students prefer to socialize with their Chinese peers because of the discourses of othering to which they are subjected. Unsurprisingly, in the interviews, the students emphasize that they did not have Italian friends, and those Italians that they do know are school acquaintances with whom they have no social ties outside of school. A typical statement illustrates our claim:

> I do not have any Italian friends who I go out with on Saturday nights. I have [Italian] school friends who I get along with, but I am very much bound to the Chinese community. I grew up with Chinese friends, have Chinese friends now, and go to Chinese afterhours school. (Laixia, female, 1.75-generation, prestige lyceum).

Interestingly, the Chinese identity position that our students' exhibit is a locally produced manifestation of Chineseness, independent of any other manifestations of Chineseness. This is clear when the students talk about their attachment/sense of belonging to their parents' place of birth and/or mainland China. They overwhelmingly state that they have no sense of belonging to either location; typical responses on their attachment/sense of belonging are:

> I can take it or leave it [Wenzhou]. (Mingyue, female, second-generation, vocational school).

I was born here in Italy and I often go to China on holidays. I only go there to see my relatives for a while. It is not that I have a really strong attachment to the place [Wenzhou]. (Songli, male, second-generation, lyceum).

I know Shanghai and that is about it. People say that it is beautiful, but I did not like it when I went there. (Yaping, female, 1.5-generation, vocational school).

However, the participants state that they find growing up in Prato *normal*, which suggests that they nurture a sense of belonging to the place:

Yes, pleasant but normal, like normal (laughter). (Feiyan, male, 1.5-generation).

It has been all quite normal for me. I went to nursery school here [Prato], I grew up here…it has all been normal. (Linli, female, second-generation).

The students did not claim a sense of belonging to Wenzhou or to mainland China because their habitus has been shaped in a different cultural location. They nurture a sense of belonging to Prato because they were born in Prato, or have been socialized in Prato. Thus, they have experienced habitus formation in Prato (albeit primarily in Chinese cultural spaces in Prato), and within a sociocultural milieu that is exclusionist toward them, as well as within a socioeconomic milieu to which they are external. Remarkably, the 1.5-generation participants who were partly schooled in Wenzhou/mainland China, and those with interrupted schooling, report a sense of belonging to Prato and not to their parents' place of birth or mainland China. This result requires further investigation in view of the fact that those students were partly socialized in China, having been partly schooled there.

The Italian identity position of the young Italian-schooled Chinese-Pratese migrants is complex. In a substantive sense, these young people feel a sense of Italian identity because they are social subjects in the Italian social field as a result of their participation in the Italian school system (Bourdieu 1990). However, the hierarchical ordering of the social subjects that characterizes the field renders them other and thus challenges their identification as Italian. Additionally, they are the children of Chinese-run business operators and workers who are external to the local Italian business networks. However, the students inadvertently claim Italian identity in discursive constructions of self in the semi-structured interviews when they are invited to self-identify:

I feel more, how can I say, I have become like an Italian. More Italian than Chinese. Because, having gone to school here, I have been influenced by the people who surround me. (Laixia, female 1.75-generation, lyceum).

Well, I would say that I am Chinese, that I have been in Italy for many years now and that I attend [name of vocational school]. (Mengyuan, female, 1.5-generation, vocational school).

Further, the participants subscribe to Italian identity when they self-represent as integrated into mainstream society by underlining their Italian language competence, since language systems have symbolic value (Bourdieu 1977, 1991). That is, in pointing out that they have Italian language competency (indexicality principle) compared with their peers who do not, the students align with the dominant identity in their situated social field:

> Well, [that] I am a girl who was born and grew up here. I speak Italian perfectly well, like all the others [Italians] and that it is also the same case with the others [Chinese-Italians]. Also, I do not have any integration problems, different to some who came here at my age, at 18. They came here and had difficulty in understanding the language. (Linli, female, second-generation, vocational school).

Notably, because of their integrated status and their Italian literacy skills, these students highlight that they belong to a select group of Chinese migrant children. This is as compared with their aforementioned peers who have never attended school in Italy, and who, these students claim, are illiterate in Italian.

Further, the interview results reveal that the students are adopting Italian values/cultural traits, which also indicates they are developing a social identity that is akin to that of the dominant cultural group (Wimmer 2008). In the interviews, one participant talks about the differences between Italians and first-generation Chinese (mirroring the view of first-generation Chinese migrants about Italians), thus manifesting identification with Italians:

> They [Italians] live too much for the day. They think too much of the present instead of thinking about the future. Although, I think they do well. (Zhiyuan, male, 1.5-generation, prestige lyceum).

This statement is not contested by the co-participants who were present during the interview, rather it is mutually agreed upon (emergence principle). This suggests that that the study group participants, in contrast to their first-generation parents, are adopting Italian values/cultural traits. Therefore, because the participants are adopting what they perceive to be Italian values/cultural traits, they are in a position to enter the symbolic boundary of the Italian social group and become Italian social subjects (Barth 1969). To test these findings, further research is required to examine whether the dominant social group accept the inclusion of these Chinese-Pratese youths as Italians.

The interviews also indicate that the students are developing Italian values/cultural traits when they align with the symbolic value that the dominant cultural group assigns to two prestigious senior secondary schools in Prato. This is evident in an exchange with Linli, a female second-generation student who attends one of the vocational schools. Here, we use Bourdieu's (1977) view that languages have symbolic value and inherent social meaning specific to the social field in which they are situated. We apply the principle to senior secondary schools in Prato. That is, the schools are awarded symbolic value/social meaning specific to their situated social field.

Interviewer: "What do you do in your free time?"

Linli: "I spend time with my sister."

Interviewer: "How old is she?"

Linli: "She is sixteen and she goes to [name of prestigious lyceum]... My younger brother is fifteen and he goes to [name of another prestigious lyceum]. He is in the second year."

Interviewer: "Are they different types of schools?"

Linli: "Yes. Yes, there are not many Chinese at [name of prestigious lyceum]... you can count them on one hand."

Interviewer: "Why?"

Linli: "Because it is hard. It is the hardest [lyceum] in Tuscany, at least in Prato."

We emphasize that the participating students' Italian identity position that we report on is self-ascribed. It is not awarded to them by the local dominant cultural group, nor by the nation-state legislation on non-EU migrants. Although the participating students' Italian identity is relatively muted, it could be a useful resource to break down the liability of outsidership experienced by Prato's Chinese business community and workers. When asked to talk about their plans for the future in the semi-structured interviews, most of the young people state their intention to work in Chinese businesses in Prato. The participants whose parents are business operators express their intent to work in positions of responsibility as administrators, merchandisers, or fashion designers in fast-fashion businesses. This is illustrated by Laixia (female, 1.75-generation, prestige lyceum), Weinan (male, 1.75-generation, prestige lyceum), and Linli (female, second-generation, vocational school).

Interviewer: "What do you think you will be doing over the next five years?"

Laixia: "I will probably go to Milan and study fashion at the Maragoni, it is a fashion institute, and then work in merchandising in my family's business."

Interviewer: "What do you think you will be doing in the next five years?"

Weinan: "In five years' time I hope to have finished university according to schedule and to be working."

Interviewer: "In which field?"

Weinan: "Economics and management, after I have graduated from Bocconi University... but you cannot really say... yes, and working in our [Chinese] businesses."

Interviewer: "How do you see yourself in five years' time?"

Linli: "With a degree. I want to study fashion in Florence. With a degree and hopefully having a good job."

Interviewer: "Would you like to be anywhere in particular, or do you think you might stay in Prato?"

Linli: "Have my own business."

Interviewer: "And in ten years' time?"

Linli: "Married."

Interviewer: "With a business?"

Linli: "Yes."

Interviewer: "And would you like to have staff?"

Linli: "Yes" (laughter).

In contrast, those participating students whose parents are workers express their intent to work as translators or interpreters in Chinese-run businesses in Prato. This is illustrated by Kexia (female, second-generation, vocational school) and Caixia (female, 1.5-generation, prestige school).

> **Interviewer**: "What do you think you might be doing in five years' time?"
>
> **Kexia**: "Me? (laughter) Working (laughter), working. I think for now I will stay in Italy, because I feel comfortable here, and because well, we work quite enough. Well, except for the current crisis, but in any case there is work for me here. I am told, 'you are a Chinese girl, you know Chinese'. Then in Prato, there are many Chinese [businesses], right? They need young people who can speak Chinese and Italian to translate. Many people have already asked me to work for them. They want to take me on."

> **Interviewer**: "What do you think you might be doing in five years' time?"
>
> **Caixia**: "After I finish school I could become an interpreter where I would use both languages—Italian and Chinese."

Our findings suggest that, evident in their self-ascribed Italian identity position, these young people can help to overcome the liability of outsidership that affects Chinese-run businesses in Prato. They can do so because they have acquired the necessary cultural capital (Italian language competence, and Italian values and traits) and the necessary social capital (acquaintances with Italian peers). That is, the social and cultural capital acquired by these young people places them in a position to develop weak ties with Italian business networks, thus gaining some degree of insidership in the local Italian business community. As Granovetter (1973) argues, weak ties are extremely important for the diffusion of information and network creation. These weak ties are also likely to contribute to the broad integration of the young Chinese population into local society.

Finally, the hybrid Chinese-Italian identity of the Chinese migrant youth we studied is translocal because it was produced in local private Chinese social spaces and in limited public Italian social spaces in Prato. The hybrid identity is a product of sociospatial dynamics and processes of simultaneity and identity formation that transcend boundaries, including beyond those of nation-states. In the specific case of the young Italian-schooled Chinese-Pratese migrants in this study, their translocal identity has been shaped within the boundary of the Italian nation-state. This is evident in the interviews in which the participating students talk about their sense of belonging to their parents' place of birth, to mainland China, and to Prato, and in our analysis that reveals that their sense of Chineseness has no affinity with manifestations of Chineseness beyond being Chinese in Prato. Further, we find that their Italian identity is produced locally.

Interestingly, the participating students' hybrid Chinese-Italian and translocal social identity that emerged was not influenced by their generation group or by their social class. Instead, it was influenced by their socialization in local Chinese and local institutional Italian social spaces. This is evident by reviewing the data we have analysed throughout the chapter, particularly the participating students' generation group and type of school attended.

5 Conclusion

The young Italian-schooled Chinese-Pratese migrants who participated in this study revealed in their linguistic practices and reflections that they had a translocal, locally produced Chinese-Italian social identity. Their Chinese identity was revealed when they self-identified; that is, when they talked about the social meaning they attached to the practice of speaking Chinese, and about the prejudice and racism they experienced. Notably, the Chinese identity of the participating students is fundamentally one that they choose through default, because they are made to feel other by legislation on non-EU citizens and by local popular exclusionist discourse on Chinese migrants. Further, this otherness is fueled by their belonging to a social group whose business practices are marked by a liability of outsidership at the local Italian level (being external to those local business networks). The participating students' Chinese identity also appeared to be exclusively locally produced. The data showed that it had no affinity with other manifestations of Chineseness, being solely constructed in Chinese social spaces in Prato. This was suggested by the participating students' non-identification with their parents' place of birth and/or with mainland China.

The participating students' Italian identity was revealed when they talked about a sense of belonging to Prato as a place, when they talked about their Italian language competency, and when they talked about their own values/cultural traits that they perceived to be typically Italian. Notably, their Italian identity is self-ascribed: not acknowledged by the local dominant group because of the exclusionist stance toward non-EU migrants in general and Chinese migrants in Prato in particular. Importantly, as a result of this identity position, the participating students possess cultural capital (in the form of knowledge of the Italian language and of Italian values/cultural traits) and social capital (through their Italian acquaintances) arising from their participation in Italian social spaces through schooling. That social and cultural capital may assist in overcoming the liability of outsidership that currently characterizes the Chinese-run businesses in Prato; particularly, the students' potential to develop weak ties to facilitate information exchange and network creation within the Italian business community.

Acknowledgments This research was partly funded by the EUOSSIC Consortium in collaboration with Monash University (Melbourne) and LUISS (Rome).

References

Alfieri M (2012) Chinese immigrants finding their digs in Italian textile town of Prato. La Stampa. Retrieved from http://www.lastampa.it/2012/07/24/esteri/lastampa-in-english/chinese-immigrants-finding-their-digs-in-italian-textile-town-of-prato-HY0qJBF4dlRYHdEjXXihyJ/pagina.html

Ambrosini M (2012) 'We are against a multi-ethnic society': policies of exclusion at the urban level in Italy. Ethnic Racial Stud. doi:10.1080/01419870.2011.644312

Baldassar L, Johanson G, McAuliffe N, Bressan M (2015) Chinese migration to the new Europe: the case of Prato. In: Baldassar L, Johanson G, McAuliffe N, Bressan M (eds) Chinese migration to Europe, Prato, Italy and beyond. Palgrave Macmillan, Hampshire

Baldassar L, Raffaetà R (2017) It's complicated, isn't it? Citizenship and ethnic identity in a mobile world. Ethnicities. Baldassar

Barth F (1969) Ethnic groups and boundaries (introduction). Retrieved from http://walk2-geographies.files.wordpress.com/2009/03/barth-introduction-ethnic-groups-and-boundaries.pdf

Bourdieu P (1977) The economics of linguistic exchanges. Soc Sci Inf 16:645–668

Bourdieu P (1986) Forms of capital. In: Richardson JG (ed) Handbook of theory and research for the sociology of education (pages?). Greenword Press, New York

Bourdieu P (1990) The logic of practice (trans: R Nice) Polity Press, Oxford

Bourdieu P (1991) Language and symbolic power (Thompson JB (ed), trans: Raymond G, Adamson M). Polity Press in association with Blackwell, Cambridge

Bracci F (2015) The 'Chinese Deviant': building the perfect enemy in a local arena. In: Baldassar L, Johanson G, McAuliffe N (eds) Chinese Migration to Europe. Prato, Italy and Beyond. Palgrave MacMillan, London, pp 83–100

Bucholtz M, Hall K (2005) Identity and interaction: a sociocultural linguistic approach. Discourse Stud 7(4–5):585–614

Cinesi in Provincia di PO (2013) Retrieved from http://www.tuttitalia.it/toscana/provincia-di-prato/statistiche/cittadini-stranieri/repubblica-popolare-cinese/. Retrieved on 27 Feb 2014

Colombi M, Guercini S, Marsden A (eds) (2002) L'imprenditoria cinese a Prato. Olschki, Firenze

Comune di Prato (2013) Patto sulla sicurezza tra Regione Toscana, Prefettura, Provincia e Comune di Prato. Retrieved from http://allegatipm.comune.prato.it/dl/20100215144120454/patto-prato-13.pdf. Retrieved on 19 Nov 2014

Comune di Prato (2014) Prato Conta a cura dell'ufficio statistica. http://statistica.comune.prato.it/?act=f&fid=6370. Retrieved 19 Nov 2014

Dei Ottati G (2009) An industrial district facing the challenges of globalization: Prato today. Eur Plan Stud 17(2):1817–1835

Granovetter MS (1973) The strength of weak ties. Am J Sociol 78(6):1360–1380

Greiner C, Sakdopolak P (2013) Translocality: concepts, applications and emerging research perspective. Geogr Compass 7(5):373–384

Latham K (2015) Media and discourse of Chinese integration in Prato, Italy: some preliminary thoughts. In: Baldassar L, Johanson G, McAuliffe N (eds) Chinese Migration to Europe. Prato, Italy and Beyond. Palgrave MacMillan, London, pp 139–158

Marsden A (2014) Chinese descendants in Italy: emergence, role and uncertain identity. J Ethnic Racial Stud 37(7):1239–1252

Ortner S (1984) Theories in anthropology since the sixties. Comp Stud Soc Hist 26:126–166

Paciocco A (2015) Constructing social identity through language: the case of Italian-schooled Chinese migrant youth in Prato. Unpublished thesis, Monash University, Melbourne

Paciocco A (forthcoming) Performing Chinese diasporic identity through Mandarin: the case of Italian-schooled Chinese migrant youth in Prato. J Lang Identity Educ

Pedone V (2013a) A journey to the West. Observations on the Italian migration to Italy. Firenze University Press, Firenze

Pedone V (2013b) *Chugo*, uscire dal Paese: breve quadro dei flussi migratori dalla Cina verso l'estero. In: Bert F, Pedone V, Valzania A (eds) Vendere e comprare. Processi di mobilità sociale dei cinesi a Prato. Pacini Editore, Pisa, pp 59–84. Pieraccini S (2008) L'Assedio cinese. Il Sole 24 Ore Spa, Milano

Provincia di Prato (2011) La scuola pratese: rapporto 2011. Osservatorio Scolastico http://osp. provincia.prato.it/pubblicazioni/Pubblicazione_ID_30.pdf

Raffaetà R, Baldassar L, Harris A (2015) Chinese immigrant youth identities and belonging in Prato, Italy: exploring the intersections between migration and youth studies. Identities Glob Stud Cult Power. http://dx.doi.org/10.1080/1070289X.2015.1024128

Rumbaut RG (2004) Ages, life stages, and generational cohorts: decomposing the immigrant first and second generations in the United States. Int Migrat Rev 38(3):1160–1205

Wimmer A (2008) The making and unmaking of ethnic boundaries: a multilevel process. Am J Sociol 113(4):970–1022

Vandrick S (2014) The role of social class in English language education. J Lang Identity Educ 13:85–91

Smartphones and Outsidership in Prato's Small Business Community

Graeme Johanson, Francesco Beghelli and Anja Fladrich

Abstract The theories of outsidership and insidership, and of foreignness, create contested discourse about the globalization of businesses, large and small. This chapter reviews the relationships between businesses, Chinese migrants, and mobile telecommunications based on available published research and on two small constructivist studies undertaken in Prato, Italy in December 2015 and May 2016. The studies generated two fresh datasets that are analyzed in the chapter. Prior studies of Prato's industrial district have been undertaken by economists, sociologists, political scientists, geographers, anthropologists, linguists, and media scholars (among others). This chapter focuses on overturning the usual representation of outsidership and foreignness in Prato. The chapter argues that many Wenzhounese outsiders (numerous hardworking micro businesspeople) insert their own portable insider networks and tight-knit practices in Prato. They thus marginalize the local textile manufacturers into the role of outsiders in their own territory. Many of the migrants from Wenzhou, China, along with their family businesses and self-selected virtual networks, tend to act independently with the assistance of smartphones. The trading conditions that they experience in Prato are similar to those in Wenzhou.

Keywords Micro business · Migrants · Wenzhou · Chinese values · Chinese guanxi · Smartphones · Grounded theory

G. Johanson (✉)
Monash University, Melbourne, Australia
e-mail: graeme.johanson@monash.edu

F. Beghelli
Finyx Srls, Prato, Italy
e-mail: fb.progettofinyx@gmail.com

A. Fladrich
Holmes Institute, Melbourne, Australia
e-mail: AFladrich@Holmes.edu.au

© Springer International Publishing Switzerland 2017
S. Guercini et al. (eds.), *Native and Immigrant Entrepreneurship*,
DOI 10.1007/978-3-319-44111-5_7

1 Wayfaring and Reflecting

Business in Prato is dominated by textile-manufacturing firms and by numerous Chinese migrants who staff and manage small businesses that make ready-to-wear fast fashion. In 2013, Prato had 50% more clothing companies than textile manufacturers (European Foundation 2013, pp. 13–31).

Prato's Chinese enclave increasingly extends to the northwest of the old city gate (Porta Pistoiese), and resembles any shopping neighborhood in China. The community appears self-sufficient, with few overt signs of interaction with Italian people in space, culture, or language. The profusion of shops in Via Pistoiese continues to expand, featuring retail clothing and services such as restaurants and hairdressers. Evidence of the increasing prosperity of the area includes new jewelry retailers selling high-end watches.

Smartphones are no longer luxury items owned only by the wealthy, and this chapter examines how smartphones enable the Chinese outsiders to become insiders in Prato. Section 2 discusses the appropriate theory and the interpretive methods behind our analysis. It considers the effects of the different Italian and Chinese approaches to business strategy, governance structure, finance methods, product quality, and marketing techniques. We introduce the two sets of interviews undertaken with Chinese micro-entrepreneurs in 2015 and 2016 that examined their smartphone use. The overarching aim was to determine the extent that Chinese entrepreneurs benefit from being ethnic and business outsiders, while at the same time importing strong, well-established insider customs.

Section 3 outlines the scope of micro businesses in Prato, and the size of their Chinese component. We explain why we undertook a second set of interviews in 2016; they provide more detail than the first set. Smartphone use is extensive across China and Italy, and the quantity of smartphone use by the Chinese entrepreneurs implies definite benefits of use. We also note the values attributed to the ties between Chinese migrants and other non-European Union (EU) migrants. While smartphones are widely used for business, the Chinese migrants in our study also used them to manage their family affairs. They are particularly suited to the establishment and maintenance of the Chinese guanxi (social networks) that provide a forum for shared beliefs, trust, conviviality, and the sense of belonging.

Chinese and Wenzhouese values are often identified as a foundation of business practice. The penultimate section of this chapter explores the relevance of these values to Wenzhouese micro businesses in Prato and to smartphone use. Many Chinese migrants aim to have a successful business in Prato. However, their trajectory is disrupted by accusations of illegality, by feelings of insecurity, by the limitations of risk-taking, by government interference, and by business fluctuations.

Finally, we explore the implications of the preceding discussions. We try to answer important but difficult questions. Have collaborations between local Italians and migrant Chinese improved in recent times? Do the insider and outsider concepts affect such collaborations? Can smartphones help to resolve differences? We propose that smartphones be developed as a fulcrum for improved collaboration among businesses. However desirable language skills may be for improved business and cultural interactions, their lack is still a considerable obstacle. To some extent, smartphone translation can assist. We recommend some future research projects.

2   Theoretical and Interpretive Conundrums

Prato is complex from social, theoretical, economic, and governance perspectives. This chapter tries to clarify some of the persistent issues pertaining to the micro businesses in Prato, to the concepts of belonging, to the lack of community collaborations, and to the roles of mobile phones.

To date, the economic theories about outsidership, foreignness, and networked interactivity are based on the analysis of specific institutions such as multi-nationals (Johanson and Vahlne 2009) and small and medium enterprises (SMEs) (Schweizer 2012). International business studies do not deal with the place-based dilemmas of business marginalization, nor with how to cope with the incompatible business cultures in Prato. Research by a dedicated group of local academics who maintain a long-term commitment to interpretation of their context is the exception (e.g., Dei Ottati 2009a, 2014; Guercini 2002, 2008). Only recently have scholars begun to explore the make-up of Industrial Districts such as Prato as independent entities (Lombardi and Sforzi 2016).

Fundamentally, we question whether studies of the liabilities of foreignness or outsidership assist in understanding an industrial city like Prato (located far from the source of Chinese revitalization). Is Prato—as the center of an Industrial District —seriously trying to resolve incongruous business strategies, structures, financing, products, and marketing techniques?

Identifying the attitudes and behaviors of local Chinese migrants should help to clarify their motivations and practical actions based on the experiences of daily living. To investigate the Chinese experiences in Prato, we adopt a constructivist research approach to understand their business outlooks and operations (Johanson and Vahlne 2009, p. 18; Schweizer 2012, p. 85).

In the last decade, the first and third authors of this chapter have spent periods in Prato observing business patterns and changes. The second author lives on site. Having previously lived in China, the third author is fluent in Mandarin. The third author undertook a research visit to the city in December 2015, which included conversations in Chinese with ten Chinese micro business managers. This visit raised questions about their lack of contact with Italian culture, the social capacity of the Chinese, and the use of mobile communication devices. In May 2016, the second author undertook a more in-depth study by interview of 20 Chinese micro-entrepreneurs, investigating their mobile phone use. Small Chinese enterprises in Prato use smartphones very extensively for business management, but even more so for the arranging their family lives and for amusement.

A high proportion (approximately 90%) of the customers in Via Pistoiese are Chinese. The first set of interviews revealed that the Chinese owners found it difficult to attract Italians shoppers. Despite speaking Italian, one interviewed shopkeeper could not sell clothes to Italians. The few Chinese clothing shops that existed inside the old city walls in 2010 have now vanished.

In 2008 we noted that the Chinese migrants in Prato used internet cafes for business services and for forging networks (Denison and Johanson 2009). By December 2015 they relied more heavily on smartphones (seven of the ten interviewees used smartphones). The most popular smartphones are Chinese brands, followed by Apple iPhones, and Samsung phones. During the first study all of the overheard conversations and the observed text messages were in Chinese. To obtain the first interview set, we interviewed ten business people, some of whom we previously interviewed for different studies. The results of the first interview led us to undertake a second interview set—detailed in Sect. 3—to understand better the value of smartphones to micro businesses.

Since the early 1980s Prato's experiences of various co-national business successes and upheavals have been charted often (European Foundation 2013; Ceccagno 2009; Lombardi and Sforzi 2016). Previous studies show the high economic and social costs of non-collaboration for the Italian and Chinese people living in Prato. The studies show evidence of abuse of power, of the absence of formal institutions promoting co-operation, of social isolation from the host country, of segregated business objectives, of low levels of trust, of avoidance of legal obligations, and of threatened value systems. Unsurprisingly these issues are described as a set of serious liabilities or burdens (Guercini and Milanesi 2016).

Initially the Chinese influx—mainly from the city of Wenzhou—into Prato was unheralded and unplanned. The Wenzhouese brought their own networks (guanxi) that functioned independently of the local networks, even bypassing them (see Sect. 4). Mobile phones acted as both convenient business tools and family organizers. To the Chinese, the smallness and/or newness of their enterprises seemed of little consequence (Singh et al. 1986; Bruderl and Schussler 1990). The Regional Institute for Economic Planning of Tuscany (IRPET) estimated that the gross domestic product (GDP) of the Prato region would decline by 22% without its Chinese contributions (Lombardi and Sforzi 2016, p. 11).

In a positive sense outsidership has a good counterpart. In international business, insidership can be characterized by trusted networks, positive relationships, social capital growth, reciprocity of values, opportunities for expansion, and ongoing learning and sharing of knowledge. These hallmarks are interrelated (Lombardi and Sforzi 2016). Typically, such desirable features trigger reliable networks, entrepreneurial attitudes, risk-taking, bold decision-making, venture capital, family support, and fresh perspectives. Each of these features suit small family-based businesses, and depend heavily on the flexibility that derives from technological efficiencies (Johanson and Vahlne 2009; Schweizer 2012).

3   How and Why Are Smartphones Used? Statistics and Interviews

We convey some of the scope of the enterprises under scrutiny by examining the number of Chinese migrants and Chinese businesses in Prato.

Thousands of Wenzhouese work in Prato (Zhang and Zhang 2016). Prato's overall population is approximately 191,150 (Istat 2015a), with about 16,918 being official Chinese migrants (Prato Municipality Statistical Office 2015). Frequent speculation in the mass media that up to one third of all of the Chinese in Prato are illegal and unregistered does not assist in making precise statements (Nadeau 2013). In Italy as a whole, the number of Chinese migrants increases by approximately 2% annually (Istat 2015b).

The European Commission defines microbusinesses as firms with fewer than ten employees, or with an annual turnover of less than €2 million (European Commission 2016). We took into account the employee numbers only in the interviews, because we did not expect to receive accurate information from the interviewees about their annual turnover.

In assessing the number of Chinese microbusinesses in Prato, Ceccagno (2012) asserted that "... *provisional data for 2011 show that 4945 Chinese businesses were active...*". More roughly Chen estimates the number at between 4000 and 7000 (Chen 2011, p. 19). China itself is characterized by high numbers of micro businesses (Liu 2008, p. 38).

In 2011, between 81 and 92% of Prato's clothing companies were Chinese-owned, depending on the source quoted (Bracci 2015, p. 86; Ceccagno 2009, p. 6; Huang 2015). Chinese businesses contribute 11% to local gross domestic product (IRPET 2015). The number of Chinese businesses in Prato grew steadily in the period 2008–2013 (Dei Ottati 2014, p. 1256; Lombardi and Sforzi 2016, p. 7), while the number of European-owned businesses shrank (a financial crisis in Europe peaked in 2009–2011).

We sought to find out how Chinese micro businesses were using smartphones. In May 2016, the second author undertook in-depth interviews with 20 micro entrepreneurs, and asked about their uses of mobile phones. He found that small Chinese enterprises in Prato use smartphones for every aspect of their businesses, and even more extensively for their family lives and for amusement.

We identified the interviewees using purposive and snowball sampling, and conducted semi-structured questions with them in Chinese. The data from both rounds of interviews (sets one and two) were analyzed using grounded theory methods (Williamson et al. 2013). The second set of interviews elicited basic facts from the participants concerning their businesses, their experiences in Prato since migration, the importance of their smartphones in business and daily lives, and their communication within the Chinese community in Prato.

We only interviewed businesses that used smartphones. The features of the cohort are notable. Eleven women and nine men participated in the second interview set. Of the 20 participants, 13 were involved in clothing and textiles, three in restaurants, and one each in a wine shop, a food shop, a travel agent, and a lamp retailer. We focused on businesses with fewer than ten employees. On average, the businesses had four employees, ranging from a one-woman firm to a firm with seven employees. On average, the participants had worked in Prato for 11 years (ranging from 2 to 20 years).

The interviewees ranked their smartphone use for various business features using a scale of one (least important) to ten (most important). On average, the group ranked their smartphone use for business purposes at eight. However, they ranked their use for social communications and family organization both at 9.4. Regarding the many possible uses of smartphones, having a friendly chat was just as important as doing business. Other studies support the dominance of social use of smartphones (Steyn 2016).

The business functions that the interviewees used their smartphones for included: advertising, checking on the competition, finding new customers, collecting useful information, gathering news, translating from Italian into Chinese, finding workers, locating accommodation, buying, selling, managing day-to-day tasks, planning, dealing with regulatory authorities, and arranging travel. One interviewee in a fast fashion business described the integration of business needs and technology and personal communications, as efficient and organized:

I have a common chat group[1] with several [of my] workers in order to manage the workflow and send information, [and] with the others we just talk [face-to-face] or have a phone call.

(19 May 2016).

Smartphones assisted some migrants with the initial migration process from China, helping to locate compatriots, accommodation, and jobs. When asked whether the smartphone assisted in settling in Prato, the Chinese interviewees commonly said that the phone made them feel *"very comfortable"*. A bag retailer explained, *"When I need support and information, WeChat[2] provides everything that I need"* (4 May 2016).

To illustrate the potential quantity of links, one interviewee (a lamp retailer) had approximately 3000 contacts in Chinese on WeChat. In contrast, another interviewee had only approximately ten contacts. The interviewees had mostly Chinese friends, with few Italian friends (5:1). Half of the interviewees (ten migrants) maintained daily contact with their friends in Prato by phone. Further, they maintained weekly, monthly, and annual conversations with their family and friends in China.

The most popular website, used by 60% of the Chinese interviewees, was *Huarenjie*, a virtual Chinatown network dedicated to Chinese people living in

---

[1]A facility that permits free-flowing conversations in the form of a short message service (SMS) (also known as a text message).

[2]A large Chinese texting service.

Europe, containing consumer information and a strong focus on Chinese enter-tainment. Others used unspecified Chinese websites.

4 Smartphones for Chinese Business and Family Ties

For Wenzhouese micro businesspeople, Europe presents a 'chessboard' of oppor-tunities (Huang 2015; Lan and Zhu 2014). Interestingly, in reference to outsiders, one interviewee (a fast fashion businessman) still kept in touch with "*friends from Africa and from Pakistan who were my classmates in high school [in Italy]*" (15 May 2016). He considered those friends at least as close to his way of life as the Italians in Prato. For him, the outsiders were his insiders.

Greece, Portugal, and Italy have the largest proportions of manufacturing micro enterprises in Europe (Schmidt and Lane 2009). One female interviewee in our second set, a major shareholder in a Chinese family micro enterprise, said that she uses her phone to "*…often share business information with friends in Prato, in other Italian cities, or European countries such as Spain*" (4 May 2016).

Micro businesses enjoy advantages over larger firms, including the ability to adapt quickly to sudden changes and/or a crisis (Donner 2010). Smartphones assist the smaller operations in many ways. One of the interviewees in the second set was the eldest son of a bag retailer in Prato. He had worked in Prato for four years, and had 100 Chinese friends there, but no Italian friends. He explained:

> When I need support and information, WeChat provides me with everything… Thanks to social networking I find solutions to my problems, such as… information on official documents.

> (9 May 2016).

Generally, smartphones assist the migrants to obtain financial loans, gather business intelligence, contact colleagues, spread advertising, check in with their boss, to keep up-to-date with personal networks, or guanxi (Xia 2012), maintain contact with suppliers and customers, monitor prices, avoid travel costs (time, money), plan face-to-face meetings, create virtual offices, and keep records for accountability (Donner 2008). Smartphones are also widely used to transmit money back to China. In 2011, China received the second-highest amount of remittance money in the world, no less than USD $66 billion (Ratha et al. 2012).

Earlier studies on the benefits of mobile phones emphasize increased produc-tivity and thus profits for micro-entrepreneurs (Donner 2005). In Shanghai, one micro businessman who was questioned kept approximately 2000 regular and occasional clients on his mobile contact list (Yuan 2012, p. 11). In addition to our interviewee who maintained 3000 contacts on WeChat, another of our interviewees (the owner of a fast fashion company) kept over 700 contacts in her smartphone.

The social values of smartphones remain under-researched (Donner 2010; Steyn 2016). Smartphones play a significant role in the family businesses, which make up 85% of all Italian enterprises (Italian Association 2016). A 37-year-old woman from south of Wenzhou, working in a sewing machine business in Prato, explained the overlap in 2011:

> My mobile is important to talk to customers about their orders, namely the colors of yarn and sewing machine models, but I also use it every night and on weekends to talk to my husband and children back in Fujian Province.

Quoted in Johanson and Fladrich (2015, p. 184).

That woman's family had not migrated with her. Transnational mothering by migrant women is increasingly serviced by mobile phone. In an analysis of research literature on women migrants and mobile phones, Lim found that the phones helped the women to cope with the severe emotional dislocation caused by migration (Lim 2014, p. 358). Children are cultivated as an insurance policy against the future of the family guanxi (Krause and Bressan 2015).

Researchers point out that it is fruitless to try to segregate personal phone calls from micro business calls, because the two are interdependent (Donner 2007). The divide articulated by Granovetter (1983) between strong and weak ties becomes indistinguishable in the case of the Wenzhouese; the strong merge into the weak, and vice versa (Johanson and Fladrich 2015, p. 187; Lan and Zhu 2014). In the West, what is personal is private, and business is discrete work. However, this is not the case for Chinese businesses, where no external agent is required for accessing insiders (Yuan 2012). With guanxi, pluralistic ties constitute a network of essential relationships underwritten by the dedication of personal time and experienced congeniality (Yuan 2012). In Prato, a serious consequence of the focus on guanxi is that it excludes other local business community members, turning the liability of outsidership on its head. Social networks become *"more dense and insular"* as mobile phones *"strengthen social ties"* (Lan and Zhu 2014, p. 627).

Mobile phones decrease the social isolation of migrants as a group: as a collective, they are well served. In a survey in Beijing, China, 69% of poor migrant laborers said that mobile phones gave them a feeling of being closer to others (Fortunati et al. 2008). In the second set of interviews, we interviewed a female clothing retailer who had 20 Chinese friends in Prato and no Italian friends. She spoke no Italian, despite living in Prato for 10 years. She talked about her daily customs:

> I live a very simple life... Every day I work for long hours so through my mobile app I can chat... When I finish working I chat with friends and I feel better.

(6 May 2016).

Mobile phones tap into the Chinese rituals for community belonging and shared beliefs (Wallis 2013), which connects with the ability to thicken small business relationships characterized by horizontal reciprocity (Dei Ottati 2014, p. 1263; Dei Ottati and Cologna 2015). Blanchard and Castagnone wrote that a Chinese person in Prato

> associates only with people one trusts, and from whom one thinks one can obtain something at the appropriate time. Everyone... is obliged to meet the requirements of an intrinsic

'code of ethics'… Guanxi bonds… are transnational and can involve both relatives and acquaintances who live in China and members of the Chinese diaspora in other countries.

Blanchard and Castagnone (2015, p. 282).

The collective network guarantees identity and security to a member, "*a thick web of market and community relations*" (Dei Ottati 2014, p. 1264) facilitated by the mobile phone (Johanson and Fladrich 2015). The Chinese ethnic enclave and the pervasive means of communication have allowed the Chinese migrants to be successful insiders in a thriving business community, while being outsiders from an ethnic perspective. In the second set, we interviewed a woman who owned a fast fashion business in Prato for the last 14 years. She described how she uses her smartphone:

My smartphone helps me to run my business… I surf the internet but only Chinese websites because I cannot read Italian… I do not feel that I belong to either the local population or the place where I live. I still have the impression that I am a foreigner.

(10 May 2016).

With 200 contacts in her phone directory, her strong interpersonal networks allowed her to defy the orthodox liability of outsidership, and to a certain extent to render the non-Chinese businesses in Prato as outsiders in their own city.

5   Rapid Adoption of Smartphones

In the ten years between 2000 and 2010, the global number of mobile phones increased from one billion to four billion (Donner 2010). Some studies briefly mention the use of modern information and communication technologies by Prato businesses (Dei Ottati 2014, pp. 1251–1265; Lan and Zhu 2014, p. 171), but no studies address the topic in-depth.

In China, 90% of people use SMS (Xia 2012), fueling the power of guanxi. SMS messages are facilitated by Chinese social media applications such as WeChat and Sina Weibo (Farrar 2012). In China, between 53 and 73% of mobile users own smartphones, depending on the source of information (Statista 2016; Nielsen 2015), with Chinese people owning 1.029 billion mobile phones in total (Statista 2016).

There are no statistics for mobile phone ownership in Prato, but our observations suggest that it is growing. A recent study in Milan showed that Chinese migrants were the heaviest users of mobile phones after the Egyptian migrants in that city (Bajardi et al. 2015, p. 5). Smartphones comprise approximately 62% of all mobile phones used in Italy (Statista 2016). Smartphone use increases by 50% annually in Europe, and by 57% annually in China (Internet Society 2014, p. 38). The faster and cheaper that smartphones become, the more they will be used as essential business tools.

6 Personal Chinese Business Motivations and External Resistance

Values affect the business conduct of outsiders and insiders in fundamental ways. For Chinese people, many values are expressed as part of guanxi. De Pretto demonstrated the unwavering strength of Chinese values among the Wenzhouese people at home and even abroad (De Pretto 2015; Johanson et al. 2013). She applied a list of behavioral expectations, enumerated as a standard Asian Values Scale, to different groups of Wenzhouese people, testing statistically the strength of adherence. Many items on her list relate to business acumen and group solidarity, and they lend themselves to reinforcement by mobile phone communications. For example, it is believed that Chinese people should submit to the wishes of the family hierarchy, should succeed in life (as a top priority) for family honor, should not deviate from social norms, and should think about the group before the individual (Kim and Hong 2004). Researchers of mobile phone use have created similar lists about the merits of mobile phones. They assess the strength of values relating to collectivism, expression of personal emotions, desire for entertainment, and meaningful communicative transactions. Survey participants in three Chinese cities frequently used SMS texting just *"to chat and kill time with my friends"*, and *"to talk about work"*. (Xia 2012, p. 137). Our second set of interviews indicated the same preferences.

Others have a different view of Wenzhouese values. Zhang and Zhang depict Wenzhouese business migrants as narcissistic, challenging, disobedient, pompous, and restless (Zhang and Zhang 2016). Some Wenzhouese migrants in Melbourne, Australia, used similar descriptions in interviews in 2013. They explained how they needed to behave differently on visits home. They identified the native Wenzhouese as pragmatic, introverted, inscrutable, conniving, parochial, poor mixers socially, and loud and noisy (Johanson et al. 2013). Among our second set of interviewees, one interviewee resisted mixing socially with compatriots in Prato, saying, *"I seldom go out with Chinese people because... they are too noisy"* (3 May 2016). Such traits are very unlike the sober Confucian behaviors explicated in formal surveys of Chinese values, although they could still assist successful entrepreneurship.

The Wenzhouese passion for productive work means that the owners of micro businesses are not very interested in civic or cultural engagement in Prato (Dei Ottati and Cologna 2015). Their collective values and loyalties lie elsewhere (Berti and Valzania 2015). Additionally, most cannot rescind formal Chinese citizenship easily.

Wenzhouese laborers in Prato may spend 18 h a day at machine work, churning out clothing for a payment of €1–€2 per hour, according to German media (Williams 2015), with no leisure time. Local Italian businesses sometimes exploit the migrants. Italian traders facilitate the penitentiary conditions in the sweatshops by requiring ever-lower prices and shorter deadlines (Dei Ottati and Cologna 2015).

One male micro entrepreneur in Turin, Italy, explained the Wenzhouese obsession with work:

Self-employment is in our culture. The Chinese do not want to be under other people...
You gamble, but you have to try. It's just our culture... First one saves a lot and puts money
aside and then one opens something... We work hard and never take a vacation.
Quoted in Blanchard and Castagnone (2015).

Business ownership brings high status in Prato. We asked the second set of interviewees whether the ownership of a smartphone also improved status. In accordance with collective values, half of the interviewees acknowledged that a big benefit of the phones was that they made them better known in the community. For the Wenzhouese, business failure and inability to repay compatriots is serious, and has been known to lead to suicide. Loss of faith in the Wenzhou business model took hold in 2012, leading to bankruptcies and self-destruction in Wenzhou itself (Volodzko 2015). Saving face (*mianzi*) is a strong Chinese value. After 10 years, 86% of Chinese businesses in Prato close down (IRPET 2013) suggesting that business ideals may be short-lived. However, closing a business can be a clever ruse, as Ceccagno explained. Some businesses close after 1 year of operation to avoid paying tax and they then re-open under another name (Ceccagno 2012, paragraphs 36, 43).

The media focuses very much on any illegal aspect of Wenzhouese life in Prato (Donadio 2010). Many journalists try to estimate of the number of illegal migrants in Prato, with 50,000 being the highest cited figure (Bracci 2015, p. 98). New arrivals are described primarily as illegal, and their behavior is censured. Chinese people are accused of smuggling billions of dollars out of Prato (Cornish 2016). Chinese-owned businesses that function in Prato outside the local laws on labor and safety at work attract the ire of the authorities (Lan and Zhu 2014). It would be naïve to think that mobile phones were not used to assist in any illegalities (Ehlers 2006).

Mobiles phones are also regarded as essential for personal security. Chinese people do not feel protected by the Pratese authorities. Prato's local Chinese people have established an alert system on WeChat to inform groups how to be protectively aware. One interviewee closes her fabric-cutting factory late in the evening, when it is already dark. Although she has lived in Prato for 10 years, she believes that "*Prato is not a safe place, so I use social networks to share news about robberies, and to identify thieves*" (16 May 2016).

In January 2016, thousands of Chinese migrants protested in Rome about the lack of Italian state care for their businesses and persons (Cardone 2016). In the following month in Prato, 2000 Chinese migrants marched for greater protection against robberies, muggings, and theft. That unprecedented number of protesters requested proper police support for security, legality, equality and justice (Tarantino 2016).

Notably, some Wenzhouese business values were shaped long ago. During China's Cultural Revolution—and the nationalization of its commerce—Wenzhou was the only part of China that managed to maintain a capitalist business model. Consequently, the Wenzhouese have endured government surveillance and harassment in China for decades. From about 1979, the manufacturing areas of Wenzhou entered a steep economic decline (Lombardi and Sforzi 2016).

Wenzhouese resistance to authority was forged in adversity. In 1995–1996, the Chinese national government sent 8000 officials to destroy 10,000 buildings near Beijing, ousting 37,000 Wenzhouese residents who worked there illegally and paid no tax (Hoy and Qiang 2003).

One journalist interviewed Luigi, a Wenzhouese businessman in Prato, who arrived poverty-stricken in 1993 with 11 other illegal migrants:

> He calls himself Luigi because it's easier for Italians to remember… Viewed as traitors [to China then, Wenzhou migrants] are now China's vanguard. They send know-how and money back to the mother country, are courted and are treated as models… Luigi spent… two years as a forced laborer, hemming pants 18 h a day and earning €500 a month under the table, ten times the average worker's wage in China.

Ehlers (2006).

Recent memories of economic deprivation and fickle authoritarian treatment at home may affect contemporary business attitudes in Prato. Self-protection is reinforced. Although treatment has improved in China, in Prato itself, the Wenzhouese migrants—whether legal or not—have continued to endure severe disruption and discrimination from the local authorities and citizens. As isolates, Prato's Wenhounese migrants closed ranks, turning to their own networks for internal support as their businesses grew. Sustaining family wealth is an embedded and enduring endeavor that defies intimidation.

One Chinese female restaurant owner with five employees described a dichotomy in her communications:

> I know some Italians, but except for work purposes we do not communicate… I do not feel I belong to Prato because the people I have contacts with are Chinese. I am more attached to the Chinese community [in Prato]… Thanks to the direct contact with relatives and [Chinese] friends, they helped to make me feel at home [in Prato]… I still have many relatives and schoolmates. I often talk to my parents [in China by phone].

(10 May 2016).

Outsidership affects this woman's way of life; but she has created her own form of portable and comfortable insidership.

7 The Future

It is easy to find anecdotal evidence of constructive cross-cultural interactions between Italian and Chinese people in Prato. These include mention of joint employees, customers, agents, computer services, business deals, complementary companies in Prato and Wenzhou, romantic friendships, and the employment of cross-cultural clothes designers, receptionists, quality controllers, translators, lawyers, and accountants. Many would like to see greater cross-cultural links, but there is slight evidence of positive collaborations. In February 2016, the deputy mayor of

Prato expressed a public hope for healing the divisions in the community (Tarantino 2016). Many commentators with a civic conscience see the need for readjustment. Recently, a Chinese journalist in London expressed (in broken English) a strong wish:

> Both the Chinese and the Italian need to make efforts to understand each other and have more efficient communication without bringing too much emotions. It has been a hard time for Italian government to rethink their law and political systems which relates to its economic recovery practices. Meanwhile, the Chinese immigrants might slow down the pace in their busy business.
>
> Huang (2015 p. 2).

Being busy precludes improved interplay. In Prato itself, one of our Chinese interviewees pointed out that an interest in learning Italian could be taken as an indicator of enthusiasm for staying in Europe:

> Attachment to Prato as a place depends on a knowledge of Italian. If you do not know [Italian] then you want to return to China. If you can speak [Italian here] one feels at home.
>
> (3 May 2016).

Many scholars and prominent Prato citizens express hopes for better collaborations between Chinese businesspeople in Prato and the local Pratese (Dei Ottati 2014). They argue that everyone would benefit, economically and socially, from increased connectivity. Perhaps mobile phones can be conscripted to the cause, by offering more cross-cultural services, such as translations, a pool of customer contacts, market intelligence, information about regulations, specialist advice, and links to professions and associations. The potential participants in situ should be consulted about their needs. We can envisage a mobile business application resembling a broad, virtual network.

A fundamental obstacle to collaboration is that Chinese migrants themselves see little purpose in non-business liaisons. Their aim is to make money, as laborers or owners, and to depart the host country. Many settle only for as long as they earn profits. They are wary of being exploited by Italian businesses and authorities. The investment that they make in Prato is not in social capital, citizenship, civic activities, or local culture, but is directed instead toward saving sufficient funds to enlarge their business networks among their co-nationals, to become bosses (*laoban*), and eventually to sell up and move back to Wenzhou as persistent luminaries. Mobile communications assist in every stage of realizing these dreams.

Change may be forced upon the Wenzhouese business community in Prato by the shrinking pool of cheap laborers available from China (Ceccagno 2012). Lan and Zhu (2014) call for more research into the consequences of slowing migration and labor supply during economic crises. There are other pressures. Stricter controls by police, and health and labor departments, and the decreasing value of the Euro, are all having an impact. Sewing firms did not grow in productivity in 2015 (Camera di Commercio Prato 2016). There are signs that the laoban are employing cheaper African and Pakistani labor in their factories rather than Chinese workers (Vannacci 2016).

Future research might also pursue the idea that mobile communication devices may impact on outsidership generally, and not just on the Wenzhouese in Prato. Mobile phones may affect all of the migrants to Europe, and their engagement with local business, including the most recent mass exodus from northern Africa and the Middle East. The principal functions of smartphones warrant further exploration, particularly with regard to group affiliation, whether it be for business or for personal identity and development (Yuan 2012, p. 16). More research could be undertaken following Johanson and Fladrich (2015, p. 179) into the nature of portable virtual migrant communities.

Further research could also undertake a comparative study into the use of mobile phones by Italian (or Prato) micro-entrepreneurs in situ.

A recent study in Milan, Italy, used the mobile phone both as a research tool and a source of data. Bajardi et al. (2015) collected data on anonymized phone calls and SMSs over a period of 2 months, then analyzed these to indicate the primary locations of the callers. They isolated the possible reasons for the identifiable clusters of communications. Bajardi et al. analyzed the dialed international codes to find that 221 countries were contacted altogether. They determined the population distribution of specific nationalities in Milan by collating the phone data with census information. Of all of the nationalities in Milan, Chinese international phone activity was the second highest, after Egyptian activity. This suggests that mobile phones serve business and social needs very well in practice. Bajardi et al. also plotted trends in the movement of remittances.

In Prato, use of mobile phones by Chinese migrants is as intensive as at home in China, with their networks reinforcing traditional values and enabling long-practiced business activities. Using the mobile phone conveniently serves the needs of Chinese guanxi norms. A Chinese business is commonly connected with a family, or a set of networked families. Therefore, the mobile phone becomes the fulcrum of daily interaction with both family members and compatriots, and with business resources, partners, know-how, the supply chain, connected traders, and wholesale and retail clients. The phone serves both audiences (family and business) well, saving time, money, and travel. Chinese people do not distinguish between personal space and doing business. A business partner is treated like family, and reciprocation is required.

The concept of outsider has limited relevance to Chinese migrant businesses. It seems that many are not aiming high—they are opportunists who fit within the niches left by bigger businesses. Chinese entrepreneurs are as ephemeral as any small business can permit, changing product focus or converting one enterprise to another in response to market vagaries or regulatory pressures. They are agile, adapting quickly to changing external influences (whether they be widespread economic growth or depression), or to vacillations in the fashion marketplace. Many send remittances home to Wenzhou by mobile phone, dodging conventional transaction fees. They have little time for leisure or cultural entertainment, and measure the investment of time in terms of marginal profits. The mobile phone enables these entrepreneurs to keep up-to-date with local and international business trends, to manage family, to organize employees, and to plan on-the-hop.

The majority of Chinese businesses in the Industrial District of Prato are small; many are family-based, with fewer than ten employees. They operate in a trading domain dominated by insiders, collective protectionism, and Chinese minds focused on business above all else. Experience of harrassment, lack of time, short-term survival, and maximizing profits constitute a heritage that animates their spirits. Smartphones provide ideal business and social tools for the hectic daily life.

References

Bajardi P, Delfino M, Panisson A, Petri G, Tizzoni M (2015) Unveiling patterns of international communities in a global city using mobile phone data. EPJ Data Sci 4(3):19. http://epjdatascience.springeropen.com/articles/10.1140/epjds/s13688-015-0041-5

Berti F, Valzania A (2015) The integration process and social mobility: examining Chinese immigration in the industrial district of Prato. In: Baldassar L, Johanson G, McAuliffe N, Bressan M (eds) Chinese migration to Europe; Prato, Italy, and beyond. Palgrave Macmillan, Houndmills

Blanchard M, Castagnone E (2015) Becoming laoban (boss): questioning the peculiarity of professional trajectories and strategies of Chinese migrant entrepreneurs. In: Baldassar L, Johanson G, McAuliffe N, Bressan M (eds) Chinese migration to Europe; Prato, Italy, and beyond. Palgrave Macmillan, Houndmills

Bracci F (2015) The 'Chinese deviant': building the perfect enemy in a local arena. In: Baldassar L, Johanson G, McAuliffe N, Bressan M (eds) Chinese migration to Europe; Prato, Italy, and beyond. Palgrave Macmillan, Houndmills

Bruderl J, Schussler R (1990) Organizational mortality: the liabilities of newness and adolescence. Adm Sci Q 35:530–547

Camera di Commercio Prato (2016) Demografia delle imprese. Dati e tabelli. Consistenza delle imprese e flussi trimestrali di iscrizione e cessazione. http://www.po.camcom.it/servizi/datistud/dmmovi.php. Accessed 24 May 2016

Cardone A (2016) Chinese community take to the streets of Rome, calling for more public security. China-Europe News. 24 January. http://news.xinhuanet.com/english/2016-01/24/c_135039076.htm. Accessed 22 May 2016

Ceccagno A (2009) Chinese migrants as apparel manufacturers in an era of perishable global fashion: new scenarios in Prato. In: Johanson G, Smyth R, French R (eds) Living outside the walls; the Chinese in Prato. Cambridge Scholars Publishing

Ceccagno A (2012) The hidden crisis: the Prato industrial district and the once thriving Chinese garment industry. Revue Europeenne des Migrations Internationales 28(4):43–65

Chen C (2011) Made in Italy (by the Chinese): economic restructuring and the politics of migration. Inter Asia Pap 20:1–34

Colombi M, Guercini S, Marsden A (2002) L'imprenditorialità cinese nel distretto industriale di Prato [Chinese entrepreneurship in the industrial district of Prato]. Olschki, Florence

Cornish N (2016) Italy's biggest Chinese community clashes with police near Florence. The Guardian. http://theguardian.com/world/2016/jul/02/italys-biggest-chinese-community-clashes-with-police-near-florence. Accessed 2 July 2016

Dei Ottati G (2009a) Italian industrial districts and the dual Chinese challenge. In: Johanson G, Smyth R, French R (eds) Living outside the walls; the Chinese in Prato. Cambridge Scholars Publishing

Dei Ottati G (2009b) Prato faces the challenges of globalisation; possible economic scenarios. Municipality of Prato Planning Office

Dei Ottati G (2013) The Chinese role of immigration in Prato: a literature review. Prato: the economic role of the Chinese community. IRPET—Regional Institute for Economic Planning Tuscany, Florence, pp 21–38

Dei Ottati G (2014) A transnational fast fashion industrial district: an analysis of the Chinese businesses in Prato. Camb J Econ, 1247–1274

Dei Ottati G, Cologna DB (2015) The Chinese in Prato and the current outlook on the Chinese-Italian experience. In: Baldassar L, Johanson G, McAuliffe N, Bressan M (eds) Chinese migration to Europe; Prato, Italy, and beyond. Palgrave Macmillan, Houndmills

Denison T, Johanson G (2009) Community connections: the Chinese community in Prato, Italy, and their use of technology. In: Johanson G, Smyth R, French R (eds) Living outside the walls; the Chinese in Prato. Cambridge Scholarly Publishing, pp 161–173

De Pretto L (2015) Adherence to Asian values amongst Wenzhouese in Wenzhou and first generation Wenzhouese migrants in Prato. In: Baldassar L, Johanson G, McAuliffe N, Bressan M (eds) Chinese migration to Europe; Prato, Italy, and beyond. Palgrave Macmillan, Houndmills

Donadio R (2010) Chinese remake the 'Made in Italy' fashion label. New York Times, 12 Sept

Donner J (2005) The mobile behaviors of Kigali's microentrepreneurs: whom they call—and why. In: Nyiri K (ed) A sense of place: the global and the local in mobile communication. Passagen Verlag, Vienna

Donner J (2007) The use of mobile phones by microentrepreneurs in Kigali, Rwanda: changes to social and business networks. Inf Technol Int Dev 3(2):3–19

Donner J (2008) Research approaches to mobile use in the developing world: a review of the literature. Inf Soc 24(3):140–159

Donner J (2010) Policy arena: a review of evidence on mobile use by micro and small enterprises in developing countries. J Int Dev 22:641–658

Ehlers F (2006) The new wave of globalization: made in Italy at Chinese prices. Spiegel Online Int, 7 Sept. http://www.spiegel.de/international/spiegel/the-new-wave-of-globalization-made-in-italy-at-chinese-prices-a-435703.html

European Commission (2016) What is an SME? http://ec.europa.eu/growth/smes/business-friendly-environment/sme-definition/index_en.htm

European Foundation for the Improvement of Living and Working Conditions (2013) Effects of restructuring at regional level and approaches to dealing with the consequences: Prato textile district, Italy. Dublin

Farrar L (2012) Smartphone explosion liberating China's migrants. 18 Sept. CNN. http://edition.cnn.com/2012/09/18/tech/china-mobile-internet-migrants/index.html

Fladrich A (2015) The integration of Chinese migrants in Italy. Ph.D. thesis, Monash University

Fortunati L, Manganelli AM, Law P, Yang S (2008) Beijing calling … mobile communication in contemporary China. Knowl Technol Policy 21:19–27

Granovetter M (1983) The strength of weak ties: a network theory revisited. Sociol Theor 1:201–233

Guercini S (2002) Profilo del vertice, processi di sviluppo e politiche di mercato dell'impresa cinese a Prato [Profile of the summit, the processes of development and China's market policies in Prato]. In: Colombi A (ed) L'imprenditoria cinese nel distretto industriale di Prato [Chinese entrepreneurs in the industrial district of Prato]. Leo S. Olschki Editore, Firenze, pp 35–70

Guercini S (2008) Imprenditorialità e rapporto con il mercato dell'impresa cinese a Prato [Entrepreneurship and relations with the market in the Chinese firm at Prato]. In: Visconti LM, Napolitano EM (eds) Cross generation marketing. Egea, Milano

Guercini S, Milanesi M (2016) Interaction approach and liabilities: a case analysis of start-up firms. J Bus Bus Mark 23(4):293–309

Hoy C, Qiang R (2003) Socioeconomic impacts of Uyghur movement to Beijing. In: Iredale RR, Bilik N, Guo F (eds) China's minorities on the move: selected case studies. M.E. Sharpe, Armonk, pp 155–174

Huang S (2015) Made in Italy while made by Chinese. Mundus Collect. 14 Aug. http://mundusjournalism2015.weebly.com/stories/made-in-italy-while-made-by-chinese

Internet Society (2014) Global internet report; open and sustainable access for all. https://www.internetsociety.org/sites/default/files/Global_Internet_Report_2014.pdf

IRPET. Instito Regionale Programmazione Economica della Toscana (2013) Prato: il Ruolo Economico della Communita Cinese. http://www.irpet.it/storage/pubblicazioneallegato/479_Prato_Cina%20volume%20Casini%20con%20cover.pdf

IRPET. Instito Regionale Programmazione Economica della Toscana (2015) Relazioni Locali e Transnazionali delle Imprese Cinesi di Prato e Loro Contributo all' Economoa della Provincia. Florence. http://www.irpet.it/storage/pubblicazioneallegato/542_Volume%20Cina%20con%20copertina.pdf

Istat (2010) Business register. http://siqual.istat.it/SIQual/visualizza.do?id=8889018

Istat (2015a) Demographic statistics: Province of Prato. http://www.urbistat.it/AdminStat/en/it/demografia/dati-sintesi/prato/100/3

Istat (2015b) Non-EU citizens: presence, new inflows and acquisition of citizenship. Istat. http://www.istat.it/en/files/2015/10/EN_Non-EU-citizens_2015.pdf?title=Foreign+residents+in+Italy+-+22+Oct+2015+-+Full+text.pdf

Italian Association of Family Businesses (2016) Family business in Italy. http://www.aidaf.it/en/aidaf-3/1650-2/

Johanson G, Fladrich A (2015) Ties that bond: mobiles phones and the Chinese in Prato. In: Baldassar L, Johanson G, McAuliffe N, Bressan M (eds) Chinese migration to Europe; Prato, Italy, and beyond. Palgrave Macmillan, Houndmills

Johanson J, Vahlne J-E (2009) The Uppsala internationalization process model revisited: from liability of foreignness to liability of outsidership. J Int Bus Stud 40:1411–1431

Johanson G, De Pretto L, Yong DX (2013) Chinese values and identity: perceptions of Wenzhou migrants. Conference paper at the 6th Chinese in Prato and 4th Wenzhouese Diaspora Symposia. Chinese migration, entrepreneurship and development in the new global economy, Monash Centre, Prato, 29–30 Oct 2013

Kim BSK, Hong S (2004) A psychometric revision of the Asian values scale using the Rasch model. Meas Eval Couns Dev 37(1):15–27

Krause EL, Bressan M (2015) 'Fistful of tears': encounters with transnational affect; Chinese immigrants and Italian fast fashion. Paper presented at the 22nd international conference of the Council of European Studies, 9 July 2015

Lan T, Zhu S (2014) Chinese apparel value chains in Europe: low-end fast fashion, regionalization, and transnational entrepreneurship in Prato, Italy. Eurasian Geogr Econ 55(2):156–174

Lee SK (2015) Bounded solidarity confirmed? How Korean immigrants' mobile communication configures their social networks. J Comput-mediated Commun 20:615–631

Lim SS (2014) Women, 'double work' and mobile media: the more things change, the more they stay the same. In: Goggin G, Hjorth L (eds) Routledge companion to mobile media. London, Routledge, pp 356–364

Liu X (2008) SME development in China: a policy perspective on SME industrial clustering. In: Lim H (ed) SME in Asia and globalization. ERIA Research Project Report, pp 37–68

Lombardi S, Sforzi F (2016) Chinese manufacturing entrepreneurship capital: evidence from Italian industrial districts. Eur Plann Stud. http://www.tandfonline.com/doi/pdf/10.1080/09654313.2016.1155538

Lombardi S, Lorenzini F, Verrecchia F, Sforzi F (2015) Chinese micro entrepreneurship in Italy: a place-based explanatory analysis. In Baldassar L, Johanson G, McAuliffe N, Bressan M (eds) Chinese migration to Europe; Prato, Italy, and beyond. Palgrave Macmillan, Houndmills

Nadeau BL (2013) Italy's garment factory slaves. The Daily Beast. 20 Aug. http://www.thedailybeast.com/witw/articles/2013/08/20/chinese-workers-trafficked-into-italy-s-garment-factories.html

Nielsen (2015) Chinese smartphone market now driven by upgrading. Nielsen. http://www.nielsen.com/cn/en/press-room/2015/Nielsen-Chinese-Smartphone-Market-Now-Driven-by-Upgrading-EN.html

Prato Municipality Statistical Office (2015) Population data, updated 31 Dec 2015

Ratha D, Aga GA, Silwal A (2012) Remittances to developing countries will surpass $400 billion in 2012. Migr Dev Brief 19. World Bank

Schmidt J, Lane N (2009) An international comparison of small business employment. Center for Economic and Policy Research, Washington, DC

Schweizer R (2012) SMEs and networks: overcoming the liability of outsidership. J Int Entrepreneurship 11(1):80–103

Singh JV, Tucker DJ, House RJ (1986) Organizational legitimacy and the liability of newness. Adm Sci Q 31:171–193

Statista (2016) Number of mobile cell phone subscribers in China from February 2015 to February 2016. The Statistics Portal. http://www.statista.com/statistics/278204/china-mobile-users-by-month/. Accessed 22 May 2016

Steyn J (2016) A critique of the claims about mobile phones and Kerala fisherman: the importance of the context of complex systems. Electron J Inf Syst Dev Countries 74(3):1–31

Tarantino N (2016) I cinesi invocano sicurezza e legalità [The Chinese call for security and legality]. Notizie di Prato. 6 Feb. http://www.notiziediprato.it/news/tutta-prato-e-scesa-in-piazza-per-dire-basta-lunghi-cortei-gia-da-questa-mattina. Accessed 24 May 2016

Vannacci C (2016) [Nella ditta di confezioni cinese sfruttati venti operai africani, tra loro molti clandestine]. In the Chinese packaging company, twenty exploited African workers, among them many illegals. Notizie di Prato. 17 May. http://www.notiziediprato.it/news/nella-ditta-di-confezioni-cinese-sfruttati-venti-operai-africani-tra-loro-molti-clandestini. Accessed 24 May 2016

Volodzko D (2015) The boss Christians of Wenzhou. The Diplomat. 6 March. http://thediplomat.com/2015/03/the-boss-christians-of-wenzhou/

Wallis C (2013) Technomobility in China. New York University Press

Williams M (2015) Tough times in Italy's little China. 10 Nov. Deutsch Vella. http://www.dw.com/en/tough-times-in-italys-little-china/a-18837330

Williamson K, Given LM, Scifleet P (2013) Qualitative data analysis. In Williamson K, Johanson G (eds) Research methods: information, systems and contexts. Tilde University Press

Xia Y (2012) Chinese use of mobile texting for social interactions: cultural implications in the use of communication technology. Intercult Commun Stud 21(2):131–150

Yuan E (2012) From 'perpetual contact' to contextualized mobility: mobile phones for social relations in Chinese society. J Int Intercult Commun 5(3):208–225

Zhang G (2015) 'Made in Italy' by Chinese in Prato: the 'Carrot and Stick' policy and Chinese migrants in Italy, 2010–11. University of Nottingham blog. 22 Oct. http://blogs.nottingham.ac.uk/chinapolicyinstitute/2015/10/22/made-in-italy-by-chinese-in-prato-the-carrot-and-stick-policy-and-chinese-migrants-in-italy-2010-11/

Zhang Y, Zhang M (2016) Can overseas migrants develop sustained entrepreneurship? Multiple case studies of Wenzhou migrants in Italy. J Chin Sociol 3(4):1–23

Liabilities of Foreignness and Outsidership in the Evolution of Immigrant Chinese Entrepreneurship

Simone Guercini and Matilde Milanesi

Abstract This chapter investigates how the immigrant Chinese companies evolve and face their liability of foreignness and liability of outsidership (concepts borrowed from the international business field) in the industrial district of Prato. The chapter adopts the perspective of the Chinese companies, investigating how those companies overcame their liabilities as they evolved within the industrial district. The immigrant Chinese companies in Prato evolved from an initial subcontractor level to become final firms engaged in diversification; this chapter analyzes the evolution in relation to the local native and immigrant communities. The industrial areas of Prato where the native and immigrant entrepreneurs coexist can generate liabilities. The immigrant Chinese entrepreneurs are insiders to their relevant global networks; however, they can experience a liability of outsidership in the local networks of the native entrepreneurs. Further, the native entrepreneurs may themselves face a liability of outsidership in the global networks in which the immigrant entrepreneurs are embedded.

Keywords Liabilities · Foreignness · Outsidership · Immigrant entrepreneurship · Chinese · Industrial district · Networks

1 Introduction

This chapter investigates how immigrant Chinese companies evolve, and how they face their liabilities of foreignness and outsidership in Prato's industrial district. We analyze the liabilities and the evolution stages of the companies, from subcontractor level to final firms engaged in diversification processes. We interpret the evolution of such companies in relation to the local native and immigrant communities.

S. Guercini (✉) · M. Milanesi
Department of Economics and Management, University of Florence, Florence, Italy
e-mail: simone.guercini@unifi.it

M. Milanesi
e-mail: matilde.milanesi@unifi.it

© Springer International Publishing Switzerland 2017
S. Guercini et al. (eds.), *Native and Immigrant Entrepreneurship*,
DOI 10.1007/978-3-319-44111-5_8

We borrow the liabilities of foreignness and outsidership concepts from management and international business literature. The liability of foreignness (LOF) is the difficulties faced by those in contexts other than their own national context, and many studies investigate this aspect (for example, Hymer 1976; Johanson and Vahlne 1977; Zaheer 1995). More recently, the international business literature stresses the growing importance of the liability of outsidership (LOO) (Johanson and Vahlne 2009) for business networks in internationalization. The LOO is the difficulties faced by those who are external to the most effective and important (social and business) international networks. That liability distinguishes the outsider actors from the insider actors.

The industrial district of Prato, in which native and immigrant entrepreneurs coexist, can facilitate the emergence of an outsidership liability in two ways. First, the immigrant Chinese entrepreneurs who are insiders in their relevant global networks can experience a LOO in the local networks. Second, the native entrepreneurs can experience a LOO in the global network in which the immigrant entrepreneurs are embedded. The chapter adopts the perspective of Chinese companies, investigating how they overcome their liabilities as they evolve within the settlement area.

Methodologically, this chapter uses extant studies on the development of Chinese entrepreneurship in the Prato area (Becattini et al. 2009; Bellandi 1996; Dei Ottati 2009, 2014; Guercini et al. 2013). We present two emblematic cases of Chinese companies settled in the Prato area to identify the empirically observed changes among Chinese companies.

2 Literature Review

2.1 The Liability of Foreignness

Internationalization liabilities are the difficulties faced by firms when they internationalize in search of new markets. The LOF is commonly studied in the international business domain. Hymer (1976) initially conceptualized the LOF as the costs of doing business abroad. That is, foreign firms incur additional costs when operating internationally, compared with local firms that have better information about their country and its economy, laws, culture, and politics. Extending the industrial organization theory to an international context, Hymer provides an alternative to the theory of international capital movements to explain and justify foreign direct investments (FDI). He argues that multinational corporations (MNCs) could overcome imperfections in factor markets by internalizing the market for intangible assets via FDI. They do this to safeguard proprietary technology from appropriation; however, it requires managing subsidiaries in host countries.

Hymer (1976) cautions that foreign subsidiaries face distinct disadvantages because national firms have better information about their country and its economy, language, law, and politics. He gives three main reasons for the LOF: (1) the foreign firms have less information than the local firms on how to do business in the foreign country; (2) the foreign firms are exposed to discrimination by governments, consumers, and suppliers, and (3) the foreign firms are exposed to foreign exchange risk. Kindleberger (1969) makes similar observations, recognizing that disadvantages could arise for the subsidiary firms because the domestic firms are closer to the "*locus of decision making and without the filter of long lines to distort communication*". The early recognition of subsidiary disadvantages by Hymer (1976) and Kindleberger (1969) were precursors of the LOF concept. Both authors view foreignness largely in terms of the economic distance related to the costs of setting up a subsidiary, implying that subsidiary disadvantages are similar to national-level barriers to entry.

Zaheer (1995) classifies LOF sources into four categories. (1) Costs directly associated with the spatial distance between the parent firm and its subsidiaries. (2) Specific costs incurred exclusively by the foreign subsidiaries owing to their unfamiliarity with the host country's environment. (3) Costs resulting from economic nationalism and a lack of legitimacy in the host country. (4) Costs from sales restrictions imposed by the home country. While this list is not exhaustive, it identifies the key sources of additional costs faced by foreign firms operating abroad. Similarly, Matsuo (2000) argues that LOFs stem from three major sources: culture and language differences, economic and political regulations, and the spatial difference between the parent company and its subsidiary.

Building on these studies, Mezias (2002) presents two additional potential sources of LOFs. First, a LOF can arise from costs that are not exclusive to foreign firms; for example, significant operating costs can affect both foreign and domestic firms. However, the foreign firms may experience these costs disproportionately because the domestic firms have learned to mitigate the costs. Mezias's second potential source of LOF is that some advantages enjoyed by domestic firms are not available to foreign subsidiaries (and do not relate to a foreign firm's cost structure). This illustrates the need to analyze more than just the costs incurred by foreign firms operating abroad. As LOF studies develop, the construct definition should expand. An LOF definition should encompass the costs that only the foreign firms incur when operating abroad, the costs that the foreign firms incur disproportionately to the domestic firms, and the benefits denied to the foreign firms that are enjoyed exclusively by the domestic firms.

Eden and Miller (2001) decompose LOF into two hazards (unfamiliarity and discrimination) that affect the foreign firms disproportionately to the local firms in the host country. Unfamiliarity hazards reflect the lack of knowledge of, or experience in, the host country that places the foreign firm at a disadvantage compared with the local firms. Discrimination hazards are represented by the discriminatory treatment inflicted on the foreign firm relative to the local firms in the host country. Discrimination hazards can arise from differential treatment by the home or host governments, by consumers, or by the general public in the host country: these are the costs of being different, of being seen as an outsider. Eden and Miller (2001) first introduced the problem of being an outsider and its related costs.

Eden and Miller (2004) argue that cultural and spatial distances drive the extent of the LOF faced by firms. Further LOF drivers include a lack of embeddedness (Miller and Richards 2002) or of international experience (Calhoun 2002), and insufficient host-market knowledge (Petersen and Pedersen 2002). While previous research focuses on the theoretical foundations of LOFs (Luo and Mezias 2002), some studies consider what determines the extent of the LOFs.

The LOF concept appears in various theoretical streams such as international expansion, social network theory, institutional theory, and the resource-based view. Researchers who draw on the LOF concept intensively apply theories of international expansion. Scholars of the internationalization process highlight the constraints faced by foreign entrants arising from insufficient knowledge and from psychic distance (Johanson and Vahlne 1977) from the host country.[1] The Uppsala model of internationalization argues that firms first internationalize to culturally proximate countries before expanding to less culturally proximate markets. The firms assume a lower LOF degree in the culturally close countries (Johanson and Vahlne 2009; Johanson and Wiedersheim-Paul 1975). The Uppsala model relates the LOF to the construct of psychic distance: "... *the larger the psychic distance the larger is the liability of foreignness*" (Johanson and Vahlne 2009, p. 1412).

Thus, LOF broadly includes all of the additional costs for the foreign entrant. However, the additional costs are separable into (1) easily identified and quantified costs, and (2) costs that are not as easily identified (Calhoun 2002). Most LOF studies focus on the former costs, with few focusing on the culturally driven aspects of the LOF such as language or local laws. Calhoun (2002) questions how the cultural differences manifest and affect the foreign firm differently from the native firms and differently in the various countries in which the foreign firm is operating. There is little focus on the less identifiable sources of LOF because firms generally enter countries that are culturally similar as measured by concepts such as psychic distance or institutional distance.

Although the primary sources of LOFs are generally accepted, it is difficult to identify a specific LOF in a focal country. It is particularly difficult to measure disadvantage exclusively. The methodological challenges (Denk et al. 2012) include matching foreign and domestic firms for comparison, ensuring that different managerial approaches are not mistaken for LOFs, addressing locational issues within host countries, and controlling for other liabilities unrelated to foreignness that may affect foreign companies settled in a certain area. Examples of the other liabilities include the liabilities of newness and smallness: firm-specific liabilities related to age and size. Companies can simultaneously face survival challenges and benefit from distinct advantages based on their age (newness) and size (smallness) (Stinchcombe 1965; Freeman et al. 1983; Aldrich and Auster 1986; Singh and Lumsden 1990). Aldrich and Auster (1986) discuss the liability of aging in older

---

[1]Psychic distance is defined as the sum of factors preventing the flow of information from and to the market, including differences in language, education, business practices, culture, and industrial development (Johanson and Vahlne 1977).

organizations that may limit the possibility of organizational transformation. Their liability of aging arises from a combination of internal and external factors. The factors include a high level of internal homogeneity that lowers the sensitivity to external changes and the consequent propensity to change, the embeddedness in surroundings, and the development of exchange relationships that limit the autonomy and ability to change.[2]

Another difficulty in measuring the LOF arises from the need for a comparison; that is, whom are foreign firms at a relative disadvantage to? While most view this as a comparison between foreign and domestic firms, the domestic firms are not the only possible referent. Buckley and Casson (1976) provide examples in their comparison of host-country production with home-country production. Further, Eden and Miller (2001) acknowledge different possible referents, noting that an MNC can benchmark a foreign subsidiary's performance against any of its operations in other countries, to assess performance and to determine resource allocation.

2.2 The Liability of Outsidership

The LOF developed in the internationalization theories, particularly in the Uppsala model on the internationalization process of the firm (Johanson and Vahlne 1977). Researchers originally viewed the internationalization process as gradual and incremental (Johanson and Wiedersheim-Paul 1975; Johanson and Vahlne 1977).

However, the network approach challenges this view by involving relationships. That is, firms may move and internationalize faster and, most importantly, adapt faster, because of a direct link (made of relationships and trust) into the network of the new environment. Several studies on the business network—dominated by members of Europe's Industrial Marketing and Purchasing Group (Gadde and Mattsson 1987; Håkansson and Snehota 1995)—view markets as networks of inter-connected and interdependent actors who engage in exchange relationships (Håkansson 1982). The challenge is to become an insider in the relevant business networks.

Those researchers consider markets as networks of relationships in which firms are linked to each other in various complex and invisible patterns. Therefore, they argue that insidership in the relevant networks is necessary for successful internationalization. To become an insider, a firm must gain trust from (and develop relationships with) members of a network, otherwise it experiences a LOO. Outsidership comes with information constraint problems, and with uncertainties regarding the network developments and the opportunities that emerge in networks

---

[2]The liabilities of newness, smallness, and aging and how they manifest in a local cross-cultural context are interesting. However, this chapter focuses mainly on the LOF and the LOO.

and business relationships (Hilmersson 2013). The main LOO issue is how to become a group member (an insider).

A LOO occurs when a firm enters a business environment without knowing who the business actors are, how they relate to each other, or what the acceptable norms of behavior are. That is, the LOO has to do with the uncertainties and difficulties associated with being an outsider to a certain network. If a firm has the advantage of already being involved within one or several business relationships in the business environment, then the firm is an insider. Insidership is a necessary condition for access to market knowledge, and for the successful development of foreign business.

During a firm's growth process, it can move from being an outsider to being an insider, thereby overcoming its LOO. In this process, a firm first enters new networks by using relationships with firms that already are engaged in the new markets or by building relationships with firms in that market. Next, the firm uses those relationships for learning about the networks in the new market. It builds trust with the firms in the network, and creates new knowledge in its interactions with the firms in the network. The firm focuses on identifying and developing new business opportunities for exploitation, and it learns about and builds status in the new market's business networks. Hence, resolving the LOO is a question of gaining knowledge and thereby opportunities because of the relationships (Vahlne and Johanson 2013).

In a resource-based view, a firm realizes that it suffers from the LOO and will then actively works toward creating relationships with others, both known and unknown, who own the resources that the firm lacks. A firm is likely to make use of weak ties (Granovetter 1973) that require a low amount of time, emotional intensity, intimacy, and reciprocity. Accordingly, the firms with a large number of weak ties will find it easier to overcome a LOO than the firms that are engaged primarily in strong ties (Sharma and Blomstermo 2003; Schweizer 2013). The weak ties are more important here because, unlike the strong ties, the other network members do not necessarily share them (Granovetter 1973).

Since the introduction of the LOO construct, many studies try to highlight possible ways to overcome the liability, focusing both on small to medium enterprises (SMEs) and MNCs (Schweizer 2013; Vahlne et al. 2012). However, few studies seek to operationalize the concept of insidership. Schweizer (2013) focuses on SMEs, and discusses how an SME actively overcomes the LOO when internationalizing its activities. He offers a process depiction consisting of four interrelated phases. He explains how a firm's internationalization process expands into new geographical areas through new networks. First, the firm must accept its outsidership roles through internal and external triggers that should lead it to realize that it suffers from the LOO. Second, the firm undertakes one of three reactions to this realization, depending on several factors that may have an impact on the firm's reaction. During this phase, the firm re-evaluates its resources and capabilities in general and its existing relationships in particular. Third, the firm re-bundles its resources and capabilities. Fourth, the firm overcomes the LOO by gaining access to a new network that can assist in leveraging the opportunities identified in the new network.

Hilmersson and Jansson (2012) question how SMEs can establish positions of insidership in foreign business networks. They argue that the firms that become insiders in the foreign market go through three distinct stages in the network entry process. The stages are represented by three network structures characterized by the degree of insidership reached. The degree of insidership includes the types of ties developed, the type of exchange taking place, and the degree of coupling in the three stages. Hilmersson and Jansson's three network structures are (1) an exposure network, (2) a formation network, and (3) a sustenance network.

In the exposure network, the potential exporters focus on finding hubs, to expose themselves to as many potential customers as possible. They want to limit the network they expose themselves to by linking up to certain entry nodes. Thus, a potential exporter initially creates both information and social contacts to expose itself to various parties of relevance to the business in the new market. The aim is to find a position in the business network through the exposure network, mainly consisting of customers and intermediaries. In the initial exposure network stage of an entrant SME, the degree of insidership is low. The exposure network is characterized by many general and weak ties, it is dominated by information exchange, and it is open and loosely coupled.

In the formation network, the exporters from mature markets develop their businesses by gradually transforming certain weak ties into stronger ones, particularly with the found intermediaries. The hubs, like agents and their social networks, are instrumental in the establishment of a number of customer relationships in the country. Therefore, the organization set gradually closes, which leads to the formation of the inter-organizational network. The formation network of the exporters from immature markets follows a similar pattern. However, it is smaller and less complex because it only involves direct relationships with a few large customers. Gradually, the social network loses its importance, usually preceded by the organizational network. The goal in the formation network is to move forward with the partners explored in the exposure network with whom sustainable business can be developed. By that stage, the SMEs have gained enough network experiential knowledge to find new customers. Therefore, in the formation network, the SMEs exploit hubs to expand their network based on their initial few nodes. In the formation network, the entering SMEs establish their positions in the local market networks. In this stage, the degree of insidership of the formation network is intermediate. The formation network is characterized by specific ties that are growing stronger, it consists of both information and social exchange; and it is a closing network.

Finally, in the sustenance network, the exporters from the mature markets establish themselves more firmly by forming a joint venture or by establishing a subsidiary. Over the long term, the business requires more structured relationships to secure production, marketing and sales, logistics, and after-sales services. The exporters from immature markets deepen their dyadic relationships through pursuing more efficient production and logistics, or by developing new dyads. In the sustenance network, the purpose is to move on with those partners with whom sustainable business can be developed, or to develop new partners. By the final, sustenance stage of the entry process, the degree of insidership of the sustenance network is high. The sustenance network is characterized by strong ties and is tightly coupled.

Foreignness and outsidership are concepts clearly borrowed from the literature of management and international business. This chapter contributes to such literature, arguing that LOFs and LOOs can be studied within a specific territory that experiences the presence of native and immigrant entrepreneurship. In cases such as Prato (see Sect. 3), the immigrant entrepreneurs can identify a LOO in the local networks, while being insiders to the global networks dominant in specific industries and markets. The native entrepreneurs can also experience a relative outsidership, and can suffer from elements attributable to foreignness. Those elements relate to the new global networks dominated by the immigrant entrepreneurs settled in the same territory as the native entrepreneurs. In other words, two communities of persons and businesses coexisting within the same context produce liabilities such as foreignness and outsidership. These liabilities are produced locally by the forces of globalization in ways that are not yet acknowledged in the research literature.

3   Methodology

This chapter investigates how immigrant Chinese companies evolve and face their liabilities of foreignness and of outsidership in the context of the industrial district of Prato. We adopt the perspective of Chinese entrepreneurship and analyze the liabilities. We examine the evolution of such companies, from subcontractor status to final firms engaged in diversification. We look for possible interpretations of the evolution of such companies in relation to the local native and immigrant communities.

To illustrate the empirical changes in the Chinese immigrant entrepreneurship in Prato's textile district, we use previously published studies on the textile/fashion companies located in the Prato area. There is a body of literature on Prato's industrial district, with some researchers spending years studying the area through in-depth interviews with local actors such as industry associations, and native and Chinese entrepreneurs. One strand of investigation is based on interviews with the owners and managers of Chinese companies established in the district since the late 1990s. That strand aims to clarify the evolution and interaction between the Chinese entrepreneurs and the native local community. Thus, data presented herein arises from that strand of investigation (Guercini 2002; Milanesi et al. 2016) combined with other studies on the Prato industrial district undertaken by the Florentine school on industrial districts (Bellandi 1996; Becattini et al. 2009; Dei Ottati 2009, 2014). Specifically, we first give an overview of the changes that affected the textile district of Prato, and then present two Chinese immigrant companies as emblematic cases of the evolution of Chinese entrepreneurship. We use fictitious names for the companies (Cloths.It and It-Style) for privacy.

This type of study benefits from an analysis conducted at the level of the individual firm (we introduce specific cases) and from information obtained directly from the entrepreneur. We use reports and other documents, when available, to ensure the data validity.

4 The Evolution of Immigrant Chinese Entrepreneurship in Prato

4.1 Prato's Textile Industry

The city of Prato was famous for the manufacture of textiles since the twelfth century, particularly wool. However, it was only with the advent of industrialization and mechanization in the mid-nineteenth century that an industrial system of related companies engaged in the supply and production of textiles emerged. Some companies refined and used recovered wool obtained from shredding old clothes and industrial scraps (combings) as a cheap and complementary resource in the production of carded wool.

After World War II, a global liberalization process commenced in the exchange of goods, capital, and people. This liberalization intensified in the 1990s, pushed by the transition of many Eastern European countries from centralized to market economies. The global Multi Fibre Arrangement on textile and garments, which imposed importation quotas, ended in 2004. Since 1974, that agreement had partially protected the European textile and garment producers from competition from developing countries. The subsequent Agreement on Textiles and Clothing administered by the World Trade Organization introduced a process of gradual liberalization in the sectors. In the early 2000s, a combination of effects accelerated the structural changes in the global textile/fashion sector. On the macroeconomic level, a long period of stagnation and recession caused a decrease in demand. This decrease was augmented by the decline of the United States (US) Dollar against the Euro, and slowed the growth of the Western economies' middle classes. The combination of an increasing international trade and the West's economic stagnation had a significant impact on the supply and use of textile and fashion products in general. The main changes included (a) the increasing international integration of the supplier/production structures. This included the use of production facilities in low-cost emerging economies, (b) the establishment of highly flexible supplier networks and the ability to cut costs through sharing resources across company borders, and (c) the establishment of international distribution networks based on certain brand names, which favored the concentration of operators (Guercini 2004).

Within this scenario, Chinese-owned firms established themselves in Prato's textile district in the early 1990s. The Chinese firms initially set up as subcontractors to the clothing industry. The presence of Chinese companies in Prato is part of a more complex phenomenon that affects many Italian industrial districts. Many migrants enter Italy from many different countries, although Chinese migrants exhibit particularly conspicuous entrepreneurial tendencies. De Marchi and Grandinetti (2014) highlight some of the main changes affecting the Italian industrial districts. These include globalization and its effects on the firm population of the industrial districts and their fabric of inter-organizational relationships, the emergence of a multi-ethnic society within the districts, the sociocultural discontinuity induced by generational turnover, and greater industry heterogeneity within the production structure of the district territories. Within this framework, the changes underway in Prato are one variant of the evolution affecting all industrial districts, in Italy and elsewhere, through globalization.

Thus, the workforce in industrial districts is increasingly multi-ethnic and heterogeneous from one district to another because of the worker migration phenomenon. The textile district in Prato represents a particular case (Dei Ottati 2009). Alongside the original district, a second district has developed consisting of businesses founded by Chinese immigrants: there are no notable connections between the two districts, or sub-districts. This phenomenon is common in other analogous districts.

The flow of migrants to Prato grew mostly through family relationships or through acquaintances with established members of the Prato Chinese community (Colombi 2002; Guercini 1999). Most of Prato's migrants are Chinese people from the province of Zhejiang, specifically from Wenzhou. Wenzhou is a manufacturing city on China's east coast that is home to thousands of family businesses specialized in the production of personal and household goods (such as garments, shoes, bags, toys, and lighting). The Wenzhounese migrants brought manufacturing skills, an entrepreneurial spirit, and access to a flexible, low-cost workforce through family and community relations—characteristics compatible with the needs of Prato's industrial district (Dei Ottati 2009). The Chinese presence in the Prato area features entrepreneurship and self-employment, driven by the Chinese work ethic. Those features were an essential element in the development of ready-to-wear apparel, especially fast fashion for women, in a setting that until then was a traditional wool textile district.

The initial Chinese-owned firms in Prato were subcontractors. Their business profile gradually broadened, as the Chinese entrepreneurs moved into ready-to-wear female fashion (Ceccagno 2003; Dei Ottati 2013). Thus, some Chinese firms evolved from subcontractors to final firms; that is, firms specializing in design and commercial activities that use other firms, mainly specialized subcontractors, for their production. Notably, most of Prato's Chinese-owned companies retain the characteristic features of the subcontractor. However, the evolution into final firms is particularly prevalent among the second-generation Chinese companies, well integrated in the local economic and social contexts.

4.2 Chinese Immigrant Companies

We consider the cases of two Chinese-owned companies in Prato, Cloths.It and It-Style. First, Cloths.It is a garment making company that operates in the clothing sector. The company was founded in 2005 by a Chinese entrepreneur who arrived in Prato in 1992 from Wenzhou. On arrival, he worked for 4 years as an employee in several Chinese companies before starting his own business as a ready-to-wear subcontractor garment maker in 1996. His first company closed after 2 years because a client did not pay him. The entrepreneur started a new women's total look fashion business in 2005. Cloths.It sells medium-to low-priced garments to mainly Italian and European retailers. Notably, Cloths.It employs Italian people as administrators and as agents to take advantage of their existing network of relationships with Italian and foreign customers. For example, one Italian agent who currently works for Cloths.It was previously an entrepreneur. When he joined Cloths.It, the company benefitted from his previously established customer relationship networks. The main customers of Cloths.It are large Italian and European retailers. The customer relationships are mostly transactional, with a few relational approaches where information is exchanged on design, production, and market choices.

Cloths.It does not currently maintain important relationships with Chinese organizations in China, although its owner thinks that the limited cultural distance with China may lead to possible future developments. Currently, the business network described by Cloths.It is largely characterized by the absence of significant direct interactions with actors in China, and by the prevalence of interactions with Italian firms.

The Cloths.It founder has diversified his business recently. Noteworthy for their importance in terms of interpersonal networks are the presence of two other businesses: a business in the agri-food industry and a clothing wholesaler, the latter managed by the owner's wife and daughter. The agri-food business includes a farm in Maremma in southern Tuscany, acquired by the Chinese entrepreneur together with an Italian partner. That business produces wine and olive oil to export to China: the Italian partner manages the production, while the Chinese entrepreneur manages the exports to China. The entrepreneur diversified into the agri-food sector because he considers that the Chinese ready-to-wear industry in Prato is now mature. Therefore, that diversification was for personal and family investment, with no apparent links to the activity of Cloths.It.

The second case that we present is It-Style, a company that produces leather and leatherette jackets. The product in this case is not women's total look ready-to-wear, as is the case in many of Prato's Chinese-owned companies. Rather, It-Style specializes in the production of a specific product, jackets. It-Style partly replaced its leather products with fabric products recently, because of the high cost of leather and because of evolving fashion trends.

It-Style's founder is one of the best-known members of the Chinese community in Prato. Like many other Chinese entrepreneurs, he arrived in Prato from Wenzhou in 1989, after spending several months in Paris. He established It-Style as a garment making company that year, producing jackets, and working mainly as a subcontractor for Italian companies located in Florence and Empoli. After ten years, the company created its own brand of jackets; however, It-Style still supplies large foreign retailers with their own private labels and Italian multi-brand stores. Several years ago, It-Style moved its manufacturing activities from Prato to China. The company opened a controlled manufacturing facility in Hangzhou (the capital of Zhejiang Province) with 200 employees. It-Style still employs 15 people in Prato (both Italian and Chinese), with the Prato office managing the design and production of samples by local manufacturing subcontractors and fabric suppliers.

The It-Style founder is promoting a large real estate investment in a location near Nanjing in China, which is proposed as a business-to-business mall for *Made in Italy* products. He promotes the project on behalf of a group of Chinese investors who own the mall. He also acts as an intermediary between the group and the Italian firms operating in the typical made in Italy sectors (such as fashion, mechanical products, home furnishings, food, and wine).

5 Discussion and Conclusion

One interpretation of the evolution of Chinese immigrant companies is that once a production base and a Chinese social setting were established in Prato, the Chinese entrepreneurs benefited from ongoing relationships with compatriots and relatives in their country of origin. Thus, they effectively belong to networks in China and in other countries in the world linked by the diaspora to Wenzhou.

The previous empirical research shows at least three stages in the evolution of Chinese entrepreneurship in Prato:

1. The arrival of many of today's most prominent entrepreneurs in the community between the late 1980s and the early 1990s. These migrants started the early Chinese entrepreneurial activities in Prato, working mostly as garment-maker subcontractors. They supplied the established manufacturing structure by providing sewing services and finished products. They neither supplied design services nor ran retail outlets.
2. The transition in the early 2000s (particularly 2000–2002) to final firms. The Chinese entrepreneurs developed a more autonomous position in the market by integrating product design into their businesses. This resulted in the restructuring of their business networks, with the identification of downstream customers and the construction of a network of production subcontractors. At this stage, their market was no longer solely local. They strengthened their intra-community relationships (between final firms and Chinese sub-contractors), and increased their connection to the global networks of fabric suppliers and customers.

3. The most recent phase, characterized by new investments and the diversification of activities (into wholesale trade, agri-food production, real estate, and commercial activities). The key resource is no longer rapid and low-cost production capabilities. The key capability is now gatekeeping between markets and between the inter-community and international cultural contexts. Product quality is also increasing in this stage.

During this evolution, the host country's resources play an important role, eventually becoming an essential aspect of the business model of the Chinese companies. Several Italian resources play a relevant and growing role in the evolving Chinese entrepreneurship. (1) Italian employees engaged in specialist functions such as design, administrative, or commercial activities, and in other less specialized functions. (2) Italian suppliers including representatives, manufacturers of goods, and providers of specific processes such as dyeing and finishing. (3) Italian customers, albeit not as dominant in terms of market share and bargaining power as they were previously. (4) Italian providers of real estate—although in the cases examined the property is mainly acquired rather than leased from Italian owners. (5) The country of origin effect. This effect is important, because for Prato's Chinese firms, the *Made in Italy* label is an important aspect of enhanced production quality.

The two liabilities considered in this chapter (foreignness and outsidership) help us to understand the evolution of Chinese immigrant entrepreneurship. In the initial evolution phase—from subcontractors to clothing manufacturers—the family relationships are prevalent. Mediation by the members of the local Chinese community enables the initial relationships with the local native actors. In the second phase—integrated firm with design and commercial activities—the entrepreneurs of mature companies are active in Prato for many years. Thus, facing the liabilities of foreignness and of perceived psychic distance from Italian actors seems to be a key factor for the future prospects of the individual entrepreneurs (and possibly the entire system of immigrant firms).

In the second phase, relationships are created directly with the end customers both locally and in foreign countries. This is attributable to a progressive reduction of the LOO through the activation of local resources. The role and the importance of local native resources increases.

In the third and final phase of evolution, the activation of the local resources as well as the use of Italian human resources (employees) enable the creation of partnerships aimed at the diversification of business activities. In this phase, the Chinese entrepreneurs benefit from their progressive insidership not only in the network of local actors, but also in the global Chinese network in which the company is embedded. It is possible to explain the three phases of evolution in relation to the LOF and the LOO. The LOF relates to national boundaries and the learning of other aspects such as the language and the culture of the host country, while the LOO relates to networks.

1. In phase one, foreignness reduces at the level of settlement in the host country, but only partly in reference to the language and culture. Initial relationships form with the natives as subcontractors; however, the outsider status remains because the migrant entrepreneurs do not know the relevant local actors or the relationships between such actors in the local context.
2. In phase two, the LOO reduces, although the networks of Chinese immigrant entrepreneurship differ somewhat to the native entrepreneurship networks. The intra-community relationships are still important; however, the Chinese companies build business relationships with local and international customers.
3. In phase three, the diversification processes mean that the Chinese companies interact with elements of the local networks (material, human, and entrepreneurial native resources).

The liabilities of foreignness and outsidership permit an interpretation of the evolution of Chinese entrepreneurship. However, they are not enough to explain every dimension of Chinese entrepreneurship in Prato because there are other elements at play that separate the two local contexts and the community dimension. From their establishment, the immigrant Chinese companies are insiders in the local Chinese community and in the Chinese community in their country of origin. However, those companies are outsiders in the native entrepreneurial community located in the host country. This condition is only partly represented by LOF and LOO, because those liabilities do not highlight the community dimension of belonging that either exists or does not exist in the different communities, and that creates separation.

References

Aldrich H, Auster ER (1986) Even dwarfs started small: liabilities of age and size and their strategic implications. Res Organ Behav 8:165–198

Becattini G, Bellandi M, De Propris L (2009) Critical nodes and contemporary reflections on industrial districts. In: Becattini G, Bellandi M, De Propris L (eds) A handbook of industrial districts. Edward Elgar, Cheltenham

Bellandi M (1996) Innovation and change in the Marshallian industrial district. Eur Plan Stud 4 (3):357–368

Buckley PJ, Casson M (1976) Future of the multinational enterprise. Springer

Calhoun MA (2002) Unpacking liability of foreignness: identifying culturally driven external and internal sources of liability for the foreign subsidiary. J Int Manag 8(3):301–321

Ceccagno A (ed) (2003) Migranti a Prato. Il distretto tessile multietnico. Milano, Franco Angeli

Colombi M (ed) (2002) L'imprenditoria cinese nel distretto industriale di Prato. Leo S. Olschki, Firenze

De Marchi V, Grandinetti R (2014) Industrial districts and the collapse of the Marshallian model: looking at the Italian experience. Competition & Change 18(1):70–87

Dei Ottati G (2009) Italian industrial district and the dual Chinese challenge. In: Smyth R, Johanson G (eds) Living outside the walls: the Chinese in Prato. Cambridge Scholars Press, Cambridge

Dei Ottati G (2013) Imprese di immigrati e distretto industriale: un'interpretazionen dello sviluppo delle imprese cinesi a Prato. Stato e mercato 2:171–202

Dei Ottati G (2014) A transnational fast fashion industrial district: an analysis of the Chinese businesses in Prato. Camb J Econ, 1–28

Denk N, Kaufmann L, Roesch JF (2012) Liabilities of foreignness revisited: a review of contemporary studies and recommendations for future research. J Int Manag 18(4):322–334

Eden L, Miller SR (2001) Opening the black box: multinationals and the costs of doing business abroad. Acad Manag Proc, C1–C6

Eden L, Miller SR (2004) Distance matters: liability of foreignness, institutional distance and ownership strategy. Adv Int Manag 16(04):187–221

Freeman J, Carroll GR, Hannan MT (1983) The liability of newness: age dependence in organizational death rates. Am Sociol Rev 48(5):692–710

Gadde LE, Mattsson LG (1987) Stability and change in network relationships. Int J Res Mark 4(1):29–41

Granovetter MS (1973) The strength of weak ties. Am J Sociol, 1360–1380

Guercini S (1999) L'impresa con vertice di nazionalità cinese nel distretto pratese: caratteri, processi di sviluppo e politiche di mercato. In: Conference "Il futuro dei distretti", University of Padua, Vicenza

Guercini S (2002) Profilo del vertice, processi di sviluppo e politiche di mercato dell'impresa cinese a Prato. In: Colombi M (ed) L'imprenditoria cinese nel distretto industriale di Prato. Leo S. Olschki, Firenze, pp 35–70

Guercini S (2004) International competitive change and strategic behaviour of Italian textile-apparel firms. J Fashion Mark Manag 8(3):320–339

Guercini S, Milanesi M, Dei Ottati G (2013) Global and local business networks in the growth of the Chinese firm in Prato. In: 6th Chinese in Prato symposium and 4th Wenzhouese diaspora symposium on Chinese migration entrepreneurship and development in the new global economy, Prato, 29–30 Oct 2013

Håkansson H (1982) International marketing and purchasing of industrial goods: an interaction approach. Wiley, Cheltenham

Håkansson H, Snehota I (1995) Developing relationships in business networks. Routledge, London

Hilmersson M (2013) The effect of international experience on the degree of SME insidership in newly opened business networks. Baltic J Manag 8(4):397–415

Hilmersson M, Jansson H (2012) International network extension processes to institutionally different markets: entry nodes and processes of exporting SMEs. Int Bus Rev 21(4):682–693

Hymer S (1976) The international operations of national firms: a study of direct foreign investment, vol 14. MIT Press, Cambridge, pp 139–155

Johanson J, Vahlne JE (1977) The internationalization process of the firm—a model of knowledge development and increasing foreign market commitments. J Int Bus Stud 8(1):23–32

Johanson J, Vahlne JE (2009) The Uppsala internationalization process model revisited: from liability of foreignness to liability of outsidership. J Int Bus Stud 40(9):1411–1431

Johanson J, Wiedersheim-Paul F (1975) The internationalization of the firm—four Swedish cases. J Manage Stud 12(3):305–323

Kindleberger CP (1969) American business abroad: six lectures on direct investment. Yale University Press, New Haven

Luo Y, Mezias JM (2002) Liabilities of foreignness: concepts, constructs, and consequences. J Int Manag 8(3):217–221

Matsuo H (2000) Liability of foreignness and the uses of expatriates in Japanese multinational corporations in the United States. Sociol Inq 70(1):88–106

Mezias JM (2002) How to identify liabilities of foreignness and assess their effects on multinational corporations. J Int Manag 8(3):265–282

Milanesi M, Guercini S, Waluszewski A (2016) A Black Swan in the district? An IMP perspective on immigrant entrepreneurship and changes in industrial districs. IMP J 10(2):243–259

Miller SR, Richards M (2002) Liability of foreignness and membership in a regional economic group: analysis of the European Union. J Int Manag 8(3):323–337

Petersen B, Pedersen T (2002) Coping with liability of foreignness: different learning engagements of entrant firms. J Int Manag 8(3):339–350

Schweizer R (2013) SMEs and networks: overcoming the liability of outsidership. J Int Entrepreneurship 11(1):80–103

Sharma DD, Blomstermo A (2003) The internationalization process of born globals: a network view. Int Bus Rev 12(6):739–753

Singh JV, Lumsden CJ (1990) Theory and research in organizational ecology. Annu Rev Sociol, 161–195

Stinchcombe AL (1965) Social structure and organizations. In March JG (ed) Handbook of organizations. RandMcNally, Chicago

Vahlne JE, Johanson J (2013) The Uppsala model on evolution of the multinational business enterprise-from internalization to coordination of networks. Int Mark Rev 30(3):189–210

Vahlne JE, Schweizer R, Johanson J (2012) Overcoming the liability of outsidership—the challenge of HQ of the global firm. J Int Manag 18(3):224–232

Zaheer S (1995) Overcoming the liability of foreignness. Acad Manag J 38(2):341–363

Liabilities in Prato's Industrial District: An Analysis of Italian and Chinese Firm Failures

Luciana Lazzeretti and Francesco Capone

Abstract Liabilities affect a firm's competitiveness. Currently, firms face increasingly fierce competition as they operate in a period of deep financial and economic recession. The industrial districts in developed countries are experiencing profound transformations because of globalization and because of competition from developing countries and local immigrant firms. This chapter examines the liabilities faced by the firms in Prato's industrial district, by analyzing the failure rates of Italian and Chinese firms. This chapter aims to contextualize the concept of liabilities in the organizational ecology theory, to propose a quantitative approach to their investigation. The chapter contributes to existing studies by considering the different liabilities a firm has to overcome to survive in an organizational population. We adopt an organizational ecology approach to study multi-population failures in Prato's industrial district in the period 1990–2012. We construct a model of the failures of Chinese and Italian firms to investigate their evolution across time. The results emphasize the importance of the position that firms hold in strategic networks, particularly at international levels (global value chains). The firms' strategic position is important against the background of the production and the social relations in the industrial district.

Keywords Liabilities · Outsidership · Firm failures · Organizational ecology · Industrial district · Prato

L. Lazzeretti (✉) · F. Capone
University of Florence, Florence, Italy
e-mail: luciana.lazzeretti@unifi.it

F. Capone
e-mail: francesco.capone@unifi.it

© Springer International Publishing Switzerland 2017
S. Guercini et al. (eds.), *Native and Immigrant Entrepreneurship*,
DOI 10.1007/978-3-319-44111-5_9

1   Introduction

Liabilities affect a firm's competitiveness. Currently, firms face increasingly fierce competition as they operate in a period of deep financial and economic recession. The industrial districts in developed countries are experiencing profound transformations because of globalization and because of competition from developing countries and local immigrant firms. This chapter examines the liabilities faced by the firms in Prato's industrial district, by analyzing the failure rates for Italian and Chinese firms.

The liability of outsidership originates in international business literature (Johanson and Vahlne 2009; Schweizer 2013), distinguishing outsiders from insiders. The liability relates to the difficulties faced by the actors who are external to the most effective and important (social and business) networks. In revisiting the Uppsala theory, Johanson and Vahlne (2009) indicate that internationalization involves taking steps to become an insider in the relevant networks of the foreign market. However, Schweizer (2013) emphasizes that a firm that tries to gain access to such networks will suffer not only from the liability of foreignness—the costs of doing business abroad (Zaheer 1995)—but also from the liability of outsidership. These liabilities arise from a lack of market-specific business knowledge and a lack of relevant network positions (Johanson and Vahlne 2009). The liability of outsidership concept is relatively new, meaning that most studies try to investigate outsidership with the aim of overcoming the liability (Schweizer 2013). Most research is devoted to case studies (Hilmersson and Jansson 2012; Muzychenko and Liesch 2015), with few quantitative, large-scale analyses.

This chapter investigates the failures of Chinese and Italian firms operating in Prato's industrial district. We combine the liabilities of outsidership and insidership concepts (from international business research) with the quantitative approach (from organizational ecology research) that introduces other liabilities such as smallness, newness, and localization. We adopt an organizational ecology approach to study multi-population failures in Prato's industrial district in the period 1990–2012. There is little research comparing the failure rates of Chinese firms with Italian firms, with the exceptions of the Regional Institute for Economic Planning of Tuscany (IRPET) (2013) and Lazzeretti and Capone (2016, 2017). Most studies investigate how the Chinese firms settled in Prato affect the Italian entrepreneurs in the area.

We depart from the traditional analysis of Prato's industrial district, which demographically investigates the organizational population dynamics and the multi-population interactions over a 50-year period (Lazzeretti and Storai 2003). From an ecological view, Prato's industrial district is a community of organizations identified by a set of different organizational populations. We analyze two populations of firms co-located in Prato's industrial district: the Italian firms operating in the textile industry and the Chinese firms that initially operated in the textile industry and then moved to the clothing industry. Thus, we analyze the evolution over time of two populations of firms that operate in the same territory in a condition of debated separation/integration.

Prato illustrates how a mature industrial district transforms through globalization and through the settlement of Chinese entrepreneurs (Dei Ottati 2009, 2013; Belussi and Sammarra 2010; Chiarvesio et al. 2010; Santini et al. 2011; Lombardi and Sforzi 2016). Prato's industrial district is unique compared with other Italian industrial districts, where the Chinese firms remained as suppliers of the Italian firms. Rather, in Prato, the Chinese firms became final firms, entering the clothing industry.

The simultaneous presence of a multi-ethnic population of Italian and Chinese firms characterize Prato's industrial district. The co-presence of these two communities of people and enterprises in the same territory generate an intense debate about this local community (Baldassar et al. 2016; Johanson et al. 2009). The debate involves scholars of local development and of management and development economics, as well as journalists and sinologists (among others). However, there is no real shared interpretation of the phenomenon.

Some contributions describe the evolution of Prato's industrial district, hypothesizing about the presence of two separate districts with poor interrelationships. Some conjecture a Chinese siege as one of the causes of the decline of and crisis in Italian firms (Pieraccini 2008). Contrastingly, others delineate the transformation of the textile industrial district into a new fashion district, partially integrated with Chinese firms (Ceccagno 2003, 2009). Thus, the Italian and Chinese firms share the same competition and face the same crises.

Dei Ottati (2013) discusses these contrasting perspectives and notes that, economically, Prato has not exploited all of the opportunities provided by the settlement of Chinese immigrants. The opportunities would arise if the two communities integrated further. Similarly, De Noni et al. (2013), invoking the opportunity to rethink the district's governance, hope for a re-emergence of districtual ecologies capable of transforming multiculturalism from a factor of conflict to a competitive factor.

Prato's situation is complex, and is important because it represents a metaphor for the post-industrial decline of industrial districts caused by globalization (Gereffi and Memedovic 2003). Thus, Prato is an interesting case study on the profound changes involving old-Europe and the emerging countries. Those emerging countries are no longer in a development phase, but are new players in the global economy.

2 Organizational Ecology and Liabilities

Organizational ecology draws on ecological and evolutionary models, emerging as an approach to study social changes and diversity (Hannan and Carroll 1992; Hannan et al. 2007). The approach aims to study long-term organizational change, focusing on the organizations' diversity and on their rise-and-decline patterns over time. Organizational ecology particularly studies the processes that influence the birth, growth, decline, and disappearance of organizations and of organizational forms.

Organizational ecology introduces several liability concepts (Lazzeretti 2006). Its most used concept refers to the liability of newness, described as the structural inertia of organizations depending on age (Hannan and Freeman 1989; Bruderl and Schussler 1990; Henderson 1999). The liability of smallness relates to size dependence (Baum and Mezias 2002), while the liability of imitation relates to imitating already established firms (Singh and Lumsden 1990). The liability of foreignness relates to the disadvantages suffered by foreign subsidiaries in comparison to domestic firms, as regards their position in the domestic market (Zaheer and Mosakowski 1997; Mezias 2002).

Departing from Stinchcombe's (1965) ideas, the liability of newness indicates that young organizations are more likely to fail than older organizations. Young firms must establish new relationships with suppliers and customers, and must learn new rules regarding competition and the business in which they are operating. Hannan and Freeman (1989) indicate that, according to the liability of newness, the relation between failure rates and age is exponential for an organization in its early years.

Regarding the liability of smallness, organizational ecology indicates that failure rates decrease for larger organizations or firms. This indicates that during their growth, the larger firms develop strong relationships with customers, suppliers, and institutions, thereby increasing their probability of surviving a crisis (Lazzeretti 2006).

The liability of imitation refers to the relationship between the establishment (or founding) of existing firms and the founding of new firms. Delacroix and Carroll (1983) say that the founding of the initial firms in a sector encourages potential entrepreneurs to create new firms by signaling a growing niche. However, as the number of new firms increases, the imitation process leads to a glut of newly founded firms and the competition for resources discourages the founding of additional firms (Singh and Lumsden 1990). This liability relates to the density dependence theory (see Sect. 2.1).

Organizational ecology also introduces the liability of localization; that is, the areas where firms are localized. For example, the level of spatial concentration in industrial districts (Becattini 1990; Becattini et al. 2009), the center-periphery theory (Baum and Mezias 1992), and the role of agglomeration economies (Van Wissen 2004).

Mezias (2002) investigates the liabilities of foreignness, and the strategies to minimize their effects in labor lawsuit judgments in the United States. He describes how foreign subsidiaries are at a disadvantage relative to domestic firms because they suffer from a liability of foreignness. There is little research on the sources of the foreign subsidiary disadvantages. Understanding the disadvantages could uncover ways to reduce the exposure to the liabilities of foreignness, and could improve the management of foreign direct investment.

The liabilities discussed in this chapter explain why and how a firm faces a higher competition in a particular situation (size, location, age, nationality) compared with the other firms in the same industry or population.

2.1 Organizational Ecology in Studying Firm Failures

Organizational ecology studies the processes that influence the birth, growth, decline, and disappearance of organizations and of organizational forms. Initially, organizational ecology looked at industrial sectors, defined as populations of enterprises (Hannan et al. 2007). Later, several contribution were devoted to the analysis of clusters and industrial districts (Staber 2001; Maggioni 2005; Lazzeretti 2006; De Propris and Lazzeretti 2009) meant as organizational populations identified by interrelated multi-populations of firms (Baum and Singh 1994).

There are many approaches to organizational evolution (Carroll and Hannan 2000). Of these, the classical density dependence theory is probably the most widely known and tested (Dobrev et al. 2006). Many studies find evidence of the positive density effect (Bogaert et al. 2014).

In the density dependence model, over time, the growth path of an industry or a cluster (called a community of organizations) is dependent on the number of firms (size) in that industry/cluster. In the model, the founding and failure rates of the firms are dependent on the size of the population (that is, the density). Two basic forces are responsible for the size dependency of foundings and failures: legitimation and competition. Both forces relate to the size of the population.

Legitimation refers to the extent that society accepts and recognizes a new organizational form or industry. Organizational ecology argues that new industries and forms flourish when they gain constitutive legitimation, meaning that their constituents and audiences understand them and accept them. This theory states that the number of organizations (density) could be a proxy for the degree of legitimation of an organizational form. Hence, the emergence of organizational forms benefits from a positive density effect: higher densities stimulate entries and depress exits (Bogaert et al. 2014).

Competition processes emerge when firm populations employ the same set of resources and work in the same business. Therefore, the competition process depends on the number of populations in a community (or organizations in a population). To clarify the competition concept, consider how the entry of an additional competitor in a system generates a process of crowding out that increases the total number of existing firms. Therefore, the competition coefficient increases with density at an increasing rate.

The competition and legitimation processes both affect population vitality, in that their founding and failure rates vary with their density rate. The rate multiplier coefficient represents the relationship between the failure (or founding) rate and the density of a population. The rate multiplier coefficient is the ratio of the failure (or founding) rate to the rate calculated for the lowest observed population density (Fig. 1).

Particularly, at low density, the decreasing failure rates have a small negative effect on density because of the legitimation process. When the density of a population peaks, it means that it has reached its carrying capacity (N^* in Fig. 1). After this point, as the competition forces intensify, the mortality rate increases and the

Fig. 1 Relationship between mortality and population density (authors' elaboration on Hannan and Carroll 1992)

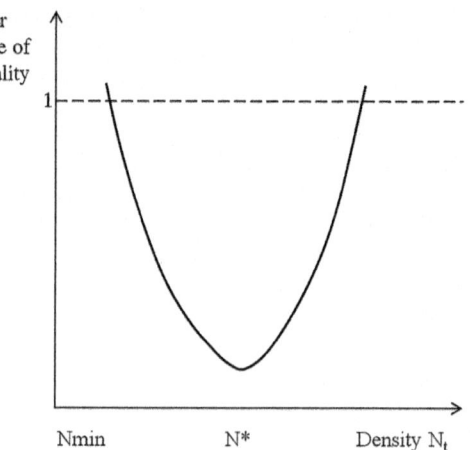

population's density falls. Hannan and Freeman (1989) find that the relationship between the density of a population and the multiplier of its failure rate is non-monotonic and U-shaped (whilst the density dependence of the founding rate is non-monotonic and inversed U-shaped) (Fig. 1).

Since its introduction in the late 1980s, the density model gained popularity and is now used in management, industrial economics, and regional sciences (Bogaert et al. 2014). Notwithstanding some initial criticisms,[1] the density model contributes to research by relating cluster life-cycle theories and ecological approaches to the economies of agglomeration.

Van Wissen (2004) compares the model of density dependence with that of agglomeration economies. He highlights the similarities between the legitimation process and some industrial district and cluster concepts, such as social capital, institutional thickness, and innovative milieu (Becattini et al. 2009). Van Wissen states that the agglomeration effects may fit neatly in the framework of the density dependence model, and that the legitimation and competition processes can have a spatial perspective.

In this case, legitimation contains the centripetal forces, and competition contains the centrifugal forces in spatial cluster formation. Wenting and Frenken (2011) analyze the global fashion design industry, and find that the legitimation processes operate locally and the competition processes operate globally. At the cluster level, Maggioni (2005) adopts the population ecology approach to study the evolution of some Italian industrial districts by considering the relationship between agglomeration economies and diseconomies. De Propris and Lazzeretti (2009) measure the

---

[1]One criticism is that the theory takes no account of firm size, whereas large and small firms clearly have very different effects in a population. A second criticism is that the theory fails to explain negative growth rates and the negative slope of the density curve beyond the peak. A third criticism is that firms differ with respect not only to size and economic activity, but also to geographical location (spatial heterogeneity) (Van Wissen 2004).

decline of Birmingham's jewelry quarter in the United Kingdom, using organizational ecology and failure dynamics. Lazzeretti (2006) applies the same approach to study the decline of the Arezzo jewelry district in Italy.

The aim of our empirical analysis is to verify the impact of the different liabilities on the failure rate of the Italian and Chinese firms in Prato's industrial district. We mainly focus on two research questions. First, how do the different liabilities affect the mortality rate of the Italian and Chinese firms? Second, which liability is the most relevant in firm mortality? We investigate this issue from an integrated perspective, combining international business concepts (insidership and outsidership) with the organizational ecology view (smallness and newness) and with the density dependence theory.

3 Research Design and Data Sources

We use several databases to reconstruct the evolution of Prato's industrial district since its foundation (1945–2011). The main data source for the company fouding rates and failure flows and the density of the two populations is the Registry of Economic Activity (REA). Prato's Chamber of Commerce (CCIAA) collects the data for the REA, and the CCIAA research office manages and analyzes the data. This database provides details on all of the foreign-owned (including Chinese) firms in the province of Prato, including their foundation and closure dates. It also provides other information related to the firms' localization, typology, and its NACE[2] codes of economic activity. Using the REA data we historically reconstructed the population of Chinese firms in Prato, from their first settlement in the early 1990s to current times. Every Pratese firm must be recorded in this registry by law.[3]

The REA database on foreign firms contains over 16,800 records in the period 1990–2011, of which 11,400 pertain to Chinese firms (almost 70%). The database registered over 11,000 foundings and 6000 failures of Chinese firms in the period. Overall, 78% of the records included in the database relate to firms operating in the textile, clothing, and leather manufacturing sectors, confirming the role played by foreign firms in Prato. Data on Italian firms were also sourced from the REA and from previous studies on Prato's industrial district since the 1940s (Lazzeretti and Storai 2003). The REA data include the density, foundings, and failures of Italian firms in the province of Prato since 1995. Data on employment are from industry and service censuses undertaken by Italy's National Institute for Statistics (ISTAT 1991, 1996, 2001, 2011), verified using CCIAA data. Export data are from the CCIAA, verified using IRPET data (2013).

---

[2]The statistical classification codes for economic activities in the European Union (EU).

[3]Notwithstanding that registration and cancellation from the REA is required by law, several authors say that Chinese firms do not always respect administrative obligations (Ceccagno 2012; Pieraccini 2008). This phenomenon is partly analysed by IRPET (2013) that estimates the relevance of the informal economy of Chinese firms in Prato's industrial district.

Herein, we define a Chinese firm in the same way as the research office of Prato's CCIAA. They define a firm as Chinese if it has an owner, a manager, or an associate of Chinese nationality. Thus, we consider all of the societies and not only individual firms.

Several authors affirm that official data do not always reflect the real numbers of founding and failing foreign firms, with Chinese firms particularly characterized by an intensely informal economy (Ceccagno 2012; Pieraccini 2008). Notably, many Chinese firms may open and close regularly to avoid paying fines and to bypass administrative and fiscal controls. This phenomenon means that some flows are over-estimated. The over-estimation is an important limitation for short period analysis; however, it should have a lesser impact in long period longitudinal studies.

4 Historical Evolution of Prato's Industrial District: Settled Chinese Firms

Chinese firms first appeared in Prato in the early 1990s, initially acting as sub-contractors to the local knitwear and garment enterprises (Dei Ottati 2013; Colombi et al. 2002). This first stage of subcontracting to the Italian textile companies represented an opportunity for the local businesses: Chinese firms provided flexible labor and low subcontracting costs. When production recovered in the 1990s, Prato's knitting mills found it difficult to source Italian workers to sew knitted garments. At that stage, the Chinese migrants started arriving in Prato (Dei Ottati 2009).

Chinese immigration to Prato initially filled the local job demands, through home working and subcontracting in knitted fabrics. The Chinese migrants later, and to a greater extent, also filled jobs in the clothing sector, whose demand would otherwise have remained unsatisfied. In the 1990s and 2000s, clothing companies grew rapidly, provoking a first shift from the textile industry (mainly knitwear). In 2011, there were 240 Chinese subcontracting clothing enterprises, working mainly for Chinese final firms (Dei Ottati 2014).

Interestingly, once the Chinese firms settled in a non-primary industry (knitwear) of the industrial district, they developed a new mode of production: fast fashion or quick fashion (Guercini 2001), which was virtually absent in Prato before their arrival. Further, the Chinese entrepreneurs later developed an entirely new industry, clothing, previously overlooked by the local entrepreneurs.

Figure 2 presents Prato's Chinese and Italian firm populations (1990–2011) subdivided by economic activity. The most important Italian trend relates to the textile industry that recorded a significant decline from approximately 7000 firms in the early 1990s to approximately 2000 firms at the end of 2011 (Fig. 2b). The number of Italian clothing companies slightly declined in the period. Contrastingly, the Chinese clothing firms grew significantly in the same period, from approximately 1000 companies in the late 1990s to approximately 3500 in 2011 (Fig. 2a).

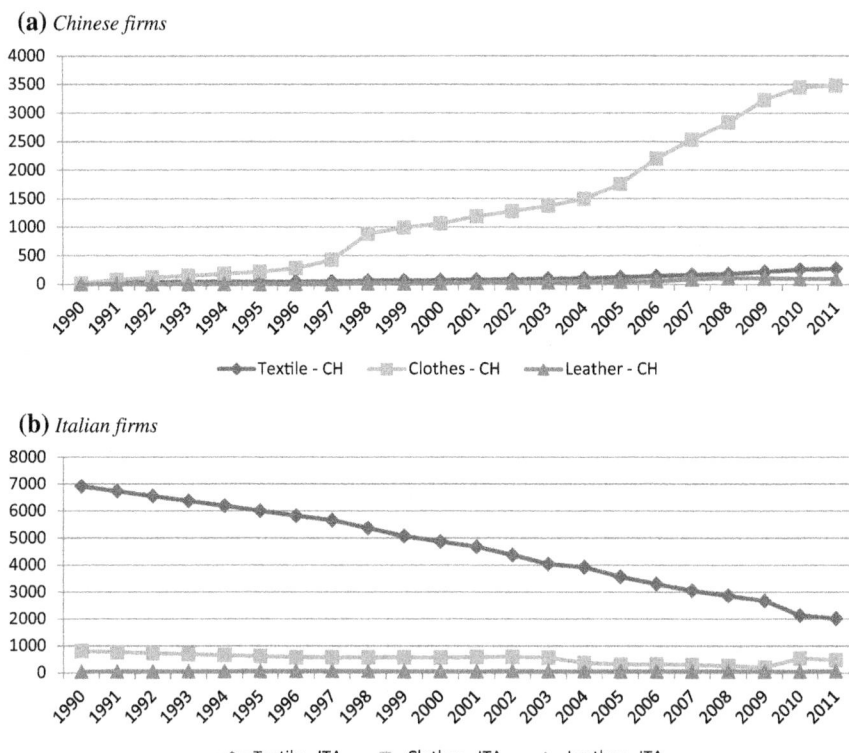

Fig. 2 Prato's Chinese (**a**) and Italian (**b**) firm numbers in the textile, clothing, and leather sectors, 1990–2011 (authors' elaboration)

Figure 3 illustrates the evolution of employment in the district, subdivided into textile and clothing activities. The results partly confirm the process already described—a deep employment crisis in textile and increased employment in clothing. Notably, the textile decline is mild after 2009, and the clothing growth is slow. The worldwide financial crisis eliminated the less efficient firms and the level of employment decreased at a reduced speed. We can partly explain the employment trends in the clothing industry by a large proportion of the Chinese workforce operating in the black economy and by its occasional employment of irregular workers.

IRPET (2013) uses different methods to try to estimate the number of Chinese employees in the informal economy in the province of Prato. From a basis of approximately 11,000 official Chinese employees, they estimate the total number of Chinese employees at 17,000–20,000. This signifies that there are 6000–9000 unregistered Chinese workers in Prato.

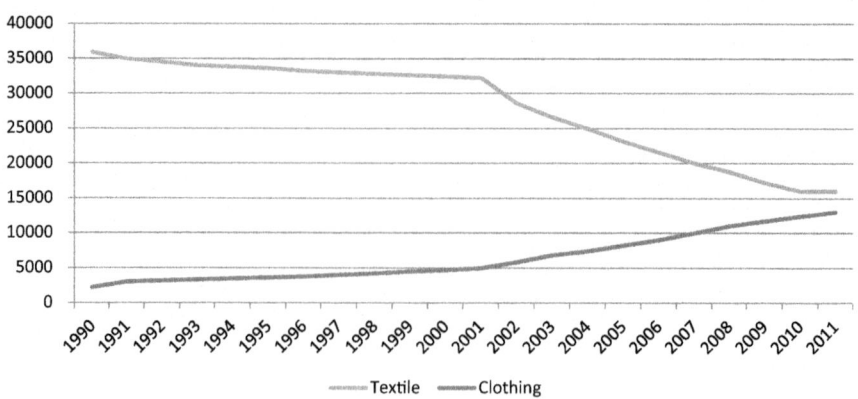

Fig. 3 Prato's total employment numbers in textile and clothing (Italian and Chinese firms), 1990–2011 (authors' elaboration of data from CCIAA Prato and of ISTAT data from 1991, 2001, and 2011)

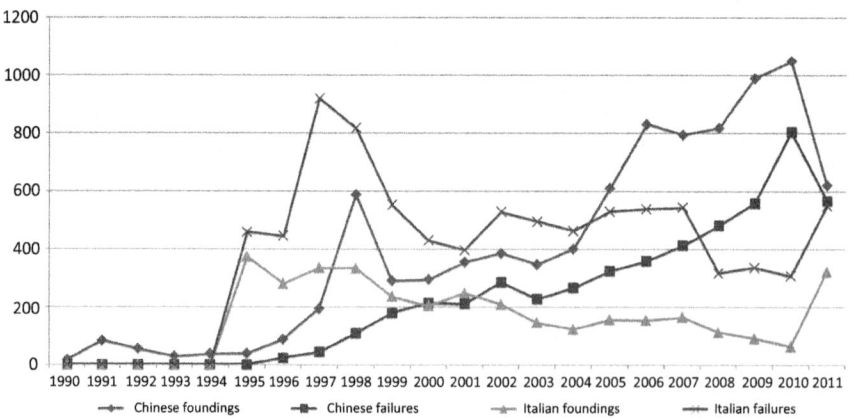

Fig. 4 Foundings and failures of Chinese and Italian firms in Prato, 1990–2011 (authors' elaboration of data from CCIAA Prato; missing Italian data pre-1994)

Figure 4 presents the foundings and failures of Chinese and Italian firms in Prato (1990–2011). As expected, more Chinese firms were founded than Italian firms. Conversely, initially more Italian firms failed than Chinese firms. The latter trend reverses in 2008.

Importantly, the overall number of firms is increasing as new firm populations develop that diversify the activities in the industrial district. Consider the number of Chinese firms operating in the import-export trade. This sub-population (approximately 400 firms in 2011) connects the Chinese firms in Prato to the Chinese global value chain. Prato's Chinese firms benefit from the low cost of raw materials imported from China (from the same ethnic community), and allow access to the

European distribution channels for finished products. This is a proxy to emphasize the increasing heterogeneity and variety of Prato's industrial district. This confirms the idea of a transformation phase for the district.

5 Firm Failures in Prato's Industrial District: Chinese Firms

This section investigates the firm failures in Prato's industrial district, focusing on Chinese firms. Most existing studies focus on the number of foundings and the founding rate (ratio of founding numbers to population size) in Prato's industrial district, generally overlooking firm mortality.

Industrial demography and organizational ecology use population pyramids to determine the overall age distribution of a population. The pyramids indicate the reproductive capabilities of the population and the likelihood of its continuation.

As noted in Sect. 4, many Chinese firms close down, more than are actually reported on. Consider the age pyramids in Fig. 5. In 1999, the oldest Chinese firm is 10 years old, and 86% of the firms are less than 5 years old. In 2005, the oldest Chinese firm is 15 years old; however, the vast majority of firms closed before reaching 10 years of age. In that year, still 84% of the firms are less than 5 years old. Finally, in 2012, the oldest Chinese firm is 20 years old; however, the majority are less than 10 years old. In 2012, still 81% of the firms are less than 5 years old.

Figure 5 shows that the Chinese firms are not actually aging, because many of them fail and are substituted by new firms. The vast majority of the firms are younger than 5 years old in each period investigated.[4]

Comparing the mortalities of Chinese firms with Italian firms further evidences this situation. Unfortunately, the REA database contains individual data for Chinese firms only—it does not contain individual data for Italian firms—therefore, we only undertake a survival analysis on the firms. Figure 6 presents the results in the form of a survival function. As shown, the number of Chinese firms decreases by half after 6 or 7 years of existence.

Compare these data with the survival analysis conducted in Randelli and Ricchiuti (2015) for firms in Tuscany in the period 1998–2010 (including both Italian- and foreign-owned firms). They find that only 25% of Tuscan firms close down within 5 years of their founding. They also find that the conditional probability of failure increases in the first 4 or 5 years of existence and then decreases. Our results show that the mortality rate of the Chinese firms in Prato is significantly more intense than the mortality rate of the Tuscan firms in Randelli and Ricchiuti's (2015) study.

---

[4]The failure numbers may be over-estimated because the REA registers firm transformations first with a failure and then with a new constitution.

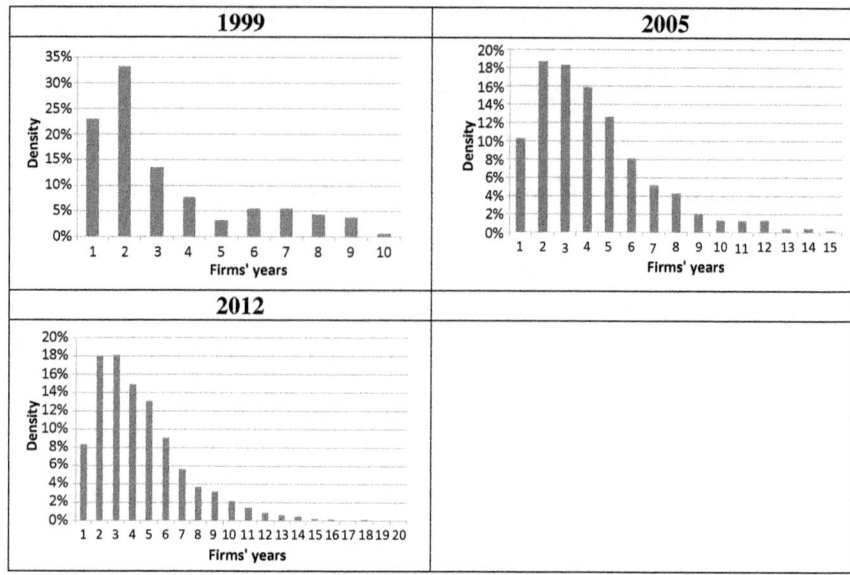

Fig. 5 Age pyramids for Chinese firms in Prato's industrial district 1999, 2005 and 2012 (authors' elaboration of data from CCIAA Prato)

Fig. 6 Survival function of Chinese firms in Prato's industrial district, 1990–2012 (authors' elaboration of data from CCIAA Prato)

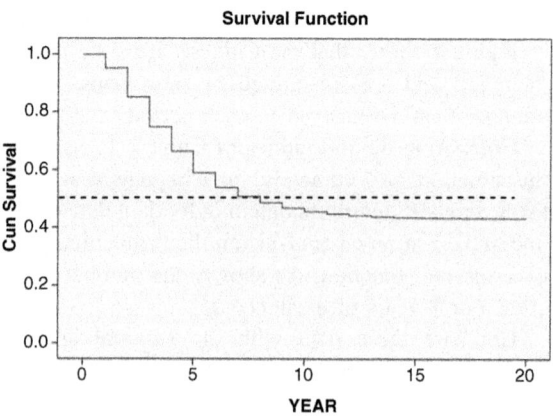

After 5 years of existence, the Chinese firms have only a 60% survival probability, whereas the Tuscan firms have a 75% survival probability. Overall, 50% of the established Chinese firms fail after 6 or 7 years, whereas it is over 10 years before 50% of the established Tuscan firms fail. This finding is particularly notable because Randelli and Ricchiuti (2015) survey the Tuscan firms solely in a crisis period (1998–2010), while we analyze the Chinese firms for the period 1990–2010. Considering the periods studied, a better result might be expected for the Chinese firms.

The findings underline the high mortality level for Chinese firms. The analyzed industrial sector (textile and clothing) does influence the results. However, there are no data to benchmark the results against the mortality of Italian firms in the textile and clothing sector. We find that the Chinese firms fail within 5 years at a fluctuating percentage of 70–90%, and never fall below these proportions.[5]

These results are in line with the few previous works (IRPET 2013) on Chinese firm mortality. Our results highlight how the Chinese firm population is characterized by a substantial mortality, a feature not fully considered in the literature. Only IRPET (2013) focuses explicitly on Chinese firm mortality, and finds that although the Chinese firms have a high mortality rate in the period under exam, the mortality of the Italian firms is even higher (p. 48), as we found (see Fig. 4).

Finally, it is important to note that the mortality of Chinese firms is routinely over-estimated by administrative sources. For example, Ceccagno (2012) reports the continuous opening and closure of Chinese firms in Prato, mainly to avoid administrative and fiscal controls, "*as a rule, these businesses close down after only one year, and reopen the activity under a different (lent) name*" (p. 51). Pieraccini (2008) observes that in the mid-2000s many Chinese firms closed down immediately after inspection to avoid paying taxes and fines. Ceccagno (2012) states that, according to some interviews, this phenomenon is worse today. Unfortunately, a clear quantification is impossible.

6 Ecological Analysis of Chinese and Italian Firm Populations

This section analyzes the failure of Italian and Chinese firms, evaluating the impact of different forms of liabilities. The study uses the basic model of density-dependent evolution (Hannan and Freeman 1989) to analyze multi-populations. In the density dependence model, the firm failure rate follows a Poisson process, so that the failure rate is a time-independent constant. As we know the number of failures per year, the failure rate model is based on a simple Poisson model:

$$F(t) = \exp\left(\theta_1 N_t + \theta_2 N_t^2 + \delta_1 F_{t-1} + \delta_2 D_{t-1} + \delta_3 \mathrm{Emp}_{\mathrm{tcloth;text}}\right.$$
$$\left. + \delta_4 \mathrm{Exports}_{\mathrm{tcloth;text}}\right) \exp\left(\sum \phi_i X_{it}\right)$$

where the two orders of density are represented by N_t and N_t^2, F_{t-1} represents previous foundings, D_{t-1} represents previous failures, X_{it} is the vector of co-variates, and the vector of parameters ϕ_i corresponds to the period variables.

We then introduce the failure rate of small and medium-sized enterprises (SMEs) to evaluate the liability of smallness, related to the size of the firm, and the failure rate at 5 years to evaluate the liability of newness. We calculate each variable for the Chinese firms.[6] We also include some control variables, including employment evolution ($Emp_{t\ text}$; $Emp_{t\ cloth}$) and export evolutions in clothing and textile in Europe and Asia ($Exports_{t\ text}$; $Exports_{t\ cloth}$).

We calculate the liability of outsidership as the difference in the failure probabilities for Chinese firms compared with Italian firms; that is, with the Chinese dummy parameters. This variable aims to estimate the difference between the insidership of the Chinese firms in the global value chain network and their relative outsidership in the local network of Italian firms. If the estimated parameter is positive, then the liability of outsidership has a greater effect than insidership in the global value chain network. If the parameter is negative, then the liability of outsidership in the local network has a greater effect than insidership. This represents a first empirical attempt to measure the phenomenon. However, we are aware that other exogenous factors could influence the mortality of Chinese and Italian firms.

We match the variables presented in Table 1 with a corresponding theoretical discussion and estimation hypotheses.

We use separate estimations in our analysis. Table 2 reports the maximum likelihood estimates of the Poisson model of density dependence for firm failures in the Italian and the Chinese firm populations. Each model analyzes the first- and second-order effects of density and includes other variables. The models compare the different probabilities of failure for Chinese firms with Italian firms, and provide an estimate of the control variables.

The analysis results are satisfactory, but do not confirm all of the hypotheses. Model 1, which estimates the first- and second-order of density and the dummy for Chinese firms, is the simplest. The first-order effect of density is not significant in each model. It is positive in models 1 and 2, and is negative in model 5. However, the parameter is not significant.

The second-order effect of density is significant and positive in model 1, emphasizing that the multiplier of the firm failure rate might be U-shaped. Consequently, the industrial district's firm populations might already be in the final stage of evolution, during which mortality is strongly influenced by competition rather than legitimation processes. These results might confirm the evolution trends of density for the firms in Prato's industrial district, as well as their mortality (see also Figs. 2 and 3). Unfortunately, a significance of the first-order parameter would be necessary to understand the direction of the curve representing the multiplier rate (Fig. 1).

The most interesting results concern the other variables involved. The Chinese dummy is negative and significant in all of the models, indicating that the Chinese firms have less probability of failure compared with the Italian firms, as expected.

---

[6]As data on employment per firm are not available, we used the legal forms for small and large firms as proxies, respectively, individual firms/partnerships and capital-based firms.

Table 1 Model variables by hypothesis (authors' elaboration)

Theoretical concept	Variables	Hypothesis (If positive higher probability of failure)
Organizational ecology hypothesis *First order of density*	Density Chinese firms	Negative
Organizational ecology hypothesis *Second order of density*	Density Chinese firms	Positive
Liability of smallness	Failures of Chinese Small (individual/partnerships) firms	Positive
Liability of newness	Failures Chinese firms below 5 years of age	Positive
Proxy for the liability of outsidership	Chinese dummy	Positive => liability of outsidership greater effect than insidership in GVC Negative => liability of outsidership greater effect than insidership in GVC
Control variables	Exports of textile in the EU	
	Exports of clothing in the EU	
	Employment textile	
	Employment cloth	

GVC Global value chain

Model 2 introduces the liabilities of smallness and newness for the Chinese firms, measured for those firms less than 5 years old. The smallness parameter is positive and significant in all of the models, highlighting that small firms have a higher probability of failure compared with other firms. The newness parameter is not significant in any model.

Model 3 introduces the evolution in textile and clothing, while model 4 estimates the evolution in exports for the period. The textile export parameter is positive in these models, meaning that there is a positive correlation between the evolution of textiles and the probability of failure. Prato's textile exports are declining (Fig. 3), thereby influencing the probability of failure of Chinese firms.

Model 4 includes the evolution of employment in textile and clothing; however, the parameters are not significant.

Model 5 represents a full model including all of the variables and showing a higher likelihood ratio. The liability of smallness, the second-order effect of density, and the liability of outsidership parameter (Chinese dummy) have the most robust results. Particularly, the liability of outsidership is the most important parameter influencing firm mortality.

Table 2 Poisson regression model estimation of failures for Chinese and Italian firms (authors' elaborations of data from CCIAA Prato)

	Model 1	Model 2	Model 3	Model 4	Model 5
Intercept	-8.236^{***}	5.889^{***}	-8.641	2.403	0.330
	(1.0329)	(0.7479)	(5.6503)	(10.9689)	(1.5146)
Density_CH	0.366	0.007			-0.75
	(0.3023)	(0.936)			(0.788)
Density_CH^2	0.660^{***}	0.011			0.088
	(0.1783)	(0.854)			(0.564)
Failures_CH_Smallness		0.904^{*}	1.142^{**}	1.244^{***}	0.939^{***}
		(0.4310)	(0.3848)	(0.3804)	(0.471)
Failures_CH_5y_Newness		0.090	-0.149	-0.259	
		(0.4339)	(0.708)	(0.3934)	
Exports textile in EU			1.032^{*}	0.356	0.482^{***}
			(0.3795)	(0.2454)	(0.1251)
Exports clothing in EU			0.493^{*}	0.008	
			(0.2129)	(0.1007)	
Employment textile				-0.127	-0.099
				(0.9662)	(0.1281)
Employment clothing				0.004	
				(0.3992)	
Chinese dummy	-3.461^{***}	-5.974^{***}	-6.106^{***}	-6.091^{***}	-5.325^{***}
	(0.423)	(0.5356)	(0.0929)	(0.0903)	(0.5062)
Degree of Freedom	3	5	5	7	6
Likelihood ratio chi-square	102.057^{***}	209.922^{***}	217.319^{***}	220.220^{***}	224.992^{***}

Standard error in brackets. Period variable omitted 2000–2011
CH Chinese
$^*p < 0.0001$; $^{**}p < 0.001$; $^{***}p < 0.01$

7 Conclusions

This chapter investigates the failure of Chinese and Italian firms in Prato's industrial district. Our aim was to investigate the evolution over time of two populations of firms operating in the same territory in a condition of debated separation/integration. We combine research concepts from international business and from organizational ecology in a quantitative study. The international business concepts include the liabilities of outsidership and insidership, while the organizational ecology concepts include the liabilities of smallness and newness. We combine the different liabilities to investigate their impact on the vital flows of firm populations in an industrial district in transformation.

We broadly consider the 20-year evolution of Chinese and Italian firms in Prato's industrial district. We focus on analyzing the failure rate for Chinese businesses, an aspect that few study. Our study objectively assesses the mortality of

Chinese firms in Prato's industrial district. We find that this population is dynamic in terms of foundings and failures, revealing high founding rates and high failure rates for the Chinese firms. The rates are high even when compared with other Tuscan (Italian and foreign) firms during a period of financial crisis.

The analysis covers a 20-year period. Prato's Chinese firms experienced a high mortality rate from the outset of their settlement; hence, the present economic downturn only seems to accentuate a phenomenon that was already underway. The reasons for this high mortality level are beyond the scope of this chapter. However, we note that the Chinese firms seemingly experienced outsidership liabilities when they first entered Prato's industrial district, regarding the relevant local networks. Subsequently, from 2008 onwards, Prato's Chinese firms suffered from the effects of the economic and financial crisis.

Contrastingly, the Italian firms have a stronger mortality and lower founding rates than the Chinese firms. This is a probable indication of how, in general, the current economic crisis challenges them both.

The ecological models are applicable to our case study, although not all of the density parameters are significant. The most interesting results emerge from analyzing the various liabilities. First, the liability of smallness is one of the most important determinants of failure, meaning that the smaller firms are more likely to fail in Prato's industrial district. This outcome is relevant for the Chinese firms in the district, as they are mainly SMEs (individual firms). We confirm that the larger firms are more able to survive across time than the smaller firms. The liability of newness is not significant in our study. This signals that the older Chinese firms in Prato's industrial distract do not compete better than the younger firms.

Finally, the liability of outsidership is the most important determinant in the analysis. This seems to evidence that for businesses (Chinese in this instance) to survive it is more significant to have a strong position in the strategic global value chain networks than in the district's local networks. This is particularly true for Prato as a mature industrial district in transformation. This result supports the earlier contributions that underline the role of globalization in supporting the competiveness of firms in industrial districts.

References

Baldassar L, Johanson G, McAuliffe N, Bressan M (eds) (2016) Chinese migration to Europe: Prato, Italy, and beyond. Palgrave Macmillan, London

Baum J, Singh J (1994) Evolutionary dynamic of organizations. Oxford University Press, New York

Baum JA, Mezias SJ (1992) Localised competition and the dynamics of Manhattan hotel industry. Adm Sci Q 37(4):580–604

Becattini G (1990) The Marshallian industrial district as a socio-economic notion. In: Pyke F, Becattini G, Sengenberger W (eds) Industrial districts and inter-firm co-operation in Italy. International Institute for Labour Studies, Geneva, pp 37–51

Becattini G, Bellandi M, De Propris L (2009) Handbook of industrial districts. Edward Elgar, Cheltenham

Belussi F, Sammarra A (2010) Business networks in clusters and industrial districts. The governance of the global value chain. Routledge, Abingdon

Bogaert S, Boone C, Negro G, Witteloostuijn A (2014) Organizational form emergence: a meta-analysis of the ecological theory of legitimation. J Manag. doi:10.1177/0149206314527129 (first published on March 25, 2014)

Bruderl J, Schussler R (1990) Organizational mortality: the liabilities of newness and adolescence. Adm Sci Q 35(3):530–547

Carroll GR, Hannan MT (2000) The demography of corporations and industries. Princeton University Press, Princeton

Ceccagno A (2009) Chinese migrants as apparel manufacturers in an era of perishable global fashion: new fashion scenarios in Prato. In: Johanson G, Smyth R, French R (eds) Living outside the walls: the Chinese in Prato. Cambridge Scholars Publishing, Cambridge, pp 42–74

Ceccagno A (2012) The hidden crisis: the Prato industrial district and the once thriving Chinese garment industry. Revue européenne des migrations internationales 28(4):43–65

Ceccagno A (ed) (2003) Migranti a Prato: Il distretto tessile multietnico. Franco Angeli, Milano

Chiarvesio M, Di Maria E, Micelli S (2010) Global value chains and open networks: the case of Italian industrial districts. Eur Plan Stud 18(3):333–350

Colombi M, Guercini S, Marsden A (2002) L'imprenditoria cinese nel distretto industriale di Prato. Olschki, Firenze

Delacroix J, Carroll GR (1983) Organizational foundings: an ecological study of the newspaper industries of Argentina and Ireland. Adm Sci Q 28(2):274–291

De Noni I, Ganzaroli A, Orsi L, Pilotti L (2013) Immigrant entrepreneurship in the Milan metropolitan area: results from an empirical analysis. Int J Econ Policy Emerg Econ 6(2): 168–188

De Propris L, Lazzeretti L (2009) Measuring the decline of a Marshallian industrial district: the Birmingham jewellery quarter. Reg Stud 43(9):1135–1154

Dei Ottati G (2009) Italian industrial districts and the dual Chinese challenge. In: Johanson G, Smyth R, French R (eds) Living outside the walls: the Chinese in Prato. Cambridge Scholars Publishing, Cambridge, pp 26–41

Dei Ottati G (2013) Il ruolo dell'immigrazione cinese a prato: una rassegna della letteratura. In: IRPET (ed) Il ruolo economico della comunità cinese. IRPET, Florence, pp 21–38

Dei Ottati G (2014) A transnational fast fashion industrial district: an analysis of the Chinese businesses in Prato. Camb J Econ 38(5):1247–1274

Dobrev SD, Ozdemir SZ, Teo AC (2006) The ecological interdependence of emergent and established organizational populations. Organ Sci 17(5):577–597

Gereffi G, Memedovic O (2003) The global apparel value chain: what prospects for upgrading by developing countries. UNIDO, Vienna

Guercini S (2001) Relation between branding and growth of the firm in new quick fashion formulas: analysis of an Italian case. J Fashion Mark Manag 5(1):69–79

Hannan MT, Carroll GR (1992) Dynamics of organizational populations: density, legitimation and competition. Oxford University Press, New York

Hannan MT, Freeman J (1989) Organizational ecology. Harvard University Press, Cambridge

Hannan MT, Polos L, Carroll GR (2007) Logics of organization theory: audiences, code, and ecologies. Princeton University Press, Princeton

Henderson AD (1999) Firm strategy and age dependence: a contingent view of the liabilities of newness, adolescence, and obsolescence. Adm Sci Q 44(2):281–314

Hilmersson M, Jansson H (2012) International network extension processes to institutionally different markets: entry nodes and processes of exporting SMEs. Int Bus Rev 21(4):682–693

IRPET (2013) Prato: il ruolo economico della comunità cinese. IRPET, Florence

ISTAT (1991) Census of Industry and Trade, Rome

ISTAT (1996) Census of Industry and Trade, Rome

ISTAT (2001) Census of Industry and Trade, Rome

ISTAT (2011) Census of Industry and Trade, Rome

Johanson G, Smyth R, French R (eds) (2009) Living outside the walls: the Chinese in Prato. Cambridge Scholars Publishing, Cambridge

Johanson J, Vahlne JE (2009) The Uppsala internationalization process model revisited: from liability of foreignness to liability of outsidership. J Int Bus Stud 40(9):1411–1431

Lazzeretti L (2006) Density dependent dynamics in Arezzo jewellery district (1947–2001): focus on foundings. Eur Plan Stud 14(4):431–458

Lazzeretti L, Capone F (2016) The transformation of the Prato industrial district: an organisational ecology analysis of the co-evolution of Italian and Chinese firms. Ann Reg Sci. doi:10.1007/s00168-016-0790-5

Lazzeretti L, Capone F (2017) Ethnic entrepreneurship in the industrial district of Prato Foundings and failures of Italian and Chinese firms. In: Hervas-Oliser JL, Belussi F (eds) Unfolding cluster evolution. Routledge, Abingdon, pp 86–105

Lazzeretti L, Storai D (2003) An ecology based interpretation of district "complexification": the Prato district evolution from 1946 to 1993. In: Belussi F, Gottardi G, Rullani E (eds) The Net-Evolution of Local Systems Knowledge creation, collective learning and variety of institutional arrangements. Kluwer, Dordrecht, pp 409–434

Lombardi S, Sforzi F (2016) Chinese manufacturing entrepreneurship capital: evidence from Italian industrial districts. European Planning Studies, 1–15

Maggioni MA (2005) The dynamics of high-tech clusters: competition, predation, synergies. In: Curzio AQ, Fortis M (eds) Research and technological innovation. Physica-Verlag, Heidelberg, pp 109–127

Mezias JM (2002) Identifying liabilities of foreignness and strategies to minimize their effects: the case of labor lawsuit judgments in the United States. Strateg Manag J 23(3):229–244

Muzychenko O, Liesch PW (2015) International opportunity identification in the internationalisation of the firm. J World Bus 50(4):704–717

Pieraccini S (2008) L'assedio Cinese: il distretto parallelo del pronto moda di Prato. Il Sole 24 Ore, Milano

Randelli F, Ricchiuti G (2015) The Survival of Tuscan Firms, Working Paper 02/2015, Dipartimento di Scienza per l'Economia e l'Impresa, UNIFI

Santini C, Rabino S, Zanni L (2011) Chinese immigrants socio-economic enclave in an Italian industrial district: the case of Prato. World Rev Entrepreneurship Manag Sustain Dev 7(1):30–51

Schweizer R (2013) SMEs and networks: overcoming the liability of outsidership. J Int Entrepreneurship 11(1):80–103

Singh J, Lumsden C (1990) Theory and research in organizational ecology. Ann Rev Sociol 16:161–195

Staber S (2001) Spatial proximity and firm survival in a declining industrial district: the case of knitwear firms in Baden-Wuttemberg. Reg Stud 35(4):329–341

Stinchcombe AL (1965) Social structure and organization. In: March JG (ed) Handbook of organizations. Rand Mc Nally, Chicago

Van Wissen L (2004) A spatial interpretation of the density dependence model in industrial demography. Small Bus Econ 22(3–4):253–264

Wenting R, Frenken K (2011) Firm entry and institutional lock-in: an organizational ecology analysis of the global fashion design industry. Ind Corp Change 20(4):1031–1048

Zaheer S, Mosakowski E (1997) The dynamics of the liability of foreignness: a global study of survival in financial services. Strateg Manag J 18(6):439–463

Zaheer S (1995) Overcoming the liability of foreignness. Acad Manag J 38(2):341–363

The Mechanism of Sustained Immigrant Entrepreneurship: Wenzhounese Immigrants in Italy

Yili Zhang and Min Zhang

Abstract This chapter focuses on the core mechanism of overseas immigrants' sustained entrepreneurship. It also analyzes how the immigrant entrepreneurs fit within the Italian culture to thereby improve their ambidextrous innovation ability and innovation performance. This chapter presents four case studies on immigrant entrepreneurs, and explores the embedding strategies in different developmental stages of entrepreneurship. The Wenzhounese immigrants who establish firms are able to develop a dynamic relationship with the Italian culture, overcoming liabilities of foreignness and liabilities of outsidership. The embedded culture plays different roles in motivating innovation at different stages of entrepreneurship. The connections between the immigrants' cluster network and their embedded culture in the regional economy evolves as the stages of entrepreneurship change. This study reveals a number of key findings that are explainable through social network theory and innovation theory. The findings offer critical insights into the study of the sustained entrepreneurship of migrants in their host countries.

Keywords Chinese immigrants · Sustained entrepreneurship · Wenzhou · Cultural embeddedness · Ambidextrous innovation

1 Introduction

As the global economy evolves, migration increases, including the accelerated spread of Chinese immigrants to different regions. The Chinese immigrants combine their social capital with the local innovation factors to create significant wealth for individuals, families, cluster networks, and even local economies.

Almost 600,000 immigrants from Wenzhou live in over 130 countries and regions around the globe. These Wenzhounese migrants are a group of *familiar strangers*, where *familiar* means that their characters and their way of working are

Y. Zhang (✉) · M. Zhang
Research Center of Wenzhounese Economy, Wenzhou University, Wenzhou, China
e-mail: yili66@163.com

© Springer International Publishing Switzerland 2017   169
S. Guercini et al. (eds.), *Native and Immigrant Entrepreneurship*,
DOI 10.1007/978-3-319-44111-5_10

well known to the group's members. A shared language and shared values mean that they effectively aggregate capital so that it increases in value. The individuals fully trust each other, facilitating the quick and cheap transfer of critical information between the network nodes. *Strangers* mean that the individuals are unfamiliar with the regional economy in which they live, the culture, and other information outside the group. The migrants generally only contact the community outside their group through economic transactions, and they tend to lack social and cultural exchanges. The barriers to accessing information make it difficult for the Wenzhounese migrants to integrate into the local society. The uncertain external environment means that the migrant start-up companies need continuous stimulation from the potential entrepreneurs.

Sustained immigrant entrepreneurship entails the integration of entrepreneurs, families, businesses, products, industry, and other elements; hence, sustainable business itself is an important part of the entrepreneurial process (Hoy and Sharma 2010). There is a recent interest in ambidextrous innovation (Lakemond and Detterfelt 2013). To sustain migrant entrepreneurship, it is critical to develop a specific environment that matches the embedded strategy, thereby promoting ambidextrous innovation. In the context of migration, ambidextrous innovation is the ability to use resources to develop both exploratory and exploitative innovation, although different skills and capabilities are required for each (Smith and Tushman 2005).

Despite the growing scope of research on embeddedness, there is a lack of collaborative study on the different dimensions of embeddedness. Research on the association between the embeddedness of cluster networks constructed by immigrants and ambidextrous innovation is particularly lacking. The existing research does not interpret the path to a viable ongoing business by immigrants. This chapter focuses on the network development of Wenzhounese immigrants in Italy, starting with industrial life cycle theory, embedded network theory, and ambidextrous innovation theory. The chapter then explores the impact of different forms of embeddedness on ambidextrous innovation at various stages of entrepreneurship.

2 Theoretical Framework

This section outlines the concepts included in our study.

2.1 Immigrant Entrepreneurship and Cluster Networks

Globalization results in increasingly frequent cross-border migration. To avoid employment barriers, many immigrants decide to start their own business rather than looking for jobs in the labor market. The disadvantages in the labor market and the unique resources of immigrant groups are the main factors driving immigrant entrepreneurship. For the migrants, establishing, maintaining, and developing social relationships within their ethnic groups is more important than accepting formal education and integrating into the mainstream society of their host country (Wang 2012). Although the internal migrant networks can gather the resources needed to start a business, they cannot provide the power required for continuous growth (Chaganti and Greene 2002).

Resources within migrant groups can promote both immigrant entrepreneurship and the formation of the industrial chain, and can eventually generate clusters. In the formation and development stages of cluster networks, the interdependence of the organizations with the cluster accelerates resource gathering and promotes the sharing of knowledge and the continuous accumulation of technology. When the cluster reaches a mature stage, such roots can cause stagnation, and innovation inertia becomes a barrier to the transformation and upgrading of industrial clusters. Some scholars believe that it is more conducive to a native cluster network's structural adjustment, optimization, and upgrading if it diverges from its original roots as soon as it enters a mature stage.

2.2 Embeddedness and Ambidextrous Innovation

Many recent innovation studies focus on ambidextrous innovation. Most studies consider that exploration and exploitation are distinct concepts: both fight for the organization's scarce resources, but the organization cannot supply both (Lavie et al. 2010). Emerging views claim that cross-border ambidextrousness and time-sequence planning can effectively resolve resource conflicts (Russo and Vurro 2010). Current research explores how to balance the relationship between exploratory and exploitative innovation and the implementation mechanism inherent in ambidextrous innovation.

When cluster networks evolve to a higher level, the connections among organizations not only generate advantages of growth and innovation but also lead to disadvantages of inertia and stagnation. Wenzhounese immigrants in Italy use guanxi (ethnic Chinese immigrant networks) as their basis for interactions. Guanxi determine that the cluster network is based on a closed network, and guanxi define the closeness of ties, the content of relationships, and the relationship quality between members. Thus, we use relationship embeddedness as a main dimension to measure social capital. Research on embedded relationships is generally interorganizational or intercluster. Granovetter believes that embeddedness in the network can measure the degree to which individuals attend to the needs and goals of others, the levels of trust, and the degree of information sharing (Granovetter 1985). Some researchers believe that weak ties promote innovation. However, others believe that such promotion is established only within a certain range. A U-shaped relationship exists between information sharing and increased individual performance. Although some studies take into account the density of the network structure, they fail to arrange the organizations within a cluster and do not consider the embeddedness of the network environment in their analytical framework. This deficiency may be the cause of the inconsistent findings.

2.3 Cultural Embeddedness and Ambidextrous Innovation

Economic behaviors can be embedded in social networks and the institution as well as in the cultural environment (Granovetter 1985). Culture and political forces have an unavoidable impact on individual behavior and on network characteristics. Thus, research has gradually incorporated cognitive embeddedness, cultural embeddedness, and institutional embeddedness into the analytical framework of embeddedness theory.

Cultural embeddedness relates to the impact of shared beliefs and values on the participants' behavior (James 2003). Cultural embeddedness thus affects the network resources and their use levels through the network behavior of the clustered firms. This results in different innovation levels and the cultural embeddedness directly determines the cluster network's course of evolution.

Innovation is a social and regional interactive process. Tacit knowledge manifests in the form of the technology and skills generated by the firms embedded in the local culture. Various contents and dimensions of cultural embeddedness encourage or restrict different types of innovative behaviors (Boschma 2005). On the one hand, the proximity of the networks helps the firms in the cluster networks to establish partnerships with other firms. While establishing trust and peripheral businesses, they can jointly access key informational resources to solve problems. On the other hand, spatial and cultural proximity have a complementary relationship that is conducive to the formation of a dense network of resources. Social and cultural proximity help to build trust between firms, to reduce opportunistic behavior, and to increase sensitivity to external information (James 2003). A constantly improving and ordered competitive market, sufficient market governance, and social and cultural networks conducive to entrepreneurship are the external conditions for entrepreneurship and for sustaining growth.

Cooperative mentality refers to the sense of active cooperation with local businesses that the participants use to maintain business contacts. Special trust implies a feeling of trust-based identity, but also a feeling of trust for the locals as reflected in the tendency to strengthen cooperation and exchanges with local businesses and employees. Concepts such as interaction frequency, emotional intensity, degree of closeness, and mutual exchange come from Granovetter's (1985) classic study. Exploratory innovation includes search, change, risk taking, and other behaviors. Exploitative innovation includes optimization, efficiency, selection, implementation, and similar behaviors.

We categorize product design, business model innovation, and new market development as the integration and recycling of resources (Boschma 2005).

Finally, by further exploring the relationship and logical order between different concepts, we highlight the main concepts of cultural embeddedness, relational embeddedness, exploitative innovation, and exploratory innovation. Cultural embeddedness includes special trust, cooperative awareness, and degree of openness. Relational embeddedness includes interaction frequency, emotional intensity, degree of closeness, and reciprocity. Exploitative innovation includes learning explicit knowledge, continuous quality improvement, and continuous management improvement. Exploratory innovation includes product design, business model innovation, and the development of new markets.

3 Methods

This chapter develops a framework that addresses cultural embeddedness, relational embeddedness, and ambidextrous innovation. Figure 1 presents our study design, in which we suggest that cultural embeddedness and relational embeddedness influence ambidextrous innovation. We explore the mechanism behind the influence that cultural and relational embeddedness have during the start-up and sustaining phases of immigrant businesses on the firms' ambidextrous innovation behaviors. We also examine the interactive patterns and the cooperative paths that arise when individuals within the social network maintain their internal social capital while seeking outside social capital.

We use a case study method for several reasons. This study focuses on how the immigrant firms embedded in cluster networks can overcome a liability of foreignness with the regional Italian culture at different stages of development. We aim to understand how to improve the achievability of immigrant entrepreneurship and how to resolve the liability of foreignness during the development of immigrant cluster networks. In drawing common conclusions from a repeated induction process, this study applies replication logic to cross-validate the propositions obtained from the different cases to obtain more-robust and more-pervasive theories (Eisenhardt and Graebner 2007).

3.1 Case Selection

We used certain criteria to select the companies for the study. First, to retain a relatively consistent external environment, the selected cases were all companies

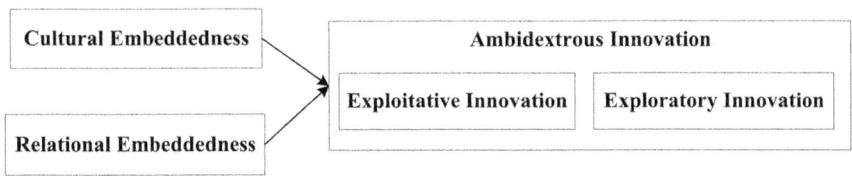

Fig. 1 Study design

established by Wenzhounese migrants in Italy that were trading for over 10 years. All of the selected cases passed through the start-up and immigrant entrepreneurship stages, tried different industries or different cities, and pursued immigrant entrepreneurship by promoting their business, resulting in better performance and development prospects in the industry in which they were currently working. Second, in their business development process, the selected companies made use of the relational resources within their network to varying degrees, and established relationships with stakeholders in Italy. Third, the selected entrepreneurs possessed certain abilities to innovate but differed in their degrees of integration with, and embedding of innovative resources in, the network. Our comparative analysis could help to reveal the internal mechanisms leading to differences in ambidextrous innovation, which would strengthen the generalizability of the research findings (Eisenhardt and Graebner 2007). Fourth, the selected entrepreneurs could provide the level of information necessary for a case study analysis, and they were willing to be part of this research. In compliance with the above criteria, this study chose four entrepreneurs, represented by the names H, ZR, X and ZY. The entrepreneurs were involved in four different industries—furniture, clothing, footwear, and designer bags, respectively.

3.2 Data Collection

The data collection methods in this study included in-depth interviews, archival records, and onsite verification. We used a range of data sources to achieve mutually complementary and to cross-validate the data (Yin 2008) to improve the validity of the cases. The chapter's authors made two trips to the University of Florence in Italy for short-term academic exchanges in 2011 and 2013. Subsequently, as visiting scholars at the University of Florence (March 2014–July 2014), we conducted in-depth research on Wenzhounese immigrant entrepreneurs in Italy. We made contact with some firms established by Wenzhounese migrants. We established the contacts through snowballing, including contacts made through the head of a chamber of commerce, through supply chain members, and through related businesses.

We primarily used face-to-face interviews. Additionally, we gathered data from Wenzhou's overseas chamber of commerce, from Chinese business newspapers, and from online media. In addition to formal interviews, this study used informal conversations to extract in-depth information and insights. This included participating in meetings held by the chamber of commerce in Italy and visiting Chinatown in Florence. We collected background information from policy documents and from academic literature to augment the data and to verify the authenticity of the respondents' answers. Finally, we gathered theoretical information using multiple sources of evidence for triangulated verification.

4 Case Discussions

This section presents the four case studies. We form basic propositions based on an independent analysis of each case. We state the relevant theories and introduce a series of propositions. We analyze whether the propositions are in line with the case studies examined to ensure the reliability of the study.

4.1 Case H: Furniture Entrepreneur

We interviewed H on 19 April 2014, in Prato, Italy. In 2001, H arrived in Italy with the help of his cousin. Over the next 2 years, H brought his younger brother and sister to Italy:

> My younger brother and my brother-in-law used to make sofas in China as well. When they first came, they did not understand the language. I understand Italian, so we cooperated. I dealt with the market, specifically dealing with the Italians. Later, my younger brother and his wife also came here. They did not make sofas at home and came here to study.

Learning from each other helped H and his relatives to master the explicit operational knowledge needed for their business and to overcome the new entrant disadvantage.

> After we all got here, the siblings separately engaged in making timber frames, cushions, sofa covers, and sofas, but in cooperation with each other.

The family members worked closely in the business and formed a clear vertical division of labor, reducing the communication and opportunity costs in the business chain and improving operational efficiency. In 2006, H and his sister cofounded a sofa factory. The embedded relationship between the family members promoted the rapid sharing of industry expertise and market information, helping H gain a comprehensive grasp of the product manufacturing technology. Expanding his expertise helped H become not just someone who knew the language but a business owner as well. He not only mastered the complete sofa production process, he was also able to control costs and to open up new marketing channels.

Strong links between family members provide emotional support and help to obtain social influence and tacit knowledge. Long-term, high-frequency communication among family members means that a family can constantly improve the quality and management in their business, while also meeting the needs of existing markets or domains (Benner and Tushman 2003). Through incremental innovations, H expanded the existing products and increased the efficiency of the existing distribution channels.

Based on the above chain of evidence, we propose:

In the start-up phase, strong individual ties in the cluster network can effectively promote exploitative innovation.

After H opened the sofa factory in 2006, the economic environment and the labor supply changed.

> Before 2007, we made couches in batches. Now each set of models only needs two copies, and the demand for an entire batch is small. Making sofas is tiresome, and it does not bring in a lot of money. Some workers moved to other jobs. Then, the inspections became stricter for immigrant firms, regarding workers, taxes, and managing product varieties. If the layout of the factory, its hygiene, or its equipment does not meet the requirements, then it will be closed.

The changing competitive environment prompted H to use his language advantage to form a stable relationship of mutual trust with the police, the landlords, and the contracted factories.

> We are very familiar with the police. The police sometimes give us a heads-up before they come, to allow us to be careful... The landlord trusts me. The rent is only €800 per month... In the past when business was good, you said how much materials were needed and the Italians gave you that quantity. Now they all know the cost. Now it only works if it is a cost-effective price.

Establishing trust between the related special interest groups helped H to focus on improving the management process through strict cost controls, and on controlling the raw materials to improve the quality and to reduce costs.

> Workers are paid by the piece. Sewing and carpentry [workers] are needed to produce a sofa. We are very clear about that so we can control the time and costs. Raw materials are under our own management.

H also focused on responding to diverse customer needs. H cooperated closely with the relevant local authorities and with individuals in Prato and made full use of his language and communication advantages. In this way, H improved the management efficiency in the sofa factory and responded effectively to the multibrand, small-batch production mode demanded by his customers. Further, the company's development innovation ability greatly improved. The factory also received offers from Prato's two largest sofa factories to provide manufacturing services.

However, with the gradual increase in production scale and during the course of business, disagreements arose in the family.

> We hired more people, recruited more people, then the job was no longer interesting. In 2010, our partnership fell apart. Each person now operates their own business exclusively and earns their own money.

H was unwilling to comment on the current relationship between his brothers and sisters because of the Wenzhounese inherent values regarding family and saving face.

Strong ties bringing resources also increase the entrepreneur's commitment to the members of the network. The network may be too steady and may thus limit innovative decisions. Overconfidence may inhibit entrepreneurial enthusiasm, or commitment to developing into a certain stage could be a barrier to sustained innovation.

Based on the above evidence, we propose:

When entering the sustaining phase and with changes in the competitive environment, the cultural embeddedness of entrepreneurs in a native cluster network can effectively promote the development of innovation, and excessive relational embeddedness may inhibit innovative decisions.

4.2 Case ZR: Clothing Entrepreneur

We interviewed ZR on 19 April 2014, in Prato. ZR arrived in Italy in 1986, and worked in various jobs including in catering and in the bag industry. He acquired basic Italian when he worked as a waiter. In subsequent years, he brought his mother and siblings to Italy. In 1993, influenced by his brother-in-law, he came to Prato and went into the clothing business by opening a factory. ZR said, "*I was scared. I had never seen the clothes, and I could only constantly ask and constantly learn.*" Fortunately, many of ZR's classmates and relatives were already in Prato. Coupled with ZR's own efforts to learn, his garment factory quickly became successful. Recalling his original intention to migrate, ZR stated:

> My family had [financial] difficulties; then I wanted to go abroad to change the living conditions for my family. When I first came, I was really frustrated. But no matter how hard it was, I was very happy.

A strong sense of responsibility and commitment to his family became ZR's motivation to learn continuously and to create value constantly for 20 years. His reputation among his peers helped ZR to acquire critical information in many industries. ZR said that he "*started everything from a mere factory worker*" who learned to use the machines himself. With his dedication and talent, ZR soon learned the relevant clothing techniques and industry terminology, and rapidly became able to work independently.

> I love to learn more than others, always willing to learn. When I worked in Milan, I learned all the basic terminology from different restaurants; later, I learned the terminology in clothing also. To settle down here, I needed at least to speak some simple Italian. I used the restaurant experience to communicate with native Italians and to learn from them... Native Italians like to work with us. Standardized decoration, good management practices: only by keeping up with these will the native Italians trust us.

His language advantage helped ZR to build trust with the Italian customers. The continuous improvement of daily management helped his factory to expand rapidly. ZR gained recognition outside of his network community because he continually expanded his industry knowledge. His strong sense of responsibility stemmed from strong ties outside of the network that promoted rapid trust building.

Based on the above chain of evidence, we propose:

In the start-up phase, strong ties within the cluster network can effectively promote the development of innovation. Cultural embeddedness in the local region can help individuals quickly access critical information outside the cluster network and gain benefits.

Changes in the environment lead to significant changes in cooperative behavior and innovation efficiency, encouraging actors to explore new patterns of norms. With ZR's growing clothing business, a number of changes occurred in the relational embeddedness in the cluster network. On the one hand, ZR's emotional attachment to his family members increased: "*I cherish my family, my children, my brother, and my brother's children; they are my life.*" On the other hand, ZR increasingly alienated external members:

> Now I really do not want to think about anything else. I just want to do my own things every day. My hobby is hiking whenever I get a chance, or planting flowers. I like the simple life. My brother says that my character is good, only that I am too low-key. More than ten years ago, the former chamber of commerce invited me to join many times, and I refused. I just follow my own principles for management.

ZR expressed worry about the current changes facing the market:

> In Prato, recruitment is more difficult. In a few more years, we will just have to shut down the company because the numbers of factories and workers are decreasing.

ZR increasingly sought external support from a network of Italian partners in whom he had full confidence, and with whom he had in-depth, open communication. These relationships helped ZR to integrate fully into the local regional clusters and culture. ZR also established a good working relationship with his Italian suppliers:

> Although all of the fabrics are made in China, we still purchase them from foreign suppliers. We do not ask the native Italian suppliers where they purchased them [the fabrics] from. Chinese people really have cheaper clothes, but the quality is also worse.

ZR appreciated the work attitude of his Italian employees:

> I hired four native Italians, an accountant, a designer, a graphic modeler, and a receptionist for clients. The designer and modeler were chosen from Italian professionally trained people. Native Italians view the job as dearer than their life; Chinese people do not. If I have to start another business, I will hire only native Italians. Native Italians take work more seriously. The Italian accountant handles all of the cash; every day I just look at the cash inflow and outflow reports. I also look for him when I need to spend money. Sometimes when the clothing prototype is finished, I just discuss the special profits with the designer.

With the professional help from Italian people, ZR's clothing business achieved deeper insights and creativity than it would otherwise have. ZR began designing styles according to customer demands. He also created a unique style for his own brand:

The designer and I first consider the needs of the customers, combined with my own feelings, and the designer quickly draws style drafts. We choose the style according to the customer demands. We quickly design, plate, and cut on the computer and then choose the right fabric sample to make a model. The designer completes a dozen drawings each day on the computer. He also adjusts the design and the models of procurement according to the fabric sample. In this way, the design is a better aesthetic fit with Italian and European customers... Our suppliers, the company decoration, and the clothing style must all comply with the customer's taste, and every piece of clothing has its own cultural heritage. The shirt brand is basically my own design.

ZR also learned lessons from developing market sales channels:

This industry is very complex. When summer has not yet begun, you need to plan immediately for the second half of the year. We are now doing next year's large customer orders; the second half of this year we have to add some individual orders. My clients are all native Italians.

In addition to mastering the industry-specific terminology, ZR used his Italian as a tool to take the initiative during negotiations. ZR relied on social integration with the Italian culture to establish trust with his Italian partners, to reduce opportunistic behaviors, and to enhance sensitivity to external information (James 2003). The symbiotic and equal relationship between partners outside of the network led to ZR acquiring tacit knowledge, forming a unique brand, completing the design of new products, and entering new markets. The integration and reformation of tacit and explicit knowledge ensured the smooth realization of new ideas and of innovation.

Based on the above chain of evidence, we propose:

During the sustained immigrant entrepreneurship phase, with the change of the competitive environment, the entrepreneurs simultaneously reduce the extent of relational embeddedness within the network and increase the degree of cultural embeddedness in the local region. They do this to effectively deal with dynamic changes in the competitive environment and to promote exploratory innovation.

4.3   Case X: Footwear Entrepreneur

We interviewed X on 25 August 2013, in Wenzhou. X moved to Italy in 2004. She had no relatives in Italy, and she made use of her husband's family network after marrying to establish her own business. She engaged in the import and export of footwear and in wholesale footwear. For the entrepreneurial process, X recalled:

The marriage gifts were more than €10,000 in cash, because a lot of my husband's friends are from Li Ao [a town in Wenzhou]. They earn a lot. Most people start their businesses by relying on the cash received at marriage. They quickly marry and then add in their savings and start their business.

The support of X's friends and relatives played a key role in the early days:

> From 2004 to 2009, my husband and I had no residency rights. If I saw the police, I fled every time. The companies we opened were under other people's names. We made an agreement on how much money to pay them, and when there were things we needed, we would let them come.

After Italy's amnesty for illegal immigrants in 2009, X began to conduct her business legitimately. However, X's business contacts within the family were limited to working together to compete against foreign competitors:

> If other people get involved, we will unite as a family through large-scale purchases and by developing a uniform price to crowd them out... We always purchased goods on our own. My husband's sister did not give us guidance. We all purchased [goods] from the same place and there was a competitive relationship; we all sourced our products in Rome. We could not all buy the same goods. It is not good for sisters and brothers. If my sister-in-law bought one brand, we had to get other brands to separate the customers... I have always run my own business separately. There is no partnership with [my husband's] brothers and sisters. My husband and I had some money, and we saw the store was cheap. With a partnership, there will certainly be no profit because [in a partnership] profits are used to purchase goods, and we cannot make money.

X believed that if she continued with the previous business model and collaborated with her family members, then it would be difficult to have independent careers.

> Italian is easy to learn. When I was in France, I using headphones to listen to French during work, and every night I stayed up to recite articles. I studied for one month and could speak the language.

With her language advantage, X established close contact with Italian customers. *"Italian people are very smart. They are very sensitive to fashion."* The communication with her Italian customers helped X to gain a deeper understanding of fashion. X's judgment of family relationships promoted her awareness of the importance of establishing relationships with local customers to expand her business. While enhancing business execution, these relationships also established a wide range of alliances.

Based on the above chain of evidence, we propose:

The financial support received from an individual's social network during the start-up phase plays an important role in the success of entrepreneurship. A language advantage can help individuals overcome information and learning bottlenecks caused by weak ties in the network. Cultural embeddedness can make up for barriers to explicit knowledge transfer during the start-up phase arising from a lack of relational embeddedness.

X believed that people from Wenzhou work faster than Italians, and that Wenzhounese entrepreneurs were more inclined to recruit workers from Wenzhou.

> In 2005 and 2006, I asked friends inside the mall [to work for me], basically I hired people through relationships. It is now difficult to recruit. Sometimes I have to ask the Christian church to help with recruitment.

X also stressed the importance of grasping fashion trends:

> Because Italy is a Mediterranean climate, the summer is long. Making boots basically means losing business. Costs rise year after year.

The changing competitive environment prompted X to instigate a series of reforms in her custom shoe making. Generally, Chinese footwear businesses first buy a shoe sample and then duplicate it. Exchanges between X and her Italian customers helped her understand the potential of considering other fashion elements, and she formed a unique aesthetic taste:

> After getting a sample, I make changes to the color or the material. It is then easy to sell these models. Even if the order is a small quantity, the domestic [Chinese] Guangzhou producers still help me make them.

Her language advantage helped X to reintegrate knowledge and to conduct specific improvements in her business. This contributed to the differentiation of her shoes, avoiding the homogenized competitive products, and led X's trade to maintain a stable growth. The uncertainty of the expected performance brought about by changes in the environment encouraged X to take the initiative and to adjust the content and sharing of cultural embeddedness. In X's case, cultural embeddedness enhanced the openness of the regional network and promoted new ideas and behavior to achieve rapid transformation.

Based on the above chain of evidence, we propose:

During the sustained immigrant entrepreneurship phase, cultural embeddedness in the local area can (and in other cases, cannot) help entrepreneurs quickly grasp changing market demands in a dynamic environment, continue to improve products, and achieve advantageous exploitative innovation.

4.4 Case ZY: Designer Bag Entrepreneur

We interviewed ZY on 18 March 2014, in Florence. In 1988, ZY immigrated to Italy with his brother and his mother. ZY's father had previously migrated there and successfully started a business earlier in the 1980s. This meant that ZY could successfully complete his studies in Italy and that he could master fluent Italian. Starting with general leather processing, ZY developed his business into an original equipment manufacturer (OEM) partner with Chanel, Bulgari, and other international designer brands. To expand the company's business and to increase the acceptance of the local people, the company began cooperating with Italian businesses in 1996:

> We started from a relatively low-end brand OEM, and then the Italians took it up for a while. Later, because of our strength in terms of quality and delivery time, we gradually won the trust of clients and gradually became the secondary agent's source of product.

ZY considered that the Italian people working with his company provided more valuable information than that offered by family members. Such information gave his business the opportunity to work directly with the top Italian brands and become a top luggage agent.

> Once the partnership is established, the Italians start ordering the simplest products in a small quantity and then gradually increase the amount and put forward higher requirements. At the same time, you must use German or Japanese machines like JUKI [expensive machines] because other production machines in the factory need to be upgraded every year, as well as [encountering costs relating to] factory management. In 2007, we were the only factory in Florence directly cooperating with the brands.

To ensure the quality of the delivered products, the designer brands sent representatives directly to ZY's production site for inspection and monitoring. One inspection type related to maintaining the brand's safety. In such inspections, the inspectors went onsite to check whether the site used black market labor. They also checked on the hygiene, health, and mental state of the workers, the cleanliness in the workshop, and for violations of intellectual property rights. Another inspection type checked the quality of the goods and the onsite processes.

> They check the quality of the production process and communicate directly with the Italian managers. They propose quality improvement requirements to ensure brand quality.

By working closely with the Italian brands, ZY continuously improved his product quality. His company regularly upgraded its equipment, so that its production techniques were comparable with other brands' OEMs. ZY wanted his company to reflect the regional characteristics:

> We hired eleven Italian employees who are responsible for quality, financial, and administrative work. They are mostly professionals. We also hired a Chinese woman as a translator who is responsible for informing the workers of technological requirements and quality requirements.

ZY's company continually improved its management processes, meaning that its customers were confident in the quality of its products. This also resulted in consistent business rules and social norms between the company and its partners. This special trust promoted the rapid embeddedness of ZY's company in the local culture. Cultural embeddedness became the internal driving force for enhancing quality and improving management.

Based on the above chain of evidence, we propose:

During the start-up phase, cultural embeddedness promotes continuous improvement in quality and management, enhancing exploratory innovation.

In 2005, ZY gradually began to participate in Italian politics and in social interactions. He subsequently established close ties with the Italian embassy in China and with the local Italian government. Through living in Italy as well as having a personal interest in wine, ZY learned the status of Italian wine in the world of wine aficionados. He identified a gap in the Italian wine market in China:

> China's wine market is slowly rising, especially in high-quality Italian wines... good quality, but compared to French wines, the promotion efforts are not enough.

In 2006, ZY began working as an agent for a midrange Italian wine brand. In early 2009, ZY performed detailed market research on China's overall wine market. He used his existing relationships to establish a top Italian wine brand, and acquired a winery in Italy. He began directly importing his wine to China. In 2010, ZY established a wine company in Shanghai in China. He invited Italian consulate personnel and business contacts to participate in wine tasting and in other promotional activities there. Using the special trust that he established within the Italian political and business world, ZY captured new business opportunities. With his reputation in the top luggage brands and his OEM experience, ZY rapidly implemented his diversification strategy and successfully expanded into the wine market. He became China's largest distributor of high-end Italian wine.

Based on the above chain of evidence, we propose:

During the sustained immigrant entrepreneurship phase, deep cultural embeddedness with the local region can help entrepreneurs implement brand strategy, develop new projects, and promote expansion into new markets; these factors are conducive to exploratory innovation.

4.5 Summary

The four cases capture the various characteristics that migrant entrepreneurship presents during the start-up and sustained-entrepreneurship phases. During the start-up phase, their economic policy was relatively loose, there was an abundant labor force, and there were mass-production demands. When entering the sustained innovation phase, their economic policy became increasingly tight, with an increasingly tight labor supply, and the customer demands were varied and smaller in quantity. Increasing competitiveness and a changing external environment jointly pushed the immigrant firms to move from the start-up phase to the sustained immigrant entrepreneurship phase. The four case studies and the propositions contained within lead to the following propositions.

Proposition 1: During the start-up phase, relational embeddedness is conducive to exploitative innovation, and cultural embeddedness helps to compensate for insufficient information that brings liabilities.
Proposition 2: During the sustained immigrant entrepreneurship phase, relational embeddedness is not conducive to exploitative innovation, and cultural embeddedness contributes to the realization of ambidextrous innovation.

5 Conclusions

5.1 Primary Findings

Our study revealed a number of key findings that are explainable through social network theory and innovation theory. Italy's Wenzhounese immigrants have built networks of entrepreneurs and industrial clusters overseas, and have accumulated valuable experience in ambidextrous innovation. Through the careful division of labor and the full exploitation of social capital, they have reduced the barriers to new entrants during the start-up phase of entrepreneurship. When the migrants succeeded in starting a business, their relational embeddedness intensified the formation of a closed network.

This study focused on the core issue of how immigrant entrepreneurs embedded in cluster networks interact and integrate with the regional Italian culture at different stages of entrepreneurship to improve their entrepreneurship. Using multicase analysis, we confirmed that changes in the external environment have an important impact on the embeddedness of Wenzhounese immigrant businesses. The interactions between immigrant firms and the regional culture can achieve integration, and can (and cannot) also promote ambidextrous innovation. The relational embeddedness of the Wenzhounese immigrant businesses in cluster networks and their cultural embeddedness in the regional economy change as the entrepreneurship phase changes, and produces different forms of coupling.

First, the entrepreneurial process and the innovation behavior of Wenzhounese immigrants are characterized by distinct phases. The phases include the early start-up phase that focuses on exploratory innovation, and the immigrant entrepreneurship phase in which ambidextrous innovation evolves. Different innovation behavior forms different path dependences on different resources. There are also different combinations of resources. In the initial entrepreneurship stage, embeddedness is mainly composed of strong ties. Entrepreneurship achieves low-cost venture copying by using observation and imitation. Strong ties promote exploitative innovation.

Cultural embeddedness in this first stage of development can also play a role in promoting innovation through two possible paths. In one path, cultural embeddedness manifests in language advantages, helping the immigrants to access critical information outside of their network and to obtain benefits. In the other path, language advantages can also help companies to overcome their liabilities of outsidership from the Italian networks. Cultural embeddedness can make up for the outsidership that causes barriers in the transmission of explicit knowledge. Both paths can lead to the coupling of embedding and cooperative relations in culture, promoting exploitative innovation in the early stages and contributing to the evolving cluster network of Wenzhounese immigrants.

When the competitive environment changes, the Wenzhounese-owned migrant companies consciously reduce the degree of relational embeddedness to implement the exploitative innovation better. However, only reducing the degree of relational embeddedness is not conducive to achieving ambidextrous innovation. Hence, cultural embeddedness could help the companies to acquire the integration advantages of exploratory and exploitative innovation. This is essential both for ongoing product upgrades and quality improvement and for the development of new products and markets. Therefore, migrant entrepreneurship needs to maintain relational embeddedness in the local network at an appropriate level. The entrepreneurs should reduce gradually the liabilities of foreignness and outsidership locally produced through the Italian culture and the native networks.

Second, the first- and second-generations of Wenzhounese migrants in Italy differ in their implementation paths of entrepreneurship. Timing also has an impact on the innovative path. Entrepreneurs H and ZR immigrated to Italy many years ago. Their network, based on kinship and geographical proximity, built a platform for sharing resources. The initial entrepreneurial path is very dependent on cooperation among family members and on information exchange between relatives and colleagues. The low-cost imitation business model becomes the most direct and effective developmental path. H had limited experience in starting a business—she had to rely on her husband's family network to enter the footwear business. The family networks helped them to cope with the potential market risks. However, strong ties come with decision-making commitments to family members that curb the innovative behavior of individuals. Therefore, by relying on cultural embeddedness, ZR achieved greater business success and development than H. Using cultural embeddedness, ZR overcame the liabilities of foreignness and outsidership from the natives' networks.

ZY belongs to the second-generation of entrepreneurs, and inherited and developed the family business. Homogeneous and redundant information in a closed network cannot provide new sources of profit. ZY relied on heterogeneous information and on innovative resources outside of the network to capture business opportunities in a timely fashion. He became successful in business by integrating resources and by breaking rigid decision-making processes rooted in values.

Third, this study found that strong ties during the start-up phase could contribute to exploitative innovation, in common with Dei Ottati (2014). The most significant contribution of this chapter is its clear revelation of the mechanism behind the impact of cultural embeddedness on ambidextrous innovation at different stages. Cultural embeddedness in the early stages of migrant entrepreneurship promotes exploratory innovation. However, the role of cultural embeddedness in exploitative innovation needs to be used. Based on immigration networks and on immigration chain theory, the expanding number of immigrants from Wenzhou will face significantly reduced risks and difficulties in starting a business in Italy in the future. Despite the current financial crisis and the high unemployment problems faced by European countries, the number of new businesses established in Italy by migrants increased in recent years. In the period 2008–2014, the number of Chinese firms in Prato increased from 4803 to 5230 (data from Prato's chamber of commerce). Migrants from China's Zhejiang Province, particularly from Wenzhou, mostly ran those firms (Johanson and Smyth 2009). As X observed:

In the past, business was just like our struggle in Shanghai; hardship and luck are what it takes. Now it relies on relationships. Whether the family is strong or not, new companies with no foundation will certainly be eliminated.

Firms in the cluster compete fiercely. New entrants must open up new markets, establish flexible business alliances, and overcome local liabilities to sustain their immigrant entrepreneurship (Guercini 2016).

5.2 Research Limits

The subject would benefit from further research. First, in the face of different environments, different industries, and different intensities of competition, the degree of various embedded relationships differ. One way to enhance the external validity of these case studies is to subdivide the role of the various embedded scenarios.

Second, the network of overseas Wenzhounese immigrants lacks an intermediary service structure that specializes in coordination and organization. Researching the core firm of the network can reveal the core business strategy that affects the entire network's ambidextrous innovation. Finally, case studies help to reveal the evolution of the relationship between the selection of the ambidextrous innovation mode and the embedded paths. Future research can use the simulation method to simulate the evolution of overseas networks and to explore the pattern of innovative cluster networks.

Notably, through their process of immigrant entrepreneurship, some successful pioneers provided a wealth of qualitative research data for this study. However, many others failed in their entrepreneurship; yet, those failed entrepreneurs had difficult experiences and accumulated rational experiences. Stories of failure can provide deep insights into the emotional choices and the rational judgements of immigrant entrepreneurs. Successful experiences are certainly valuable, but experiences of failure are indispensable. Accordingly, follow-up studies should investigate the typical cases of failed entrepreneurship or cases of continuous transformation in the entrepreneurial process. These will provide a vivid and comprehensive picture of the true paths of immigrant entrepreneurship and integration.

References

Benner MJ, Tushman ML (2003) Exploitation, exploration, and process management: the productivity dilemma revisited. Acad Manag Rev 28(2):238–256

Boschma R (2005) Proximity and innovation: a critical assessment. Reg Stud 39(1):61–74

Chaganti R, Greene PG (2002) Who are ethnic entrepreneurs? A study of entrepreneursapos; ethnic involvement and business characteristics. J Small Bus Manage 40(2):126–143

Dei Ottati G (2014) A transnational fast fashion industrial district: an analysis of the Chinese businesses in Prato. Camb J Econ 38(5):1247–1274

Eisenhardt KM, Graebner ME (2007) Theory building from cases: opportunities and challenges. Acad Manag J 50(1):25–32

Granovetter M (1985) Economic action and social structure: the problem of embeddedness. Am J Sociol 91(3):481–510

Guercini S (2016) Local liabilities between immigrant and native entrepreneurship in industrial districts and global value chains. Paper presented at the workshop "evolving industrial districts within global and regional value chains and the role of manufacturing and innovation capabilities". University of Padova, Padova, 7 April

Hoy F, Sharma P (2010) Entrepreneurial family firms. J New Bus Ideas Trends 8(1):66–68

James A (2003) Regional culture, corporate strategy and high tech innovation: Salt Lake City. PhD dissertation, University of Cambridge

Johanson G, Smyth R, Trench R (eds) (2009) Living outside the walls: The Chinese in Prato, Cambridge Scholars Publishing

Lakemond N, Detterfelt J (2013) Counterbalancing exploitative knowledge search during environmental dynamism: reinforcing new ideas for existing products. Creat Innov Manag 22 (4):420–434

Lavie D, Stettner U, Tushman ML (2010) Exploration and exploitation within and across organizations. Acad Manag Ann 4(1):109–155

Russo A, Vurro C (2010) Cross-boundary ambidexterity: balancing exploration and exploitation in the fuel cell industry. Eur Manag Rev 7(1):30–45

Smith WK, Tushman M (2005) Managing strategic contradictions: a top management model for Managing Innovation Streams. Organ Sci 16(5):522–536

Wang QF (2012) Ethnic entrepreneurship studies in geography: a review. Geogr Compass 6 (4):227–240

Yin RK (2008) Case study research: design and methods, 2nd edn. Sage, Thousand Oaks, CA

Understanding Chinese Immigrants in Prato's Industrial District: Benefits to Local Entrepreneurs

Xander Ong and Susan Freeman

Abstract This chapter provides an encompassing description of Chinese living overseas, particularly immigrant Chinese entrepreneurs, the influence of guanxi, and the vast international Chinese networks they leverage to internationalize. Chinese networks can be a double-edged sword, both enabling and constricting their further development in the host markets. Chinese immigrant networks can form enclaves, such as the one in Prato. While these enclaves support new Chinese immigrants socially and economically, they can be inaccessible to the local entrepreneurs. Thus, there is value in proactively encouraging collaborative opportunities between local entrepreneurs and Chinese immigrants. The international Chinese resources and networks could be valuable to the native entrepreneurs in Italy and to others around the world.

Keywords Chinese immigrants · Local policymakers · Native entrepreneurs · Guanxi · Ethnic enclave · Industrial district

1 Introduction

China's overseas business community is a major force in Asia's economic growth and increasingly in the global economy. However, research on the internationalization process and on ethnic Chinese immigrant entrepreneurship overwhelmingly focuses on firms from developed countries. An alternative focus, is the Chinese immigrants in Prato's industrial district. Those individuals are part of a global phenomenon of Chinese immigrants some of whom have become transnational entrepreneurs. China's government is interested in maintaining the vibrancy of and

X. Ong
Department of Management, Monash University, Caulfield Campus, Melbourne, Australia
e-mail: xander.monash@gmail.com

S. Freeman (✉)
School of Commerce, University of South Australia, Adelaide, Australia
e-mail: susan.freeman@unisa.edu.au

© Springer International Publishing Switzerland 2017   189
S. Guercini et al. (eds.), *Native and Immigrant Entrepreneurship*,
DOI 10.1007/978-3-319-44111-5_11

improving the legitimacy of its overseas communities. The socioeconomic links of the overseas Chinese play a vital role in the influence of China as a leading global player. It is important to understand what drives new ventures from emerging economies such as China to internationalize into developed economies. This chapter presents relevant literature on *guanxi* (ethnic Chinese immigrant networks), and on the enclave economy. We hope such information will provide insights for researchers, policymakers, and industry players as they seek to understand deeply the Chinese business community in Prato.

The social network concept is similar to guanxi in the Chinese business community, whereby reciprocity, trust, and interdependencies are highly valued through the effective use of social capital. We use a constructive approach that seeks to highlight the benefits to the local native entrepreneurs of associating with Chinese immigrants by examining background literature on the Chinese and on their overseas Chinese networks. Particularly, the chapter provides new perspectives on social capital between local entrepreneurs and overseas Chinese immigrants. It also suggests how the global phenomenon of Chinese immigrants can assist a local economy, such as Prato.

The Chinese migrants rely on guanxi for their social relationships, meaning that those transnational entrepreneurs operate in a distinctive social structure that differs from a Western social network. It is important to understand clearly their impact from a macro-global perspective. Many researchers regard a Chinese immigrant enclave economy as the outcome of an ethnic economy, bounded by co-ethnicity and location—we show why this is not necessarily a negative for the local native community within an industrial district.

The resources of an enclave economy are usually ethnically exclusive; hence, we propose greater efforts by local policymakers, such as in Prato's industrial district, to promote inter-ethnic interactions. We suggest that more exchanges of resources between ethnic groups (such as Chinese immigrants and their native Pratese counterparts) will drive and encourage the international entrepreneurial links between native firms and Chinese firms, into China. Thus, this chapter suggests why a constructive approach that promotes the benefits to the native Pratese entrepreneurs in associating with the Chinese immigrant entrepreneurs will provide new business opportunities as the differences among Chinese immigrant entrepreneurs and their social networks is clarified.

2   Ethnic Chinese Networks

Ethnic Chinese networks are among the most dynamic in the world and are rapidly growing economically. Ethnic Chinese networks are:

> Built upon ethnic ties… across national boundaries… The powerful networks also explain why… Chinese economies [in South East Asia] performed better than other Asian

economies during the Asian financial crisis… [Ethnic Chinese networks play an] important role in the new millennium and the study of those networks warrants special attention.

Peng (2000, p. 229)

Successful ethnic Chinese businesses thrive in Asia and increasingly in many other parts of the world (Ahlstrom et al. 2010). As an ethnic group, the population of overseas Chinese is larger and culturally more coherent than are the overseas Indians and the other major ethnic diasporas (Peng 2000). Chinese business communities worldwide are perceived as a transnational community with shared tacit knowledge based on mutual trust and a perception of shared culture, common descent, and ethnic affiliation (Dahles 2010).

Much of the success of China and Southeast Asia is attributable to Confucianism (the teachings of Confucius, 551–478 BC) that underlines the determination, thrift, scholarship, and hard work of Confucian societies (Yeung and Tung 1996). One critical Confucian virtue, ren, stresses the morality of treating others the way we want to be treated (Storz 1999). Storz (1999) suggested that the reciprocity highlighted in relationships by Confucius is guided by morality, virtue, humanity, and love. Confucianism's emphasis on the individual's virtue, reciprocity in relationships, and harmony in social structures (Ip 2009) has widely influenced Chinese management, business ethics, and activities (Lin and Ho 2009). Confucian dynamism, which reflects the work ethics prescribed by Confucianism, underpins Chinese societies worldwide (Ji and Dimitratos 2013). Confucian dynamism is:

The acceptance of the legitimacy of hierarchy and the valuing of perseverance and thrift, all without undue emphasis on tradition and social obligations which could impede business initiative.

Franke et al. (1991, p. 167)

Confucian dynamism values social structure and order, long-term orientation, respect for tradition, perseverance, and reciprocity (Hofstede and Bond 1988; Minkov and Hofstede 2012). Ji and Dimitratos (2013) found that Confucian dynamism influences the entry mode choices of Chinese private firms. Decision makers with strong Confucian values, such as a preference for stability, thrift, and long-term orientation, tend to favor non-equity modes of market entry with low risk and low commitment levels.

Despite the overseas Chinese business community being viewed as a major force in Asia's economic growth (Dahles 2010) and increasingly in the global economy (Ahlstrom et al. 2010), research on the internationalization process overwhelmingly focuses on firms from developed countries (Liu et al. 2008). Limited research considers how Chinese firms undertake internationalization (Xie and Amine 2009). Chinese internationalization is becoming increasingly relevant and hence warrants further study (Saad and Koh 2010). Yamakawa et al. (2013) called for further research on what drives the new ventures from emerging economies such as China to internationalize into developed economies.

To explain the context of the chapter, the province of Prato, which is located close to Florence in Italy, has the highest concentration of Chinese immigrants of any Italian province, despite being the smallest province (Johanson et al. 2009). Officially, approximately 12% of Italy's 145,000 Chinese migrants reside in Prato, with the unofficial figure being larger. One estimate suggests that one in five Chinese workers is an undocumented illegal migrant (Nielsen et al. 2012). Prato is an historic center of textile production. In the 1980s, Prato innovated from producing carded wool fabrics of medium quality to producing new fibres and textile materials, such as viscose, silk, and cotton (Dei Ottati 2009a). However, because of international competitive pressure, the number of Pratese textile firms decreased substantially in the period 1991–2005 (Dei Ottati 2009a). In response, some Italian fast fashion firms changed their business model from one relying on the domestic market to one dealing internationally with overseas suppliers and manufacturers (Runfola and Guercini 2013). The international competition led to a reduction in the final product prices. This decreased the subcontractors' prices and resulted in many such businesses becoming unviable (Dei Ottati 2009b).

Negative sentiments toward the Chinese-dominated Pratese fast fashion industry worsened as Prato's textile industry declined (Dei Ottati 2009a). Despite the argument that the Chinese in Prato are *"fundamental to the competitiveness of [the] 'Made in Italy' [brand]"* (Denison et al. 2009, p. 10), this community was seen as a threat by many in the local Italian community and as socially and economically unsustainable (Dei Ottati 2009a). Therefore, there is a need to understand Prato's ethnic Chinese business community clearly.

As ethnic Chinese businesses venture abroad, most rely on their elaborate and complex networks and relationships to gain entry to and access resources in foreign markets (Chen and Chen 1998). Relationships and social networks are critical in the facilitation of business operations in a Chinese-based society (Tsang 1998). The social networks of Chinese immigrants are crucial as they internationalize into China, their country of origin (Chung and Tung 2013). The ethnic Chinese relationships, heavily influenced by their history and culture, give rise to unique concepts such as guanxi (Dunning and Kim 2007; Su and Littlefield 2001; Yunxia and Allee Mengzi 2007).

Other cultures have concepts similar to guanxi because of their emphasis on relationships. Some examples include *wasta* in Arab nations, *jeitinho* in Brazil (Smith et al. 2011), and *blat* in Russia (Michailova and Worm 2003). We first discuss guanxi before examining the internationalization of ethnic Chinese businesses and the potential liabilities of ethnic Chinese networks.

2.1 Guanxi

Guanxi, rooted in thousands of years of Chinese tradition, is *"ubiquitous and plays a crucial role in daily life"* (Tsang 1998, p. 65), and significantly affects business activities (Yen et al. 2011). Chinese managers spend considerable time and resources building their networks, and rely on them for their business operations (Wong 1998; Zhao and Hsu 2007).

Despite China's integration into the global economy and the increased adoption of international business practices by Chinese managers (Nolan 2011), the emphasis on guanxi is still evident in Chinese international business exchanges (Shuang et al. 2012). Faure and Fang (2008) did not consider China's economic progress as catching up with Western business practices. Rather, they considered it a "... *collection of new cultural elements, sedimentation of those elements within the Chinese system, then digestion and finally re-use within the Chinese metabolism*" (p. 206). As the exchanges between the West and the East increase, we need a greater understanding of guanxi (Yen et al. 2011).

Many studies on guanxi attempt to dissect and obtain a deep understanding of the concept; however, "... *how guanxi is related to business and what kind of role guanxi plays in business operations remain largely unknown...*" (Fan 2002, p. 374). Guanxi is multifaceted and complex (Guo and Chang 2010). Usually conceptualized at the individual level, guanxi is also relevant at an organizational level, becoming a valuable organizational resource (Li and Sheng 2011). A "... *plethora of implicit and explicit definitions of guanxi...*" make it difficult to understand and discuss the concept (Chen et al. 2013). For example, Hutchings and Weir (2006) stated that guanxi "... *is a relationship between two people expected, more or less to give as good as they get...*" (p. 143). Seung Ho and Luo described guanxi as an:

> Intricate and pervasive relational network that contains implicit mutual obligations, assurances, and understanding... [that] has been pervasive for centuries in every aspect of Chinese social and organizational activities.
>
> Seung Ho and Luo (2001, p. 455)

Tsui and Farh (1997) suggested that guanxi is "*a certain type of interpersonal relationship, one that is personal and built on a particularistic criteria*" (p. 59). However, So and Walker argued that:

> A one line definition for guanxi is misleading because the very reason the Chinese word guanxi is used in English text, instead of saying 'particularistic ties', is because a simple English translation is insufficient to bring out the special nature of guanxi.
>
> So and Walker (2006, p. 4)

Guo and Chang (2010) suggested that the guanxi concept often becomes unclear in the attempts to define it, because the definitions consider multiple dimensions. Therefore, for the purpose of this chapter, we use the following definition:

> Guanxi is an evolving Chinese version of social networks that creates and transmits social capital via distinct and complex rules of personal interaction; it is the strategic establishing, developing and maintaining of informal relationships bound by culturally unique forms of trust and reciprocal obligation.
>
> Guo and Chang (2010, p. 14)

Reciprocity, trust, and social obligations underpin guanxi primarily (Luo 2007; Tsui and Farh 1997). Table 1 lists the main aspects of guanxi: bases, dimensions, and principles (Luo 2007).

Table 1 Guanxi bases, dimensions, and principles (adapted from Luo 2007)

Bases	Dimensions	Principles
Locality/dialect	Mianzi (face)	Transferable
Kinship	Renqing (unpaid obligations)	Reciprocal
Workplace	Ganqing (affection)	Intangible
Blood	Xinren (trust)	Utilitarian
Social	Kexin (credibility)	Long-term
	Tiaohe (harmony)	Personal
		Contextual

As a further explanation, Barnes et al. pointed out that:

The concept of social networks is very much in congruence with research on guanxi—whereby reciprocity, trust and interdependencies are highly valued through the effective use of social capital.

Barnes et al. (2011, p. 511)

A social exchange perspective highlights the ongoing exchanges between network actors (Chetty and Blankenburg Holm 2000; Hailén et al. 1991) and the process of slowly building relationships with high trust and commitment levels (Sasi and Arenius 2008). However, Gao et al. (2010) argued that, in contrast with Westerners, the Chinese have a stronger emphasis on differentiated relationships and tend to treat people differently based on their relationship status. This cultural tendency frequently translates into Chinese business practices that differ from Western business practices (Boisot and Child 1996). Thus, the emphasis of guanxi on social relationships leads to a distinctive social structure that differs from a Western social network (Guo and Chang 2010).

We argue that because of robust family ties and an accumulation of relational values, the Chinese business networks differ substantially to the European and North American business networks, and even to other Asian business network counterparts, such as the Japanese *keiretsu* and the Korean *chaebol* (Todeva 2007). It takes considerable time to develop relationships with the foreign ethnic Chinese and to learn about the Chinese market (Gao et al. 2012). A guanxi network is an exclusive circle of members, with limited access to both Chinese and non-Chinese members (Gao et al. 2014). Su and Littlefield (2001) suggested that the outsiders to guanxi networks can use intermediaries to enter and develop guanxi networks. Gao et al. (2014) referred to the intermediaries as the guanxi gatekeepers, thereby emphasizing the role that the intermediaries play in bridging the structural holes (guanxi gates) that outsiders often find hard to overcome.

The terms guanxi and trust are sometimes interchangeable in the literature when describing the business practices of Chinese private firms (Qin 2011). Trust is an important factor in business success, especially when there is a difference in how actors perceive trust and act based on trust (Ertug et al. 2013).

There are two main forms of trust: (1) affect-based trust founded on interpersonal concern or care and (2) cognition-based trust founded on the perception of another's reliability and trustworthiness (McAllister 1995). Chinese people only slightly separate their business and personal lives (Kwock et al. 2013). Chua et al. (2009) found that the Chinese are more likely than are the Americans to mix social-emotional concerns with economic behavior. Compared with American managers, Chinese managers place more cognition-based trust on the actors socially embedded in their own networks. In other words, a Chinese manager tends to trust a socially connected actor in business. However, American managers have more separation with any relevant affect-based and cognition-based trust than have Chinese managers (Chua et al. 2009). Additionally, the Chinese managers distribute the affect-based trust broadly across their networks, while the affect-based trust of the American managers tends to be stronger within cohesive groups of friends. Chua et al.'s (2009) study highlights the instrumental aspects that Chinese managers place on social ties and the influences that network members have on the perceived trust of others.

Despite the wealth of literature on guanxi, most studies primarily examine guanxi among Chinese people or the influence of guanxi in China (Chen et al. 2013). However, the influence of guanxi on business practices extends not only domestically in China, but also to foreign markets where Chinese people have influence (Chua et al. 2009).

2.2 Internationalization of Ethnic Chinese Businesses

Chinese outward foreign direct investment increased substantially in the past decade (Gao et al. 2013). Xie and Amine (2009) asserted that guanxi is a critical factor in the internationalization of ethnic Chinese firms. Ethnic Chinese networks consist of tens of millions of ethnic Chinese people across the world (Yeung 2006) and have a significant impact on bilateral trade between countries (Rauch and Trindade 2002). However, ethnic Chinese networks are not homogeneous, because many historical and cultural contexts influence their decisions, operations, and outcomes (Ahlstrom et al. 2010). Many perceive the overseas Chinese as a single ethnic group, because of their similar physical appearance and their assumed shared culture, values, and customs. However, they are often distinct because of differences in dialect, region, country of birth, or ancestral origin (Salaff 2005).

Todeva (2007) suggested that there are three main streams of Chinese networks. The streams vary mainly according to their context: business networks in mainland China, business networks formed by overseas Chinese immigrants, and Chinese business networks across regions connecting overseas and mainland Chinese communities. A great diversity is evident within ethnic Chinese networks. Therefore, the distinctions and variations are important despite the literature often clustering them as a single group. While past research emphasizes the cohesiveness of ethnic networks, Ilhan-Nas et al. (2011) suggested that future studies should examine the conflicts and the differentiations within the ethnic networks.

As outward foreign direct investment from China increases (Luo et al. 2010; Yeung 2006), we need to clearly understand how these firms internationalize (Yamakawa et al. 2008). Xie and Amine (2009) identified the factors that influence internationalization in a qualitative study of eight Chinese entrepreneurs. First, memberships in broad domestic social and business networks provide access to valuable information. The entrepreneurs have exclusive information and benefits from their ethnic Chinese ties that a non-Chinese entrepreneur would not have (Xie and Amine 2009). Second, the Chinese entrepreneurs entering psychically distant markets can overcome the relevant challenges by receiving support from ethnic Chinese ties or from people with whom they have guanxi. Finally, Chinese entrepreneurs who enter geographically distant but culturally close ethnic Chinese markets can enhance their position by building their social networks with the local ethnic Chinese. In contrast, in their study of 109 Chinese textile firms, Ciravegna et al. (2014) found that firms gain most foreign market entry opportunities proactively through events such as trade fairs, rather than through social ties. Thus, Chinese-run firms internationalize in a number of ways, influenced by a myriad of factors.

Research also shows that the Chinese sometimes exhibit short-term transactional behaviors, especially toward foreigners, as compared with the time-consuming, guanxi-building processes that an ethnic Chinese person often undergoes in relationships with other ethnic Chinese people (Styles and Ambler 2003). Guanxi with a fellow ethnic Chinese person may comprise tedious cultural practices that may not always lead to positive outcomes for the business. In contrast, short-term transactions with foreigners might be less time-consuming, yet more fruitful. For example, Seung Ho and Luo (2001) stressed that guanxi cultivation can be very costly and may not be worth the time and resources invested. Therefore, in some cases, it may be more advantageous to have a non-ethnic/ethnic interaction than an ethnic/ethnic interaction. Having considered the role of guanxi in Chinese business interactions (Gao et al. 2012), we now discuss the literature examining ethnic Chinese immigrant entrepreneurship.

3   Ethnic Chinese Immigrant Entrepreneurship

There is a gradual increase in the research on immigrant and ethnic entrepreneurship (Cavusgil et al. 2011). However, despite the increase in the number of immigrant-owned businesses in many countries (Yang and Wang 2011), the literature on immigrant entrepreneurship is still limited (Yang et al. 2012b). The terms ethnic entrepreneurship, immigrant entrepreneurs, and immigrant ethnic entrepreneurship are interchangeable in the literature (Chand and Ghorbani 2011). Ethnic entrepreneurship emphasises the connections and the regular interactions among people of common migration experiences or national background (Waldinger et al. 1990). The ties between these immigrants of common ethnicity sometimes lead to business ownership, and is termed ethnic entrepreneurship (Valdez 2008). Therefore, ethnic entrepreneurs are actors who start businesses in their countries of settlement and become self-employed (Kloosterman and Rath 2003). Zhou (2004, p. 1040) further defined ethnic entrepreneurs as follows:

> Ethnic entrepreneurs are often referred to as simultaneously owners and managers (or operators) of their own businesses, whose group membership is tied to a common cultural heritage or origin and is known to out-group members as having such traits; more importantly, they are intrinsically intertwined in particular social structures in which individual behavior, social relations and economic transactions are constrained.
>
> Zhou (2004, p. 1040)

Thus, embeddedness underlines ethnic entrepreneurship. Embeddedness is the interconnection between the social relationships and the economic actions of common ethnic actors. Research examines the antecedents and the consequences of the emergence of ethnic entrepreneurship (Ilhan-Nas et al. 2011). Immigrants face many market disadvantages, such as exclusion from the mainstream market and the lack of relevant language skills (Zhou 2004). These disadvantages create group cohesion among the ethnic groups and allow them to draw from the pooled resources within the community, resulting in the emergence of ethnic entrepreneurs (Yang et al. 2012a).

Traditionally, ethnic entrepreneurs are the petty traders, merchants, dealers, and shopkeepers who conduct business in restaurants, laundries, newsstands, and taxis (Zhou 2004; Zhou and Cho 2010). However, ethnic entrepreneurs now bypass these traditional occupations and venture into professional services, high-tech industries, and transnational corporations (Fong and Luk 2007; Zhou and Cho 2010). Sometimes the ethnic groups choose to become entrepreneurs, other times they set up small businesses because they cannot find employment (Ibrahim and Galt 2011). Empirical evidence suggests that the Chinese immigrants are more likely to seek self-employment than are the native people in the host country, because of dis-crimination in the mainstream labor market and because of the disadvantages (such as having poor command of the native language) associated with an immigrant status (Mata and Pendakur 1999). For example, the Filipino immigrants in the United States (US) are more proficient in English than are the Korean immigrants. Thus, the Filipino immigrants assimilate better into mainstream institutions than do the Koreans, leading to fewer incentives for self-employment (Zhou 2004). The immigrants who learn and become fluent in the native language do so for greater economic returns (Zhou 2004).

Ethnic entrepreneurship is an option for addressing unemployment, because it creates job opportunities for individuals, in or out of the ethnic group (Zhou 2004). Additionally, ethnic entrepreneurship can provide a higher earning advantage over other forms of employment, while relieving the pressure on the mainstream labor market by providing employment for the immigrants (Zhou and Cho 2010). The entrepreneurial spirit passes to other ethnic group members as the successful ethnic entrepreneurs become mentors and role models to the aspiring entrepreneurs (Zhou 1992).

Beyond the study of ethnic entrepreneurs as a disadvantaged group, research now investigates the successes of their transnational activities (Ma et al. 2013). Transnational entrepreneurs are those immigrants whose successes are dependent on their connections in another country (Portes et al. 1999). Hence, the research on immigrant transnational businesses needs to examine industrial structures and social networks as part of the context to understand how and why these two processes facilitate immigrant entrepreneurial cross-border cooperation. Additionally, we support the premise that:

> Regional industrial structure and embedded social networks, rather than the multinational firm, should be the focus in the study of transnational business. The complementary regional industrial structures allow economic and technological collaboration between these two regions while the social networks help coordinate these transnational (cross-regional) collaborations.
>
> Hsu and Saxenian (2000, p. 1991)

The literature increasingly highlights the importance of ethnic networks for entrepreneurial success (Yang et al. 2012a). Ethnic networks provide entrepreneurs with necessary resources, such as information, opportunities, and loans (Zhou 2004). Immigrant entrepreneurs are increasingly transnational because of their unique social networks and their connections with their country of origin (Ma et al. 2013). Immigrant entrepreneurs often use ethnic ties to identify foreign market opportunities (Smans et al. 2014).

The growing number of ethnic Chinese entrepreneurs evident in many developed countries may be because of the widespread global dispersion of ethnic Chinese networks (Yang and Wang 2011). In response to various institutional environments, ethnic Chinese immigrant entrepreneurs often use guanxi to reduce the costs involved in identifying and developing opportunities and for contract enforcement (Yang et al. 2010; Ilhan-Nas et al. 2011). However, guanxi can also lead to negative organizational and social consequences, such as market fragmentation and opportunistic behavior (Lin and Si 2010). While guanxi drives ethnic Chinese networks, it also comes with potential liabilities.

4   Liabilities of Chinese Networks

Guanxi or relationships within ethnic Chinese networks may come with liabilities (Chen and Chen 2009; Dahles 2010; Fan 2002; Li et al. 2008; Li and Sheng 2011; Lin and Si 2010; Luo 2008; Zhuang et al. 2010). Similar to the embeddedness concept, guanxi has contradictory and paradoxical effects (Chen et al. 2013). Guanxi can be both beneficial and detrimental to further business development. The ethnic Chinese networks are both a valued resource for internationalization, and a liability to the broader business economy (Peng 2000).

While guanxi can operate as a governance mechanism in the less institutionalized Chinese economy, it has negative aspects (Gu et al. 2008). Chen and Chen (2009) warned that, although guanxi often benefits the parties involved, it may have negative consequences for the parties and for those not involved. For example, some Hong Kong managers view guanxi as time-consuming, costly and, sometimes, corrupt (Yi and Ellis 2000). Guanxi can lead to the overburdening of reciprocal obligations, to overdependence on certain actors, and to overemphasis on group cohesion that reduce the competitiveness of firms (Gu et al. 2008). Actors with good guanxi between themselves might cooperate for their own mutual benefits at the expense of outsiders (Chen and Chen 2009). For instance, special connections with officials fostered through guanxi can sometimes lead to corruption, which enhances the anti-Chinese sentiments that can lead to violence (Peng 2000). When private and public resources are intermingled in guanxi exchanges, acts can be unethical, infringing upon public ethics and the rule of law, benefitting the privileged at the expense of the community (Chen et al. 2013).

Although guanxi emphasizes drawing on established connections to secure favors (Luo 2007; Yunxia and Allee Mengzi 2007) and can involve cronyism (Fan 2002), it does not necessarily equate with cronyism and corruption (Chen et al. 2013). Guanxi may lead to favoritism, but is not itself favoritism or cronyism (Khatri et al. 2006).

While most literature examines the positive or negative aspects of guanxi, Faure and Fang (2008) argued that the ability to manage paradoxes is China's most important cultural characteristic that enables and supports China's prolific economic growth. The double-edged characteristic of guanxi needs further research to provide a balanced understanding of guanxi's functions and its consequences that are inherent in ethnic Chinese networks (Chen et al. 2013).

The resources and benefits of ethnic Chinese networks can be limited to insiders (Leung et al. 2008). A high concentration of ethnic networks within a locality could lead to the formation of an enclave economy, such as the Chinese enclave in Prato.

5 Enclave Economy

Zhou and Cho (2010, p. 86) explained that "*the enclave economy is a special case of ethnic economy, one that is bounded by coethnicity and location*". Particularly in the early developmental stages, an enclave economy requires a high physical concentration of co-ethnic clientele, a limited level of institutional completeness, and easy access to ethnic resources, such as ethnic labor and access to credit and information (Zhou and Cho 2010). The geographic clustering of economic activities and the diversification of ethnic businesses are some of the main characteristics of an enclave economy. Bounded solidarity, created through the virtue of foreign status, is prominent among immigrants of similar ethnicity (Zhou 2004).

The natives' perception of the foreigners as culturally distant increases the perception of common origin, shared cultural heritage, and mutual obligations among co-ethnic owners, workers, and customers (Portes and Zhou 1992). An enclave economy persists because of the network structures of ethnic and immigrant ties that provide opportunities (Logan et al. 2003). Ilhan-Nas et al. suggest that some ethnic entrepreneurs are:

> Forced to demonstrate opportunity-seeking behavior because they have actually been subject to discrimination, language barriers and incompatible education or training.
>
> Ilhan-Nas et al. (2011, p. 623)

In some societies:

> Racial exclusion and discrimination erect structural barriers to prevent immigrants from competing with the native born on an equal basis in the mainstream economy.
>
> Zhou (2004, p. 1047)

As a result, the immigrants take up jobs that the locals do not desire or they carve out market niches for themselves (Zhou 2004). The market for ethnic entrepreneurs usually begins within the ethnic community, because ethnic communities have unique needs and preferences best served by people who share and know them (Aldrich and Waldinger 1990). Thus, the needs of the ethnic consumers are usually unmet by the native-owned businesses and thereby become business opportunities for the ethnic entrepreneurs. Additionally, because of the limited availability of low-cost housing to some migrant groups, the ethnic groups geographically concentrate and create geographically clustered ethnic-specific needs (Cologna 2005; Fairchild 2010). The geographically concentrated ethnic market and its ethnic entrepreneurial opportunities facilitate the further clustering of migrants (Aldrich and Waldinger 1990). Thus, ethnic entrepreneurship sometimes results in ethnic enclaves supporting the entrepreneurial activities of their ethnic members, providing them with the necessary resources to "*confront economic discrimination and competition*" (Ilhan-Nas et al. 2011, p. 623).

An enclave economy also has its disadvantages (Ilhan-Nas et al. 2011). The jobs in enclave economies sometimes command low wages and long work hours (Logan et al. 2003). Xie and Gough (2011) studied US legal immigrant data from 2004 and discovered that immigrants working in ethnic enclaves usually have lower overall earnings than do the immigrants working in the mainstream economy.

A successful enclave economy brings about social capital with resources that may not equally benefit another group sharing the same neighborhood (Zhou and Cho 2010). An enclave's labor and capital market may shelter its ethnic group members from competition by other ethnic groups and from government surveillance and regulations (Ilhan-Nas et al. 2011). An underground economy can result from an ethnic enclave (Cologna 2005). As the resources of an enclave economy are usually ethnically exclusive, policymakers are encouraged to promote inter-ethnic interactions to increase the exchanges of resources between ethnic groups (Zhou and Cho 2010). Although enclave economies provide ethnic entrepreneurs with the strong ties and support needed in the growth stage, resources outside of the ethnic network are necessary for sustained growth (Yang et al. 2012b).

The growth potential of the ethnic businesses can be constrained by the ethnic market itself because of the limited ethnic population (Aldrich and Waldinger 1990). As businesses develop, more weak ties are required to facilitate development through new opportunities. Ethnic entrepreneurs have to leverage customers beyond the ethnic community for continued growth (Aldrich and Waldinger 1990). Studies on immigrant entrepreneurship highlight the issue of immigrant businesses having too many intra-ethnic ties and too few inter-ethnic ties (for example, Danzer and Yaman 2013; Eran 2002; Ndofor and Priem 2011). When there are insufficient new ties leading to new opportunities, then overembeddedness can occur (Uzzi 1997).

Barberis and Aureli (2010) suggested that the Chinese enclave economy in Prato's industrial district is overembedded. The Chinese enclave economy in Prato produces fast fashion garments. The enclave has access to low-cost ethnic labor willing to work long hours, which some argue is unsustainable (Dei Ottati 2009a). Further, social conflicts arise between the enclave economy and the local population. Dei Ottati (2009b) described how insufficient meaningful dialogues between the diverse populations enhance the levels of mistrust and conflict. The separateness of the Chinese enclave economy from the local economy socially and economically makes it challenging for social and economic integration (Dei Ottati 2009a). The intertwined social relationships and economic actions in Prato's industrial district further highlight the value of studying the interactions between distinct networks, including ethnic based networks, using embeddedness.

6 Conclusion

To explain the challenges in the interactions between foreign Chinese immigrants in Prato's industrial district and local (host) market networks, this chapter discusses the concepts of immigrant entrepreneurs and the local native community, networks and guanxi, social capital, ethnic enclaves, and future economic and social policy directions. Drawing on a constructive approach that seeks to highlight the benefits to native entrepreneurs in associating with Chinese immigrants, this chapter examines the background literature on the Chinese, and their overseas Chinese networks.

We provide a new perspective of the influence and impact of social capital on native entrepreneurs and on Chinese immigrants. We examine how the global phenomenon of Chinese immigrant entrepreneurs can assist China to benefit economically from inward and outward trade and investment. The emphasis of guanxi on social relationships leads to a distinctive social structure of transnational entrepreneurs that differs from a Western social network. This helps to explain the impact of Chinese immigrant entrepreneurs from a macro-global perspective. Many regard a Chinese immigrant enclave economy as the outcome of an ethnic economy, bounded by coethnicity and location. We show why this is not necessarily a negative for the local native community.

Finally, as the resources of an enclave economy are usually ethnically exclusive, we propose enhanced efforts by local policymakers, such as in Prato's industrial district, to promote inter-ethnic interactions. This is achievable, for example, through trade-based exhibitions, through informal chamber of commerce seminars and workshops, and through social and cultural exchange activities to encourage positive interactions. Enhancing the exchanges of resources between ethnic groups, such as Chinese immigrants and their local Pratese counterparts, will drive and encourage the international entrepreneurial links between native firms and Chinese firms. The links will extend into China and to other markets where the Chinese diaspora operates. Thus, this chapter shows why a constructive approach that clearly explains the benefits to native entrepreneurs in building social ties and business networks with Chinese immigrant entrepreneurs, will provide new business opportunities, both locally and trans-globally, as the differences among Chinese immigrant entrepreneurs and their social networks become clear.

We offer several limitations of the chapter and provide guidance for future research on Chinese immigrant entrepreneurship within foreign industrial districts. First, while the chapter offers a detailed literature review, we need further research to build and support our body of knowledge, especially from the Chinese and Italian perspectives. We acknowledge that while our literature review is helpful, it is not complete. Future research might consider studies in Chinese on Italy or on Europe, as well as studies in Italian. Those perspectives could provide confirming and contrasting perspectives that would be valuable in explicating the cross-cultural dimensions, especially as they relate to affect-based and cogitative-based trust in ethnic enclaves.

To expand the knowledge base on guanxi, comparisons are possible between Italian business practices/models that highlight European practices rather than American practices. Additionally, the Chinese in Prato come from diverse backgrounds and origins, and form diverse groups and associations in Italy. We need further research on associations (their specific purposes and their international linkages) to understand the growth of international entrepreneurship through social ties and ethnic ties outside China and other ethnic Chinese markets. Some research suggests that guanxi is an important way to find employment before migration. It would be interesting to consider how that relates to necessity based and opportunity based international immigrant entrepreneurship. Finally, some studies suggest that guanxi encourages the perpetuation overseas of fixed Chinese class structures and employment favoritism. It would be interesting to establish whether this is so, and how extensive it is Prato, or whether immigrant entrepreneurship moderates this relationship.

References

Ahlstrom D, S-j Chen, Yeh K (2010) Managing in ethnic Chinese communities: culture, institutions, and context. Asia Pacific J Manag 27(3):341–354. doi:10.1007/s10490-010-9218-4

Aldrich HE, Waldinger R (1990) Ethnicity and entrepreneurship. Ann Rev Sociol 16(1):111–135. doi:10.1146/annurev.so.16.080190.000551

Barberis E, Aureli S (2010) The role of Chinese SMEs in Italian industrial districts. Urbino University. http://works.bepress.com/selena_aureli/1. Accessed 18 Nov 2012

Barnes BR, Yen D, Zhou L (2011) Investigating guanxi dimensions and relationship outcomes: insights from Sino-Anglo business relationships. Ind Mark Manage 40(4):510–521. doi:10.1016/j.indmarman.2010.12.007

Boisot M, Child J (1996) From fiefs to clans and network capitalism: explaining China's emerging economic order. Adm Sci Q 41(4):600–628

Cavusgil T, Nayir DZ, Hellstern G-M, Dalgic T, Cavusgil E (2011) International ethnic entrepreneurship. Int Bus Rev 20(6):591–592. doi:10.1016/j.ibusrev.2011.09.004

Chand M, Ghorbani M (2011) National culture, networks and ethnic entrepreneurship: a comparison of the Indian and Chinese immigrants in the US. Int Bus Rev 20(6):593–606. doi:10.1016/j.ibusrev.2011.02.009

Chen H, Chen T-J (1998) Network linkages and location choice in foreign direct investment. J Int Bus Stud 29(3):445–467

Chen CC, Chen XP (2009) Negative externalities of close guanxi within organizations. Asia Pacific J Manag 26(1):37–53

Chen CC, Chen XP, Huang S (2013) Chinese Guanxi: an integrative review and new directions for future research. Manag Organ Rev 9(1):167–207

Chetty S, Blankenburg Holm D (2000) Internationalisation of small to medium-sized manufacturing firms: a network approach. Int Bus Rev 9(1):77–93. doi:10.1016/S0969-5931(99)00030-X

Chua RYJ, Morris MW, Ingram P (2009) Guanxi vs networking: distinctive configurations of affect- and cognition-based trust in the networks of Chinese vs American managers. J Int Bus Stud 40(3):490–508

Chung HFL, Tung RL (2013) Immigrant social networks and foreign entry: Australia and New Zealand firms in the European Union and Greater China. Int Bus Rev 22(1):18–31. doi:10.1016/j.ibusrev.2012.01.005

Ciravegna L, Majano SB, Zhan G (2014) The inception of internationalization of small and medium enterprises: The role of activeness and networks. J Bus Res 67(6):1081–1089. doi:10.1016/j.jbusres.2013.06.002

Cologna D (2005) Chinese immigrant entrepreneurs in Italy: strengths and weaknesses of an ethnic enclave economy. In: Spaan E, Hillmann F, Naerssen ALv (eds) Asian migrants and European labour markets: patterns and processes of immigrant labour market insertion in Europe. Routledge, New York

Dahles H (2010) Ethnic Chinese enterprises and the embeddedness of failure. J Enterp Communities 4(2):184–198

Danzer AM, Yaman F (2013) Do ethnic enclaves impede immigrants' integration? Evidence from a quasi-experimental social-interaction approach. Rev Int Econ 21(2):311–325

Dei Ottati G (2009a) An industrial district facing the challenges of globalization: Prato today. Eur Plan Stud 17(12):1817–1835

Dei Ottati G (2009b) Italian industrial districts and the dual Chinese challenge. In: Johanson G, Smyth R, French R (eds) Living outside the walls: the Chinese in Prato. Cambridge Scholars, Newcastle, pp 26–41

Denison T, Arunachalam D, Johanson G, Smyth R (2009) The Chinese community in Prato. In: Johanson G, Smyth R, French R (eds) Living outside the walls: the Chinese in Prato. Cambridge Scholars, Newcastle, pp 2–20

Dunning JH, Kim C (2007) The cultural roots of Guanxi: an exploratory study. World Econ 30 (2):329–341

Eran R (2002) Conclusion: the economic context, embeddedness and immigrant entrepreneurs. Intl J Entrep Behav Res 8(1):162–167

Ertug G, Cuypers IRP, Noorderhaven NG, Bensaou BM (2013) Trust between international joint venture partners: effects of home countries. J Int Bus Stud 44(3):263–282. doi:10.1057/jibs. 2013.6

Fairchild GB (2010) Intergenerational ethnic enclave influences on the likelihood of being self-employed. J Bus Ventur 25(3):290–304. doi:10.1016/j.jbusvent.2008.10.003

Fan Y (2002) Guanxi's consequences: personal gains at social cost. J Bus Ethics 38(4):371

Faure GO, Fang T (2008) Changing Chinese values: keeping up with paradoxes. Int Bus Rev 17 (2):194–207

Fong E, Luk C (2007) Chinese ethnic business: global and local perspectives. Routledge, London

Franke RH, Hofstede G, Bond MH (1991) Cultural roots of economic performance: a research note. Strateg Manag J 12(S1):165–173. doi:10.1002/smj.4250120912

Gao H, Ballantyne D, Knight JG (2010) Paradoxes and guanxi dilemmas in emerging Chinese-Western intercultural relationships. Ind Mark Manage 39(2):264–272. doi:10.1016/j. indmarman.2008.11.001

Gao H, Knight JG, Ballantyne D (2012) Guanxi as a gateway in Chinese-Western business relationships. J of Bus & Ind Mark 27(6):456–467

Gao H, Knight JG, Yang Z, Ballantyne D (2014) Toward a gatekeeping perspective of insider–outsider relationship development in China. J World Bus 49(3):312–320. doi:10.1016/j.jwb. 2013.06.002

Gao L, Liu X, Zou H (2013) The role of human mobility in promoting Chinese outward FDI: a neglected factor? Int Bus Rev. 22(2):437–449.

Gu FF, Hung K, Tse DK (2008) When does guanxi matter? Issues of capitalization and its dark sides. J Mark 72(4):12–28

Guo C, Chang A (2010) The challenge of defining guanxi in a contemporary business context: a review. In: 7th Asian Academy of management conference, Macau, China, 14 Dec 2010

Hailén L, Johanson J, Seyed-Mohamed N (1991) Interfirm adaptation in business relationships. J Market 55(2):29–37

Hofstede G, Bond MH (1988) The confucius connection: from cultural roots to economic growth. Org Dyn 16(4):5–21

Hsu J-Y, Saxenian A (2000) The limits of guanxi capitalism: transnational collaboration between Taiwan and the USA. Environ Plan A 32(11):1991–2005. doi:10.1068/a3376

Hutchings K, Weir D (2006) Guanxi and wasta: a comparison. Thunderbird Intl Bus Rev 48 (1):141–156

Ibrahim G, Galt V (2011) Explaining ethnic entrepreneurship: an evolutionary economics approach. Int Bus Rev 20(6):607–613. doi:10.1016/j.ibusrev.2011.02.010

Ilhan-Nas T, Sahin K, Cilingir Z (2011) International ethnic entrepreneurship: antecedents, outcomes and environmental context. Int Bus Rev 20(6):614–626. doi:10.1016/j.ibusrev.2011. 02.011

Ip P (2009) Is confucianism good for business ethics in China? J Bus Ethics 88(3):463–476. doi:10.1007/s10551-009-0120-2

Ji J, Dimitratos P (2013) Confucian dynamism and Dunning's framework: direct and moderation associations in internationalized Chinese private firms. J Bus Res 66(12):2375–2382. doi:10. 1016/j.jbusres.2013.05.023

Johanson G, Smyth R, French R (2009) Living outside the walls: the Chinese in Prato. Cambridge Scholars, Newcastle

Khatri N, Tsang EWK, Begley TM (2006) Cronyism: a cross-cultural analysis. J Int Bus Stud 37 (1):61–75

Kloosterman R, Rath J (2003) Immigrant entrepreneurs: venturing abroad in the age of globalization. Berg, New York

Kwock B, James MX, Tsui ASC (2013) Doing business in China: what is the use of having a contract? The rule of law and guanxi when doing business in China. J Bus Stud Q 4(4):56–67

Leung TKP, Heung VCS, Wong YH (2008) Cronyism: one possible consequence of guanxi for an insider: how to obtain and maintain it? Eur J Mark 42(1):23–34. doi:10.1108/03090560810840899

Li JJ, Sheng S (2011) When does guanxi bolster or damage firm profitability? The contingent effects of firm- and market-level characteristics. Ind Mark Manage 40(4):561–568. doi:10.1016/j.indmarman.2010.12.012

Li JJ, Poppo L, Zhou KZ (2008) Do managerial ties in China always produce value? Competition, uncertainty, and domestic vs. foreign firms. Strateg Manag J 29(4):383–400

Lin L-H, Ho Y-L (2009) Confucian dynamism, culture and ethical changes in Chinese societies—a comparative study of China, Taiwan, and Hong Kong. Intl J Hum Resour Manag 20(11):2402–2417. doi:10.1080/09585190903239757

Lin J, Si S (2010) Can guanxi be a problem? Contexts, ties, and some unfavorable consequences of social capital in China. Asia Pacific J Manag 27(3):561–581. doi:10.1007/s10490-010-9198-4

Liu X, Xiao W, Huang X (2008) Bounded entrepreneurship and internationalisation of indigenous Chinese private-owned firms. Int Bus Rev 17(4):488–508. doi:10.1016/j.ibusrev.2008.02.014

Logan JR, Alba RD, Stults BJ (2003) Enclaves and entrepreneurs: assessing the payoff for immigrants and minorities. Int Migrat Rev 37(2):344–388. doi:10.2307/30037842

Luo Y (2007) Guanxi and business, 2nd edn. World Scientific, New Jersey

Luo Y (2008) The changing Chinese culture and business behavior: the perspective of intertwinement between guanxi and corruption. Int Bus Rev 17(2): 188–193

Luo Y, Xue Q, Han B (2010) How emerging market governments promote outward FDI: experience from China. J World Bus 45(1):68–79. doi:10.1016/j.jwb.2009.04.003

Ma Z, Zhao S, Wang T, Lee Y (2013) An overview of contemporary ethnic entrepreneurship studies: themes and relationships. Intl J Entrep Behav Res 19(1):32–52

Mata F, Pendakur R (1999) Immigration, labor force integration and the pursuit of self-employment. Int Migrat Rev 33(2):378–402

McAllister DJ (1995) Affect- and cognition-based trust as foundations for interpersonal cooperation in organizations. Acad Manag J 38(1):24–59. doi:10.2307/256727

Michailova S, Worm V (2003) Personal networking in Russia and China: Blat and Guanxi. Eur Manag J 21(4):509–519

Minkov M, Hofstede G (2012) Hofstede"s fifth dimension: new evidence from the world values survey. J Cross Cult Psychol 43(1):3–14

Ndofor HA, Priem RL (2011) Immigrant entrepreneurs, the ethnic enclave strategy, and venture performance. J Manag 37(3):790–818. doi:10.1177/0149206309345020

Nielsen I, Paritski O, Smyth R (2012) A minority-status perspective on intergroup relations: a study of an ethnic chinese population in a small Italian town. Urb Stud 49(2):307–318. doi:10.1177/0042098010397396

Nolan J (2011) Good guanxi and bad guanxi: Western bankers and the role of network practices in institutional change in China. Intl J Hum Resour Manag 22(16):3357–3372. doi:10.1080/09585192.2011.586869

Peng D (2000) Ethnic Chinese business networks and the Asia-Pacific economic integration. J Asian Afr Stud 35(2):229–250. doi:10.1177/002190960003500202

Portes A, Guarnizo LE, Landolt P (1999) The study of transnationalism: Pitfalls and promise of an emergent research field. Ethnic Racial Stud 22(2):217–237

Portes A, Zhou M (1992) Gaining the upper hand: Economic mobility among immigrant and domestic minorities. Ethnic Racial Stud 15(4):491–522

Qin Z (2011) Models of trust-sharing in Chinese private enterprises. Econ Model 28 (3):1017–1029. doi:10.1016/j.econmod.2010.11.013

Rauch JE, Trindade V (2002) Ethnic Chinese networks in international trade. Rev Econ Stat 84(1):116–130

Runfola A, Guercini S (2013) Fast fashion companies coping with internationalization: driving the change or changing the model? J Fashion Market Manag 17(2):190–205. doi:10.1108/JFMM-10-2011-0075

Saad I, Koh J (2010) Maintaining racial harmony imperative to Singapore's survival: MFA. Channel News Asia, 28 April

Salaff JW (2005) Cluster introduction: Subethnicity in the Chinese diaspora. Intl Migr 43(3):3–7. doi:10.1111/j.1468-2435.2005.00323.x

Sasi V, Arenius P (2008) International new ventures and social networks: advantage or liability? Eur Manag J 26(6):400–411. doi:10.1016/j.emj.2008.09.008

Seung Ho P, Luo Y (2001) Guanxi and organizational dynamics: organizational networking in Chinese firms. Strateg Manag J 22(5):455–477

Smith PB, Huang HJ, Harb C, Torres C (2011) How distinctive are indigenous ways of achieving influence? A comparative study of Guanxi, Wasta, Jeitinho, and "Pulling Strings". J Cross Cult Psychol. doi:10.1177/0022022110381430

So YL, Walker A (2006) Explaining guanxi: the Chinese business network. Routledge, London

Storz ML (1999) Dancing with dragons: chopsticks people revealed for global business. Glob Bus Strateg, Ashburton

Styles C, Ambler T (2003) The coexistence of transaction and relational marketing: insights from the Chinese business context. Ind Mark Manage 32(8):633–642

Su C, Littlefield JE (2001) Entering Guanxi: a business ethical dilemma in mainland China? J Bus Ethics 33(3):199–210

Todeva E (2007) Business networks in China: legacies and practice. In: Clegg S, Wang K, Berrell M (eds) Business networks and strategic alliances in China. E. Elgar, Cheltenham, Northampton, pp 182–208

Tsang EWK (1998) Can Guanxi be a source of sustained competitive advantage for doing business in China? Acad Manag Exec 12(2):64–73

Tsui AS, J-lL Farh (1997) Where guanxi matters: Relational demography and guanxi in the Chinese context. Work Occup 24:56–79

Uzzi B (1997) Social structure and competition in interfirm networks: the paradox of embeddedness. Adm Sci Q 42(1):35–67

Valdez Z (2008) The effect of social capital on White, Korean, Mexican and Black business owners' earnings in the US. J Ethnic Migr Stud 34(6):955–973. doi:10.1080/13691830802211265

Waldinger RD, Aldrich H, Ward R (1990) Ethnic entrepreneurs: Immigrant business in industrial societies. Sage series on race and ethnic relations, vol 1. Sage Publications, Newbury Park, Calif

Wong YH (1998) Relationship marketing in China: the magic and myth of Guanxi? J Intl Market & Market Res 23(1):3–14

Xie YH, Amine LS (2009) Social networks and the internationalization of Chinese entrepreneurs. Glob Bus Organ Excell 29(1):61–78. doi:10.1002/joe.20299

Xie Y, Gough M (2011) Ethnic enclaves and the earnings of immigrants. Demography 48 (4):1293–1315

Yamakawa Y, Peng MW, Deeds DL (2008) What drives new ventures to internationalize from emerging to developed economies? Entrepr: Theor Pract 32(1):59–82

Yamakawa Y, Khavul S, Peng MW, Deeds DL (2013) Venturing from emerging economies. Strateg Entrep J 7(3):181–196. doi:10.1002/Sej.1158

Yang H, Lin Z, Lin Y (2010) A multilevel framework of firm boundaries: Firm characteristics, dyadic differences, and network attributes. Strateg Manag J 31(3): 237–261. doi:10.1002/smj.815

Yang Z, Wang CL (2011) Guanxi as a governance mechanism in business markets: Its characteristics, relevant theories, and future research directions. Ind Mark Manag 40(4): 492–495. doi:10.1016/j.indmarman.2010.12.004

Yang J-p, Tang L-p, Lu Z-p (2012a) Social network's impact on new venture performance—an empirical research of Zhejiang entrepreneurs. In: Zhang L, Zhang C (eds) Engineering education and management, vol 111. Lecture Notes in Electrical Engineering. Springer, Berlin, pp 27–34. doi:10.1007/978-3-642-24823-8_5

Yang X, Ho E-H, Chang A (2012b) Integrating the resource-based view and transaction cost economics in immigrant business performance. Asia Pacific J Manag 29(3):753–772. doi:10. 1007/s10490-010-9236-2

Yen DA, Barnes BR, Wang CL (2011) The measurement of guanxi: introducing the GRX scale. Ind Mark Manag 40(1):97–108. doi:10.1016/j.indmarman.2010.09.014

Yeung HWC (2006) Change and continuity in Southeast Asian ethnic Chinese business. Asia Pacific J Manag 23(3):229–254

Yeung IYM, Tung RL (1996) Achieving business success in Confucian societies: The importance of Guanxi (connections). Org Dyn 25(2):54–65

Yi LM, Ellis P (2000) Insider-Outsider perspectives of guanxi. Bus Horiz 43(1):25

Yunxia Z, Allee Mengzi Z (2007) Understanding Guanxi (connections) from business leaders' perspectives. Bus Commun Q 70(3):385–389

Zhao H, Hsu C-C (2007) Social ties and foreign market entry: an empirical inquiry. Manag Intl Rev 47(6):815–844. doi:10.1007/s11575-007-0054-9

Zhou M (1992) Chinatown: the socioeconomic potential of an urban enclave. Conflicts in urban and regional development. Temple University Press, Philadelphia

Zhou M (2004) Revisiting ethnic entrepreneurship: convergencies, controversies, and conceptual advancements. Int Migrat Rev 38(3):1040–1074. doi:10.1111/j.1747-7379.2004.tb00228.x

Zhou M, Cho M (2010) Noneconomic effects of ethnic entrepreneurship: A focused look at the Chinese and Korean enclave economies in Los Angeles. Thunderbird Intl Bus Rev 52(2): 83–96. doi:10.1002/tie.20316

Zhuang G, Xi Y, Tsang ASL (2010) Power, conflict, and cooperation: the impact of guanxi in Chinese marketing channels. Ind Mark Manag 39(1):137–149. doi:10.1016/j.indmarman.2008. 07.002

Concluding Remarks: The Benefits of Overcoming Local Liabilities

Simone Guercini, Gabi Dei Ottati, Loretta Baldassar
and Graeme Johanson

Abstract This concluding chapter summarizes the main results emerging from the book, and highlights the positive aspects to the phenomenon of new forces arriving in an industrial territory. The term native entrepreneurship suggests that the culture of the incumbent community may no longer be the dominant one in the settlement context. This is because globalization endows the transnational communities with a position of strength and/or certain advantages. This chapter briefly summarizes the contributions emerging from the previous chapters. We consider the connections between the contributions, including identifying the most obvious liabilities, and assessing the related costs and the potential benefits. The main finding emerging from the book is that the relationship between native and immigrant entrepreneurship is challenging. The relationship is associated both with local liabilities and with great opportunities. Overcoming the separations between the communities in a settlement presents risks; however, it is necessary and can offer important benefits.

Keywords Local liability · Overcoming separation · Globalization · Immigrant entrepreneurship · Native entrepreneurship · Interaction

S. Guercini (✉) · G. Dei Ottati
University of Florence, Florence, Italy
e-mail: simone.guercini@unifi.it

G. Dei Ottati
e-mail: gabi.dei@unifi.it

L. Baldassar
University of Western Australia, Perth, Italy
e-mail: loretta.baldassar@uwa.edu.au

G. Johanson
Monash University, Melbourne, Australia
e-mail: graeme.johanson@monash.edu

© Springer International Publishing Switzerland 2017
S. Guercini et al. (eds.), *Native and Immigrant Entrepreneurship*,
DOI 10.1007/978-3-319-44111-5_12

> Even in the Old World progressive industrial districts gain much from the immigration of workers to whom all methods of manufacture are new; and who readily betake themselves to the newest processes, and work these to the best of their power.
>
> Marshall (1920, p. 104)

The immigration of workers mentioned by Marshall in this quotation is not the same as the migration associated with the emergence of entrepreneurship. However, it offers the opportunity to highlight a positive potential in the phenomenon of new forces arriving in an industrial local system. This positivity is important, because it partly offsets the many challenges related to the interactions between native and immigrant entrepreneurship that emerge throughout this book.

The main theme of the book is the relationships between native and immigrant entrepreneurship, and it contains contributions from scholars of management, economics, sociology, and anthropology. We understand that adopting a multidisciplinary approach presents some difficulties for the reader, and that the terminology and methodological choices vary in the book's chapters. However, the multidisciplinary approach makes it possible to present different perspectives (as described in the Introduction). We followed the approach of the early theorists on human development who had both economic and sociological interests and who shared common foundational concerns. We particularly refer to the insider and outsider concepts that appear throughout the book. These concepts are of interest to both economists and sociologists and constitute a large component of the liability concerns (see the previous chapters authored by Guercini, Dei Ottati, Baldassar and Johanson).

The book aims to document and describe the local liabilities perceived by entrepreneurs because of the presence of separation in a local context between two or more communities. In this sense, the book offers useful insights. Multidisciplinary contributions are particularly suited to migration studies, and produce important results. We define local liabilities as the observed liabilities involved in the separation between communities at the local level. "*Local liabilities emerge locally where two (or more) separate communities (of persons and firms) exist*" (Guercini 2016). The term *local* refers to a social space. The greater the separation between the communities sharing the place, the greater the local liability. The focus on entrepreneurial liabilities anticipates the study of possible ways to overcome the liabilities, including their antecedents and consequences.

The main finding emerging from this book is that the relationship between native and immigrant entrepreneurship is challenging, and at the same time is associated with local liabilities and with great opportunities. The choice of the term *native* to qualify the entrepreneurship established in its place of origin has different meanings in the management and economics literature, and in anthropology and sociology. The use of the term native suggests that the culture of the incumbent community may no longer be the dominant one in the settlement context, given the position of strength and/or the advantage of the transnational communities through globalization (see chapter by Guercini, Dei Ottati, Baldassar and Johanson). In this case, the native culture may no longer provide an advantage when globalization processes assume centrality over the culture and rules of the host country. This also applies locally for developed and industrialized countries affected by significant immigration flows (see chapter by Barberis and Violante).

By considering the emblematic case of Prato, the book offers some unique comparisons between native and immigrant entrepreneurship. Immigrant entrepreneurship contributes significantly to the generation of value added in different local contexts. Prato is an excellent case study, particularly for Chinese entrepreneurial immigration (see chapter by Biasi and Rosignoli). We focus on entrepreneurship of Chinese origin that is significantly (but not exclusively) concentrated in the fast fashion industry (see chapter by Becucci).

Although immigration can make a positive contribution to an economy, in the local context there may be separation conditions. This book highlights the existence and the force of local liabilities as economic and social costs associated with separation. In other words, a local liability is the costs related to the presence of two or more communities in the same place, and relates to the distance between the cultures. This is ultimately the concept of local liability.

To evaluate the effect of local liabilities, we note that in the globalized world, migration processes are not separate from other phenomena that affect international trade and investment flows. Immigrant entrepreneurship relates to these phenomena, as highlighted in the chapter by Barberis and Violante in this volume. This means that the liabilities can arise locally in terms of foreignness and outsidership in inter-community relations between native and immigrant entrepreneurship; however, the liabilities are matched by the benefits of limited psychic distance and insidership in social and business networks at a transnational level. This seems particularly clear for the Chinese immigrant entrepreneurship in Prato, as evidenced in the book (see chapter by Barberis and Violante).

In the specific context of Prato, the Chinese community has a perceptible impact on total output or gross domestic product (chapter by Biasi and Rosignoli). The Chinese community generates significant transfers abroad, while stimulating consumption and affecting the real estate and industrial markets (chapter by Biasi and Rosignoli and chapter by Becucci).

Why is the case of Prato emblematic? Prato has been a famous and paradigmatic case of an Italian industrial district. Prato was a reality exposed to globalization—it specializes in a single industry (textile) and it experienced international competition mainly exporting its production worldwide. The literature on industrial districts focuses on the effects of belonging to a local community of people and firms. The effects of the local presence of separate communities is not a traditional part of the industrial district model (Becattini 1990; Dei Ottati 1994). Migration driven by globalization results in the presence of different communities in a local context that are often separated. The theme of separation between communities sometimes intersects with the theme of change or crisis in specific local development (as in some Italian industrial districts). The relevant literature on international business liabilities and on industrial districts present both similarities and differences. Many of the international business and industrial district concepts used in this book are not new to sociology or anthropology, particularly the notions of insiders/outsiders, trust, and the relational approach. Clearly, anthropology and sociology perspectives focus on individual and social collectivities, while business economics focuses on firms and markets.

In both international business and industrial district analyses, firms are immersed in networks, through which they build relationships of trust and discover profit opportunities—the potential and limits of a firm's success depend on the network of relationships in which it is embedded. Some international business literature considers the economic relationships between firms that create social relationships (Cavusgil and Knight 2015). That research strand stresses that the process of building trust is essentially social and based on a common history; however, the commitment to the relationship is not influenced exclusively by the immediate prospect of profit. A second international business literature strand (Johanson and Vahlne 2009) argues that building relationships can be a gradual, time-consuming process that requires social and informal interactions. This is consistent with the vision of the industrial district. However, when the entrepreneurs (employees) belong to the same community, the situation is different. In the latter case, the shared social culture includes norms of behavior and, when the industrial district functions properly, the community punishes those who transgress (Brusco 1999).

In the international business literature, a firm overcomes the liability of outsidership if it becomes an insider in some relevant network. The firm becomes an insider to acquire the knowledge, general and specific, related to the foreign market that it intends to enter. In the industrial district, the individual firm first embeds in a community of people (social context) that share its own culture and institutions. This includes implicit rules of behavior and relative social and economic sanctions and rewards. Hence, the industrial district is a web of business networks, more or less integrated, including all of the firms of the district (Becattini 1990). In the industrial district model, most of the relevant information circulates throughout the system because there is a sharing of both cognitive codes (industry culture) and behavioral codes (social culture). In a thriving industrial district, the basis of trust comes from belonging to the same community (bounded solidarity), but also importantly from personal reputation gained through repeated business interactions (Dei Ottati 1994).

The local liabilities in the industrial district may be similar to those liabilities found in the international business literature (foreignness, outsidership). However, they are not identical because they arise from migration and from the coexistence of two communities in a local context. Many questions remain. For example, what is the relationship between firms located in the same place when entrepreneurship is apparent in both of the communities? What are the antecedents and consequences of local liabilities? How can the liabilities be overcome? The inter-community relationships (between immigrants and natives) are a key point.

The local liability is the cost that arises when the members of each community suffer from the separation through a lack of integration. Prato does not lack relationships between Chinese and Italian firms and people. However, the roles played change in the various phases of the Chinese presence (Milanesi et al. 2016). The natives and the immigrants interacted from the beginning (Guercini 2001); however, at first there was a pure market interaction with an asymmetry of power in favor of the natives (Dei Ottati 2014). When the immigrant entrepreneurs became final marketers in the fast fashion sector (see chapters by Becucci, chapter by Guercini and Milanesi, and chapter by Zhang and Zhang), inter-community relationships reduced. Today, the Chinese entrepreneurs have many transactions and in some cases relationships with native Italians, including with customers, with agents, and with service providers, in addition to their relationships with their employees and people with whom they conduct joint business.

This book shows that the integration process between natives and Chinese immigrants in Prato appears slow and is limited to a few cases. This level of integration is insufficient to overcome the barriers that separate both communities of people, and both sets of firms. With the aim of creating a platform for interaction, official institutions can help to overcome the highlighted local liabilities. Overcoming the separation of the communities can offer benefits (to the extent that they are perceived by the communities) that are sufficient to offset the costs of integration. What hampers the overcoming of local liabilities? We must consider several aspects. (1) The distrust of the people in both communities in the local context. (2) The will expressed in the policies of other actors (for example, the public policy makers in the country of origin). (3) The role of the actors in the international value chains that can push the separation (for example, to maintain the conditions of cost advantage).

Therefore, the social relationships between the members of the community affect the business relationships. In addition, these social and business relationships also change over time and can be significantly influenced by the maturation and development of the younger generations. The study reported in the chapter authored by Paciocco and Baldassar highlights selected samples of young Italian-schooled Chinese migrants who present a complex mixed Chinese-Italian identity. Their experiences of mixed identities are often difficult and this is typical of the translocal migrant contexts. However, their cross cultural competencies can also offer important opportunities for overcoming local liabilities, particularly if associated with a sense of belonging in Prato and the will to stay and work for Chinese-run firms (chapter by Paciocco and Baldassar).

The role of new communication technologies and their popularity in the communities of origin and settlement may maintain the effects of separation. The mass use of new technologies, such as smartphones, tends to favor the agile connections of migrants with their own culture. Those effects can renew the translocal character over time, making it easy for the migrants to use their known heritage (including business practices) from their home territory (chapter by Johanson, Beghelli and Fladrich). Network communications allow the current migrants to take their roots with them. They negotiate two worlds at once, that of their country of origin and that of their new settlement (chapter by Johanson, Beghelli and Fladrich).

Given these conditions, the coexistence at a local level between native and immigrant entrepreneurship can be associated with liabilities perceived by both groups of firms. Although Prato's immigrant Chinese entrepreneurs are insiders in the transnational networks, they can perceive liabilities of foreignness in their settlement context and liabilities of outsidership from the local networks of natives. In turn, the local native entrepreneurs can be outsiders to the translocal networks of the immigrants (chapter authored by Guercini and Milanesi). The chapter by Lazzeretti and Capone analyzes the liabilities tested by immigrant entrepreneurship in the light of organizational ecology theory, assuming a competition for resources between the two communities. We then present an analysis based on case studies, offering hypotheses about the sustainability of immigrant entrepreneurship requiring a development of innovation capability (ambidexterous organization) that can benefit from a process of overcoming local liabilities. Finally, the chapter authored by Ong and Freeman focuses on the outsidership of local native entrepreneurs from the networks of Chinese immigrants, considering the value that can be generated for the native Italian firms by exceeding this liability of outsidership. In addressing this issue, native local entrepreneurship can benefit from the overcoming of local liabilities, taking into account the characteristics of the Chinese social networks (guanxi), of their strengths but also of the limitations and problems associated with them (chapter by Ong and Freeman).

Expanding the horizon to global value chains (Gereffi 1999; Cattaneo et al. 2010), the competitive position of alternative chains may involve other elements. The ethnographic study of Chinese fast fashion firms in Prato touches on the existing separation between the business entrepreneurship of the immigrant and native communities (see the chapter authored by Becucci). Such a study also explains how important transaction flows can be, affecting access to resources available to natives (real estate, technical skills, professional expertise, established trade channels), even in the presence of a persistent separation between the communities. In other words, the separation appears strong on the cultural level rather than on the transactional level.

Direct competition does not appear, at least in the cases examined, because native and immigrant entrepreneurship operate in different industries and/or global value chains (Gereffi 1999) or in different positions within the same industry. However, there is indirect competition and cultural separation—not limited to belonging to different cultures but extending also to the development of specific business cultures and market visions—that limits the development of business opportunities together. Therefore, the Chinese focus on large production volumes rather than on profit margins and the living conditions accepted by the Chinese workforce consequently lead to competitive factors at different levels and distances.

In understanding how to overcome the liabilities, the chapters in this book present several useful contributions. The chapters help to: (1) identify the most obvious liabilities; (2) assess the costs (and benefits) associated with separation; (3) understand the benefits that derive from the overcoming of local liabilities; and (4) understand the direction of the processes in place in individual firms, in the business context, and in the community of people.

Importantly, this book documents the separation condition that can characterize two or more business communities coexisting in the same local context. The separation condition causes liabilities, similar to those recognized in international businesses (chapter by Guercini and Milanesi). Specifically, this book documents that a strong and persistent separation between the two communities dominates the case studied. From the firms' perspective, this separation is a source of costs pertaining to acquiring the knowledge that is available from the members of the other community. Conducting business in a context where other communities exist involves incurring specific costs for accessing resources. This is not just true for immigrant entrepreneurship. It also relates to the native entrepreneurship rooted to the settlement place because of the growth of opportunities accessible to transnational networks through globalization.

The simultaneous presence of different communities in the same place generates transaction occasions. However, in this respect, there are high costs because of the absence of knowledge and trust (Williamson 1975). This is unsurprising because the cost argument underpins the liability concept. For example, the liability of foreignness is the costs that must support the foreign subsidiaries of a multinational corporation (Hymer 1960; Zaheer 1995). In multinational enterprises, the subsidiaries face additional costs over those faced by the local competitors to deal with international markets. That liability is a measurable phenomenon based on the additional costs recorded by the foreigners (the outsiders). The additional costs incurred as part of both native and immigrant entrepreneurship testify to the existence of local liabilities, and derive from the lack of knowledge available about the other community present in the same place.

To define the concept of separation, we refer to the literature on the response to the stress of acculturation (Berry et al. 1987). However, to produce local liabilities, the individual entrepreneurs do not have to feel an acculturation stress. It is sufficient that they face de facto a disadvantage in the networks because of the separation condition with respect to the context of the other business community coexisting in the same place.

Although separation is the dominant condition in the relationship between native and immigrant entrepreneurship, in our case the separation is never complete. Some relationships are long lasting between the individual enterprises and the individual entrepreneurs of the two communities. Moreover, it is precisely in these opportunities for exchange that businesses feel the additional costs related to local liabilities. However, these are fixed costs, which once incurred do not reoccur (Hymer 1960). Even incomplete separation does not seem sustainable with the evolution of immigrant entrepreneurship, both relating to the character of the younger generation (chapter by Paciocco and Baldassar) and ensuring sustainable entrepreneurship in terms of the capacity to innovate (chapter by Zhang and Zhang). Therefore, overcoming the separation is necessary; this can present risks but it can also offer important advantages. This is true in the industrial districts for the integration of the labor force, as Marshall stated in the quotation at the beginning of this chapter. Although immigration is a source of stress, it also requires learning, or it can be the origin of a process of learning. Learning is an important part of entrepreneurship and of entrepreneurial networks. For example, moving from separation to integration can help to identify and seize opportunities otherwise not achieved because of the psychic distance (see previous chapters authored by Guercini, Dei Ottati, Baldassar and Johanson).

In conclusion, the local liabilities imply additional costs associated with the presence of entrepreneurship embedded in different cultures. The liabilities also offer opportunities and economic and social benefits for the development of businesses and of local contexts. Thus, the concept of local liabilities refers to the costs of separation between natives and immigrants in the development of local networks of people and firms. Acculturative stress can absorb resources and generate costs. However, it also supports intense learning and sustained development, and provides a competitive advantage for firms in a local context in the globalization process.

References

Becattini G (1990) The Marshallian industrial. In: Pyke F, Becattini G, Sengenberger W (eds) Industrial districts and inter-firm co-operation in Italy (pp 125–154). International Institute for Labour Studies, Geneva

Berry JW, Kim U, Minde T, Mok D (1987) Comparative studies of acculturative stress. Intl Migr Rev 491–511

Brusco S (1999) The rules of the game in industrial districts. In: Grandori A (ed) Interfirm networks: organization and industrial competitiveness. Routledge, London

Cattaneo O, Gereffi G, Staritz C (2010) Global value chains in a post-crisis world. A development perspective. The World Bank, Washington

Cavusgil ST, Knight G (2015) The born global firm: An entrepreneurial and capabilities perspective on early and rapid internationalization. J Int Bus Stud 46(1):3–16

Dei Ottati G (1994) Trust, interlinking transactions and credit in the industrial district. Camb J Econ 18:529–546

Dei Ottati G (2014) A transnational fast fashion industrial district: an analysis of the Chinese businesses in Prato. Camb J Econ 38:1247–1274

Gereffi G (1999) International trade and industrial upgrading in the apparel commodity chain. J Int Econ 48:37–70

Guercini S (2001) Relation between branding and growth of the firm in new quick fashion formulas: analysis of an Italian case. J Fashion Market Manag 5(1):69–79

Guercini S (2016) Local liabilities between immigrant and native entrepreneurship in industrial districts and global value chains, paper presented at the workshop "evolving industrial districts within global and regional value chains and the role of manufacturing and innovation capabilities". University of Padova, Padova, 7 April

Hymer SH (1960) The international operations of national firms: a study of direct foreign investment. Ph.D. dissertation, published in 1976. MIT Press, Cambridge

Johanson J, Vahlne JE (2009) The Uppsala internationalization process model revisited: From liability of foreignness to liability of outsidership. J Int Bus Stud 40(9):1411–1431

Marshall A (1920) Industry and trade. A study of industrial technique and business organization; and of their influences on the condition of various classes and nations, 3rd edn. London, Macmillan

Milanesi M, Guercini S, Waluszewski S (2016) A Black Swan in the district? An IMP perspective on immigrant entrepreneurship and changes in industrial districts. IMP J 10(2):243–259

Williamson OE (1975) Markets and hierarchies: analysis and antitrust implications. The Free Press, New York

Zaheer S (1995) Overcoming the liability of foreignness. Acad Manag J 38(2):341–363

Printed by Printforce, the Netherlands